WANTON WORDS

RHETORIC AND SEXUALITY IN
ENGLISH RENAISSANCE DRAMA

Wanton Words

Rhetoric and Sexuality in English Renaissance Drama

MADHAVI MENON

UNIVERSITY OF TORONTO PRESS
Toronto Buffalo London

ISBN 0-8020-8837-6

Printed on acid-free paper

National Library of Canada Cataloguing in Publication

Menon, Madhavi
    Wanton words : rhetoric and sexuality in English Renaissance
drama / Madhavi Menon.

    Includes bibliographical references and index.
    ISBN 0-8020-8837-6

    1. Sex in literature.   2. Sex and language – England – History –
16th century.   3. English drama – Early modern and Elizabethan –
1500–1600 – History and criticism.   I. Title.

    PR649.R46M45 2003   822'.3093538   C2003-902982-4

University of Toronto Press acknowledges the financial assistance to its
publishing program of the Canada Council for the Arts and the Ontario
Arts Council.

University of Toronto Press acknowledges the financial support for its
publishing activities of the Government of Canada through the Book
Publishing Industry Development Program (BPIDP).

For Amma, Achan, and Kalyani

Contents

Acknowledgments   ix

Foreplay   3

1 Setting the Stage: Metaphor   5

2 Performance Anxiety: Metonymy, *Richard II*, *The Roaring Girl*   35

3 First Night: Metalepsis, *Romeo and Juliet*, *All's Well that Ends Well*   68

4 Cast in Order of Appearance: Catachresis, *Othello*, *King John*   94

5 Encore! Allegory, *Volpone*, *The Tempest*   124

After Words: *Henry VIII* and the Ends of History   157

Notes   173

Bibliography   211

Index   231

Acknowledgments

Like every good Indian, I have a large family of friends and relatives to thank, not only for love and support during the years it took to write this book, but also for putting up with the wantonness of my words.

Like every bad Indian who leaves home, this family extends to different corners of the globe. In Delhi, necessary love and sensible interest have always been expressed by Kripa Chetsingh, Mark Amritanand, Barkha Dutt, Ritin Rai, Deepshikha Sarin, Shweta Kumar, Suparna Sharma, and Poonam Saxena. Friends from Delhi, no longer in Delhi, but who always remind me of home, include Shekhar Aiyar, Amitabh Dubey, and Chitralekha Zutshi. Food and love and hospitality have been provided in generous proportions by Bhavna Kanodia, Pallavi Rastogi, and Elora Chowdhury, all of whom are constant and loving reminders of what it means to have a home away from home. In London, Kavita Nayar has been a part of my work for a long time; Freyan Panthaki was my early co-explorer into the possibilities of *Twelfth Night*. In Auckland, Stella and Norman Harris, Miriam Harris, Naomi Harris, and Ian Narev, convinced me with care and cake that the world looks better upside down.

In Boston, I first made the acquaintance of someone whose brilliance, love, friendship, support, warmth, and generosity knows no bounds, and without whom not one word of these pages would have been written. Lee Edelman is friend, adviser, critic, and above all, He Without Whom Life Cannot Be Lived. I am astonished at the good fortune that brought me to his door, and grateful that the door was open. For suggesting that I look at Shakespeare awry, for laughing at my Anglo-Indian pronunciation, for trying my food, for overlooking my foibles, for improving my drafts, for teasing me mercilessly, for modelling intellectual rigour and professional behaviour, for making life away from home worthwhile, I would like to offer unending love and gratitude, poor return as it is, to Lee Edelman.

Also in Boston, I met my fellow traveller and kindred spirit, Judith Brown, who has always listened, lectured, and loved me. She has fed me gastronomically and intellectually, borne my tantrums, and saved me from many a cross-cultural gaffe. I have depended on her during all the years of living in this sometimes strange land, always trusting her Canadianness to recognize its strangeness with me.

At Tufts University, I would like to acknowledge the feedback and support extended by the Medieval-Renaissance Reading Group, especially Judith Haber, Kevin Dunn, Christian Sheridan, Cheryl Smith, and Stephanie Gaynor. Samina Najmi was never part of my reading group but was always part of my life. Christian Sheridan, John Kucich, and Melissa Baker happily adjusted to my foreign ways and willingly endured both my tirades and my laughter.

Several friends and colleagues have read parts of this book at various stages, recommended changes, and listened to my thinking as it developed; without these friends, both I and this book would have been much the worse. I would like to thank Jeff Masten for his unfailing wit and astonishing wisdom, Henry Turner for his uncanny ability to get to the heart of an argument, Judith Haber for asking me to take risks, and Kevin Dunn for always making sense. Heartfelt gratitude for love, support, and advice also to Rebecca Walkowitz, Andy Parker, Marge Garber, Emily Bartels, Bruce Boehrer, Joe Litvak, Ellis Hanson, Dominic Doyle, and Rob Odom. Jonathan Goldberg had nothing to do with this book, but this book would not have been possible without his breathtaking work on Renaissance sexuality.

In Ithaca, I would like to thank Asma Barlas and Ulises Mejias for being immediately warm and sustainedly rigorous: they make intellectual conversation a delight even when the rest of Ithaca freezes. I am also grateful to my colleagues at Ithaca College, especially Sondra Guttman and Greg Tomso, who have seen me through thick and thin. An Ithaca College summer faculty research grant in 2001 enabled me to work on this book; funds from the Provost's office made its publication possible. Dean Howard Erlich and Provost Peter Bardaglio have always recognized the importance of monetary resources to the scholarly life, and for that recognition, I am immensely grateful.

My students are a constant source of pleasure and deserve a special debt of gratitude for listening and questioning and demanding with as much attention as they have. In particular, the fabulous Ashley Shelden has created a standard of intelligence, scepticism, and love that will be impossible to replace.

At the University of Toronto Press, I am grateful to Kristen Pederson Chew, Suzanne Rancourt, Miriam Skey, and Barb Porter for shepherding my wanton words through the system. I am also enormously grateful to Rick Rambuss and Stephen Guy-Bray, the two readers of my manuscript whose uncannily astute suggestions are everywhere reflected in this book.

My relatives in various parts of the world are responsible for fostering my argumentative spirit, and even though the words 'queer theory' might carry little or no meaning for them, have always revelled in my immersion in it. I would like to thank my grandmother, Kalyanikutty Amma, my aunts, Nalini B. Menon and Sushila Nayar, my cousins Gita Muralidharan, Maya Gopinadh, Gopal Menon, Siddharth and Bharat Jairaj, and my niece and nephews, Rajeev and Nandini Gopinadh, Jai and Arvind Menon.

This book is a small token of the enormous love and gratitude I owe my parents, Indira and Mohan Chander Menon, and my sister, Kalyani Menon. They have known and put up with me for longer than anyone else in my life and have saved me on innumerable occasions, often from others, mostly from myself, and always with fierce support and unquestioning love. My sister is my champion in the world, and I never leave home without her. My parents, on the other hand, never leave me without a home. Almost effortlessly, my mother taught me how to think, my father taught me how to love my work, and my sister taught me how to write: without them, this book would not have been possible. It is, therefore, both indebted and dedicated to them.

Finally and fully, this book, my life, and all the dessert in the world would be as nothing without Jonathan Gil Harris. He has read every page several times, argued several points every time, suggested changes, applauded ideas, cooked food, calmed tempers, parted frays, argued concepts, challenged decisions, printed pages, walked miles, run errands, shared discoveries, assuaged homesickness, and embodied brilliance. He has delighted in my delights, and sorrowed in my sorrows; above all, he showed me at a crucial juncture in my life that every apparent end is but a new beginning. This book is also and always, for Gil, with admiration, joy, and infinite love.

WANTON WORDS

Foreplay

HOLOFERNES: What is the figure? What is the figure?
MOTH: Horns.

Love's Labour's Lost, V.i.64–5[1]

In a frenzied play of wits involving the letters of the alphabet, Holo-fernes and Moth outline an idea of language that this book will take as axiomatic. Responding to a pedantic question about a constitutive fig-ure of speech ('What is the figure? What is the figure?'), Moth puns on a stock source of Renaissance humour and horror: horns. Referring both to the pedant's book covered with a sheet of horn, and to the pop-ular symbol of cuckoldry, Moth's reply yokes together concepts that are often thought of separately: language and sexuality, tropes and the body. The delight of copulation, the inevitability of its excess, and the resultant fear of bastardy combine to give one word the power of an entire narrative. And that powerful narrative is brought into focus by Moth as a *figure of speech* irrevocably linked with sexuality.

This understanding of rhetoric is not new to *Love's Labour's Lost*, nor does it become old after it. Rather, the mutual imbrication of language and sexuality looms conceptually large in several handbooks of rheto-ric that were in circulation in Renaissance England and which, along with texts of Renaissance drama, will be the focus of this study. These handbooks – Quintilian's *Institutio Oratoria*, the pseudo-Ciceronian *Rhetorica ad Herennium*, Erasmus's *Copia Verborum ac Rerum* – were reg-ularly prescribed texts in grammar school syllabi, and reflect the sheer emphasis on language that marked academic endeavours of the time. The Latin texts were also reborn as English ones – Thomas Wilson's

Arte of Rhetorique, George Puttenham's *Arte of English Poesie*, Abraham Fraunce's *Arcadian Rhetoric* – and the flirtation with words approached Holofernes-like proportions. These handbooks of rhetoric, I suggest, display in common with Shakespeare's early play an uncanny tendency to talk about sexuality in the same breath as they talk about language. *Love's Labour's Lost* deals almost entirely with the corruption of words – not only with words as corruptible by stock characters like the pedant and the braggart, but also with words as *generators* of corruption. That this corruption is fundamentally of a sexual nature is made clear by little Moth's multifaceted reply: the figure of speech is horns.

Often read as an exercise in what Hamlet languidly calls 'words, words, words,'[2] *Love's Labour's Lost* exemplifies early in Shakespeare's career the surprisingly insistent link between rhetorical language and figural sexuality that this book will explore. From Quintilian's explanation of metaphor – which itself draws on metaphors of castration and excretion – to Puttenham's description of metalepsis as a kind of Medean corruption, classical and Renaissance handbooks of rhetoric continually align their subject matter with issues that deal with unregulated bodily desire that Jonathan Goldberg describes as 'incapable of exact definition.'[3] Throughout this book I argue that a discussion of 'sexuality' in the Renaissance, far from being anachronistic, is strongly marked by theoretical ideas about language that were in circulation at the time. The handbooks of rhetoric, whose aim it is to define *linguistic* effects, end up also describing *sexual* effects that offer a surprising insight into the nature and concept of early modern desire. Such an insight forces us to both move back 'our' boundaries of sexuality, and move forward 'their' ideas of language. Above all, it compels us to modify the way in which we now speak of the history of sexuality.[4]

1

Setting the Stage: Metaphor

They that dally nicely with words may quickly make them wanton.
William Shakespeare, *Twelfth Night*, III.i.15

The word *Cove*, or *Cofe*, or *Cuffin* signifies a Man, a Fellow, etc., but differs
something in his property, according as it meets with other words: for a Gentleman is called a *Gentry Cove* or *Cofe*; A good fellow is a *Bene Cofe*; a Churl is
called a *Queer Cuffin*, *Queer* signifies naught and *Cuffin*, as I said before, a Man.
And in *Canting* they term a Justice of Peace, because he punisheth them belike,
by no other name than by *Queer Cuffin* – that is to say, a Churl or a Naughty
man. And so *Ken* signifying a House, they call a Prison a *Queer ken* – that is to
say, an ill house.
Thomas Dekker, *Lantern and Candle-Light*[1]

Questions of precise terminology have been at the heart of debates on
Renaissance sexuality at least since the time of Alan Bray, whose pioneering study, *Homosexuality in Renaissance England*, concludes that
there was no such thing as homosexuality in Renaissance England. His
term of choice, as it has been for most studies of Renaissance sexuality,
is 'sodomy,' indicating forcefully that our current terms for sexualities
did not connote specific identities in the sixteenth century.[2] This difference in terminology has in turn been taken to indicate a conceptual difference between sexual regimes, marking the Renaissance as forever
alienated from the present day, and opening up an area of inquiry in
which 'sodomy' is treated differently from 'homosexuality.' But this
notion of conceptual and practical difference reckons without the rhetorical formulation of sexuality, the differential structuring of words,

both now and then.[3] Even as terminology is accepted as the marker of difference between sexual regimes, insufficient attention is paid to terms themselves.[4]

While Foucault's famous history has allowed scholars of Renaissance sexuality to 'date' their sexual regimes, I will argue that despite the relative terminological newness of 'sexuality,' literary discourses have for a while imparted an understanding of sexuality bound not to historical specificity but rather to rhetorical dexterity.[5] I take as pivotal scepticism of the kind articulated by Jonathan Goldberg in *Sodometries*, where he asserts that the Foucauldian insistence on the sodomite's not being a homosexual 'ignores not only the persistence of the sodomite as a means of defining homosexuality, but also how unstable the modern regime of supposedly discrete identities is.' He adds that 'certain risks – including the risk of dehistoricizing (if we take Foucault's schema to *be* history) – also have ... to be chanced.'[6] The stakes inherent in taking this chance are clear: it will require rethinking the paradigms within which we currently theorize sexuality. I suggest that historical specificity might not be the best basis from which to approach an analysis of sexuality. Rather, we should set our sights, along with Moth, on rhetorical agility, taking our cue from the handbooks of rhetoric in which sexuality is insistently displayed as a rhetorical effect.[7] Such theorizing would entail introducing the idea of rhetoric into the almost exclusively medico-juridical story of Renaissance sexuality, and insisting that we think simultaneously of language and sexuality, of 'scenes that are sexually invested because they are graphically invested,' of sites of inappropriate rhetoric, rather than correct terminology.[8]

This graphic Renaissance investment in sexuality is made clear by Feste in this chapter's epigraph from *Twelfth Night*. The Fool suggests there is a quick way to make words wanton and that this way lies in 'dalliance,' a word denoting both trivial conversation and amorous play, reinforcing Moth's suspicion that words are themselves wanton. Such linguistic and sexual performativity falls under the purview of rhetoric, not only because rhetoric is traditionally concerned with the linguistic arts of persuasion, but also because traditional codifications of these arts of persuasion share Feste's fear of wordy wantonness. Rhetoric is the study of linguistic dalliance – of wanton words – and dabbles in definitional exactitude without ever achieving it. Feste's 'fear' is that words will always be wanton even and especially when seeking controlled purity; this rhetorical wantonness is in opposition to other schemas – historical or philosophical – that might equally seek to establish conceptual and chronological coherence in the realms of dalliance. Paul de Man suggests that 'even when considered at the furthest remove from the platitudes of positivistic historicism, [history] is still the history of an understanding of which the possibility is taken for granted.'[9] Unlike this version of history, the material of rhetoric undermines its own investment in coherence by being linguistically and sexually wanton. For Feste, such linguistic performativity inheres in considerations of sexuality, and vice versa.[10] The history of sexuality for him is always also a history of rhetoricity.

Thomas Dekker echoes this understanding of rhetoric in his conycatching pamphlet from which this chapter's second epigraph is taken, and adds a twist of queerness to the mix of words and wantonness. Dekker makes clear that 'queerness' is a term with a history, but rather than providing us with a new date from which to write our histories of sexuality, this queerness emphasizes a link between itself and language that cannot rely on chronology to eke out its story. Dekker's pamphlet uses the Tower of Babel as a metaphor for the corruption of the world; in keeping with his metaphor, the 'corruption' so excoriated stems from a multiplicity of tongues, with the language of canting coming in for particular flak. At first, Dekker acknowledges that canting – which a play like *The Roaring Girl* presents as an alien and foreign tongue – in fact bears a logical resemblance to 'real' words, mostly Latin. The aim of Dekker's pamphlet is to provide readers with an adumbrated canting 'dictionary,' by which 'small stamps you may judge the greater.'[11] And the chiefest of these 'small stamps' bears a 'queer' imprint. Within the space of three sentences, 'queer' slides from being 'naught' to being an abuse of legality to being an 'ill' house. Queerness thus moves from being a signifier of no thing (Macbeth's 'signifying nothing') to a badge of defiance against the law to a house of ill repute. During this slide, the rolling stone of queerness gathers the moss of illegality, illness, and illegibility, strikingly approximating our 'modern' sense of the term. This early 'modernity' not only pushes us into rethinking our historical approaches to sexuality, but it also emphasizes a rhetorical dexterity inseparable from the idea of queerness. The text that deals with the evolution of language and the increasing diminution of meaning also deals with queerness. In other words, a historical understanding of 'queerness' is inextricable from a rhetorical understanding of language. Far from implying the 'transhistoricity' of language, rhetoric pushes at the boundaries of chronological history and makes us rethink our assumptions about language and sexual identity. As we will see, rhetoric's ability to provide a point of convergence for historically disparate material is a feature that marked Renaissance understandings of the subject. While my emphasis in the following pages will not be on tracing a 'queer' sexuality, I will nonetheless highlight the queerness of a rhetorical process that grafts its inability to define boundaries onto the body's transgressive desires, a rhetorical queerness which, as Lee Edelman suggests, 'can never define an identity; [but] can only ever disturb one.'[12]

Such a lack of fixity, as several scholars including Margreta de Grazia have pointed out, inheres in the very designation of the 'Renaissance,' a term that was 'not in general use before 1800, a good two or three centuries after the time in history that they were devised to designate.'[13] Belated, slippery, and anachronistic terminology marks the Renaissance even as it marks both rhetoric and sexuality. Choosing historically correct descriptive terms in the face of such impropriety perversely allows us to forget about rhetorical perversity. At once announcing a re-birth (of classical sensibilities) and a pre-birth (of so-called 'modern' sensibilities), the 'Renaissance' is never about itself and embodies instead a duality amply suited to the task of studying both rhetoric and sexuality. This duality, which is also a source of infinite variety, has recently been a subject of some speculation, mostly centred on how to explain it away. In her essay 'Renaissance/Early Modern Studies,' Leah Marcus states that 'while the boundaries of the Renaissance tend to push toward earlier and earlier chronological beginnings, early modern tends to creep up on the present. Scholars of the early modern period have devoted relatively little energy to the contestations of points of origin, much more to the issue of defining a terminus.'[14] The problem with such a distinction between defining origins and termini is that far from being two separate endeavours, both derive their energy from the identical impulse of delineating and making clear discrete periods of history. Such a distinction ignores the ambivalence within the term 'Renaissance' and seeks instead to range abroad in order to arrive at a more culturally and historically 'accurate' term. But the Renaissance, rather than referencing a fixed period of time, refers, quite literally, to the concept of a *re*-birth. The rebirth of classical literature and art that it might have sought to represent is made all the more interesting by the fact that this rebirth is also a *reiteration*. The repeatability of the 'Renaissance' ensures not only that it looks both forward and back, but also that it is impossible to fix its range of operations.[15] With its emphasis on reiterability, repetition, and rebirth, the Renaissance nullifies the project of truth-telling and suggests instead the rhetorical activity of arguing *in utramque partem,* on both sides of a question; ideally, we should all always be situated in the 'Renaissance,' whose insistence on a lack of moral and historical fixity provides us with a historical period that seriously challenges the basis of history, pointing to what Hayden White has called 'the poetic *act,*' the linguistic and theoretical basis, of the historical impulse.[16]

Such an approach to 'Renaissance' literature requires an ability to think beyond chronological and verifiable boundaries of textual production, an ability that I suggest should extend also to thinking about sexuality, especially as the term takes its place in the province of rhetorical reiteration. In her introduction to *Bodies That Matter* – the text that arguably made reiteration fashionable – Judith Butler states:

> [The] texts that form the focus of this inquiry come from diverse traditions of writing: Plato's *Timaeus,* Freud's 'On Narcissism,' writings by Jacques Lacan, stories by Willa Cather, Nella Larsen's novella *Passing,* Jennie Livingston's film *Paris Is Burning,* and essays in recent sexual theory and politics, as well as texts in radical democratic theory. The historical range of materials is not meant to suggest that a single heterosexualizing imperative persists in each of these contexts, but only that the instability produced by the effort to fix the site of the sexed body challenges the boundaries of discursive intelligibility in each of these contexts.[17]

Butler's introduction sounds like an uncanny reflection, 405 years later, of the title page to Abraham Fraunce's book: 'The Arcadian Rhetorike: Or The Praecepts of Rhetorike made plaine by examples, Greeke, Latin, English, Italian, French, Spanish, out of Homers Ilias, and Odissea, Virgils Aeglogs, Georgikes, and Aeneis, Sir Philip Sydneis Arcadia, Songs and Sonnets, Torquato T'assoes Goffredo, Aminta, Torrismondo, Salust his Judith, and both his Semaines, Boscan and Garcilassoes Sonets and Aeglogs. By Abraham Fraunce.' This catalogue of texts is pressed into the service of explicating rhetoric despite the fact that its components derive from different genres, languages, time periods, and countries; like Butler's description of her project, it details a relation to history that emphasizes the camaraderie of texts attempting similar *theoretical* enterprises. For both Butler and Fraunce, scholarship lies not in historical accuracy or verifiability, but rather in tracing the history of ideas as it manifests itself over time. This book similarly attempts to trace the history of sexuality by examining both classical and Renaissance rhetorical handbooks; even though they do not use the term 'sexuality,' their treatment of rhetoric continually hovers over the body and its desires, implicating each body of knowledge in the other's theoretical domain. Even as Marcus is sceptical about using the term 'Renaissance' because it suggests 'the possibility of renewed identity and therefore of essential similarity between two poles separated in time,'[18] it is precisely that understanding of cultural – and sexual – fluidity that I want to invoke in my interrogation, not just of rhetoric, but also of Renaissance drama.

In his *Apology for Actors*, Thomas Heywood makes the connection between oratory and acting that is repeated in several Renaissance texts and Tudor humanist curricula. Defending the practice of cross-dressing on the stage, Heywood notes that even the most learned of institutions – the university – allows drama within its portals because it serves a very specific purpose:

> It teacheth audacity to the bashfull grammarian, beeing newly admitted into the private colledge, and, after matriculated and entered as a member of the University, and makes him a bold sophister, to argue pro et contra to compose his syllogysmes, cathegoricke, or hypotheticke (simple or compound), to reason and frame a sufficient argument to prove his questions, or to defend any axioma, to distinguish of any dilemma, and be able to moderate in any argumentation whatsoever. (28–9)

The drama is at once the teacher and beneficiary of rhetoric. The shy scholar expands his repertoire with exposure to dramatic boldness and drama benefits from the scholar's ability to 'moderate in any argumentation whatsoever.' The necessity for the good actor to also be a good rhetor (and vice versa) is a theme Heywood reiterates with reference to gesture, facial expression, etc. In this passage, he uses rhetoric to come to the defence of drama because dramatic cross-dressing is an issue that needs to be *interpreted* by someone with knowledge of 'syllogysmes [and] cathegoricke[s].' Rhetoric, in other words, is necessary to lay and justify the very foundations of the theatre. And not just any foundation; in this text, that groundwork relates specifically to what the antitheatricalists would characterize as sexual perversion.

Even as Heywood uses the necessary connection between drama and rhetoric as an argument in favour of the theatre, however, several other Renaissance scholars make the same connection but arrive at opposite conclusions (itself a rhetorical feat). In his meditation on 'The

Causes of the Corruption of the Arts' (1531), Spanish humanist Juan Luis Vives notes that among the many reasons for the decline of oratory in the Roman empire is the fact that

> Men brought into the forum things that would have been more suitable for the stage. Thus, the nature of public speaking was profoundly changed; from being healthy, sober, and severe, it became extravagant and voluptuous, as if, having taken off its manly clothes, it had put on a woman's. The people themselves gathered in the forum and the courts not, as before, in order to consider what was transpiring and whether it was credible or not ... but as if they were going to be entertained in the theater.[19]

In this version of events, the theatre is presented as the antithesis of responsible ('manly') rhetoric, so much so that the stage becomes the repository of all that rhetoric *should not be*. The insistence on conflating the theatre with 'fallen' sexuality is a trend I will discuss later in this chapter; for now, suffice it to say that Vives is responding sharply to the slide from the responsible to the frivolous as rhetoric begins to resemble drama. At the other 'end' of the Renaissance, Margaret Cavendish has something similar to say about the theatre. In her *Blazing World* (1666), the Duchess of Newcastle engages in a conversation about plays with the Emperor and Empress of the Blazing World:

> The Empress asked, are those good plays that are made so methodically and artificially? The Duchess answered, they were good according to the judgement of the age, or mode of the nation, but not according to her judgement; for truly, said she, in my opinion, their plays will prove a nursery of whining lovers, and not an academy or school for wise, witty, noble, and well-behaved men. But I, replied the Emperor, desire such a theatre as may make wise men; and will have such descriptions as are natural, not artificial. If Your Majesty be of that opinion, said the Duchess's soul, then my plays may be acted in your Blazing World, when they cannot be acted in the Blinking World of Wit ... (220)

In keeping with the generic imperative of Utopian literature, *The Blazing World* tries to present an ideal situation in stark contrast to the situation of the 'real' world, here described as the 'Blinking World of Wit.' In this latter world, the theatre explicitly does *not* cater to the production of wise men and, by extension, is not produced by wise men either. This lack of 'wisdom' parallels the lack of 'credibility' in Vives's description of the Roman Empire, and once again expresses an anxiety that theatre is the enemy, rather than the friend, of nobility. The Duchess of Newcastle swears from the depths of her soul that as it exists, the theatre (which excludes her productions) is an effeminate 'nursery' rather than a manly 'academy.' This nursery produces the 'whining lovers' of *Love's Labour's Lost* rather than 'noble men,' abusing scholarship even as it remains a site of learning. Dramatic abuse tellingly slips, in the Emperor's words, into an abuse against 'nature' itself, inserting artifice into what should have been a purely natural space. The threat of drama quickly snowballs into a crime against Nature, testifying both to the perceived impact of the theatre, and to the vehemence of the response it engendered, a vehemence that, as we shall see, becomes vituperative in the antitheatrical tracts. The inevitable duality of a form at once popular and excoriated has been discussed at some length by Wayne Rebhorn, who notes that 'the Roman rejection of bad rhetoric as theater continue[d] in the Middle Ages ... In the Renaissance such statements proliferate[d], just as the theater [was] undergo[ing] an enormous development.'[20] This proliferation of drama, paralleled by a proliferation of interest in rhetoric books, both originated in, and is reflected by, the Tudor curriculum, in which, as Kent Cartwright observes, 'students studied and performed plays to a degree difficult to explain.'[21]

The difficulty of explaining the popularity of rhetoric and drama in Renaissance England is a difficulty that inheres in the idea of performance itself and in the difficulty of pinning down the limits of performance. This performative mobility parallels Renaissance reiterability and rhetorical instability to form the focus of this book. In the rhetorical handbooks, the desire for language exists simultaneously as the desire *of* language; the desire to shape language into a usable tool has to reckon with the startling fact that language has a desire of its own that is not always compliant. Linguistic desire becomes recognizable only as an entity that does not dare speak its name, not because it does not have one, but precisely because it has one too many. This introductory chapter will look at the first of those names – itself double – in order to outline how and why the study of rhetoric carries over into a study of the body and its desires.

The Meta Four: Quintilian, Cicero, Wilson, Puttenham

The process of carrying over is (literally and etymologically) carried out by metaphor, which transports meaning beyond the grammatically and historically delineated limit of language.[22] Most handbooks of rhetoric give pride of place to metaphor as the 'most beautiful of tropes,' and as the basis for understanding the system of tropes in its entirety.[23] I will focus on the definition of metaphor in four texts – two classical, and two English – in an attempt to bring together various strands in circulation during the sixteenth century in England.

In his *Institutio Oratoria* which, along with Cicero's *De Oratore* and Erasmus's *De Copia Verborum ac Rerum*, formed the classical core curriculum of the English grammar school, Quintilian describes metaphor as being

> ... the commonest and most beautiful of tropes ... For if it be correctly and appropriately applied it is quite impossible for its effect to be commonplace, mean or unpleasing. It adds to the copiousness of language by the interchange of words and by borrowing, and finally succeeds in the supremely difficult task of providing a name for everything. A noun or a verb is transferred from the place to which it properly belongs to another where there is either no *literal* term or the *transferred* is better than the *literal*. We do this either because it is necessary or to make our meaning clearer or, as I have already said, to produce a decorative effect. When it secures none of these results, our metaphor will be out of place. (VIII.vi.4–7)

This definition of metaphor states that it is the primary agent of rhetoric and embodies the beauty of tropological language. This beauty can only be achieved, however, if metaphor is used with *propriety*. Like a banquet at which one is strictly forbidden either to eat the wrong things or indulge excessively in the good ones, metaphor too needs to be used sparingly in order to obtain the maximum effect. But if 'propriety' is to be the hallmark of metaphor, then surely metaphor cannot properly continue to be a trope since tropological language is by definition something that 'turns' the sense of 'proper' language. The stress on propriety, which Quintilian sees as the *only* means by which metaphor can continue to function in a pleasing manner, is already recognized as lost in its definition. Metaphor as trope attempts to erase its own tropological nature by falling back on the discourse of propriety, but there is no such thing, we are forced to conclude, as a *proper* metaphor. Anticipating such a conclusion, Quintilian states that 'propriety is [itself] capable of more than one interpretation. In its primary sense it means calling things by their right names, and is consequently sometimes to be *avoided*, for our language must not be obscene, unseemly or mean' (VIII.i.2, emphasis mine). The primary role of metaphor, which is to act properly, cannot follow the primary sense of propriety, because that would mean acting improperly. Quintilian seizes on impropriety as the hallmark of the proper and states that metaphor can be pressed into service precisely to *avoid* propriety, which in this sense only heralds obscenity. However, the emphasis on the appropriateness (and hence the beauty) of metaphor is everywhere undermined by its function of transference, which if anything, gives obscenity free reign rather than reining it in. If Quintilian hopes to avoid the corruptions of metaphor and only retain its beauty, then he has either to disavow the boundary-breaking capacity that defines metaphor, or else give up altogether on the desire to govern metaphor 'properly.'

Interestingly, he does neither, but skilfully distances himself from the category of textual corruption by seeking comfort instead in the terminology of precision. The *Institutio* starts out by addressing the niceties of legal situations and in Book VIII, it treats figurative language in the manner of a legal document by *listing* its components and *classifying* them according to well-defined principles of division.[24] The desire to appropriate rhetoric as a practical art prompts an attempt to fix the meaning of tropes, but this proves to be more difficult than the project envisages. The emphasis on near-scientific rigour tries both to provide a verifiable basis for ordering a slippery language and to stem the sliding tendencies of *what* is being described: namely, ornaments of speech. The doubleness that metaphor ensures is reduced to singularity by its 'proper' and scientific application. Quintilian sternly prescribes that 'metaphor should always either occupy a place already vacant, or if it fills the room of something else, should be more impressive [and less obscene?] that that which it displaces' (VIII.6.18). As Paul Ricoeur points out, this censure castigates metaphor both for being a name that belongs elsewhere *and* for taking the place of the word that properly 'belongs.'[25] This double alienation is doubly suspect because it is seen as only one step in a series of infinite regressions in which language, or poetry, to follow Plato, is at an ever-increasing remove from the ideal Form.

Quintilian is not alone among classical rhetoricians in his quest for perfect metaphoric purity. The pseudo-Ciceronian *Ad Herennium* begins with an address to the book's recipient by the author, who notes that there are 'good grounds in wishing to learn rhetoric, for it is true that copiousness and facility in expression bear abundant fruit, if controlled by *proper* knowledge and a strict discipline of the mind' (I.1, emphasis mine).[26] The author, however, makes it abundantly clear that most of his time is spent in the active pursuit of philosophy, and that writing a rhetorical handbook reflects a deviation from his normal ways. As though to exemplify his distaste for the 'merely' ornamental, he begins by dealing with 'forensic cases' of language and the first mention of metaphor is as a 'subtype of legal issue.'

When he defines it as a trope, the author continues to cling to the notion of 'strict discipline': metaphor 'occurs when a word applying to one thing is transferred to another, because the similarity seems to justify this transference ... They say that a metaphor ought to be restrained, so as to be a transition with good reason to a kindred thing, and not seem an indiscriminate, reckless, and precipitate leap to an unlike thing' (IV.xxxiv.46). The piling high of metaphoric adjectives ('indiscriminate, reckless, precipitate') and the deflection of responsibility ('they say') are in stark contrast to the sober language that precedes this section of the text. The difference between 'being' and 'seeming' is aligned, on the one hand, with the desirable properties of metaphor ('a transition with good reason'), and on the other, with the fear that it involves an 'indiscriminate and reckless ... leap' into the unknown. Metaphor, which should, properly speaking, *be* all that is good and beautiful and pure, only *seems* to be so; the *Ad Herennium* demonstrates the corrupting effect of metaphor even as it lays down the law for its governance. The distinction between philosophy and rhetoric that the author starts out with comes to unpleasant life when his text loses the precision of philosophical (and legal) rigour to wallow in the depths of rhetorical insecurity. The desire for truth is tainted by a love of ornament and this love marks the futility of ever trying to distinguish the one from the other.

These classical lessons of rhetorical excess and the desire for containment were handed down to pupils in medieval and then Renaissance England. Medieval rhetoric was broadly divided into four schools – Aristotelian, Ciceronian, Grammatical, and Sophistic. Of these, the most important classical author was Cicero, whose youthful *De Inventione* (written when he was nineteen) and the more complete, pseudo-Ciceronian *Rhetorica ad Herennium*, were the texts most commonly admired, by both other writers and school curricula; another member of the Ciceronian school to acquire some standing was Quintilian. This medieval investment in the Ciceronian rather than the Aristotelian school of rhetoric, in the figurative rather than the philosophical mode of argumentation and ornamentation, was passed down to Renaissance England where rhetoricians started writing their own handbooks on the subject. Quintilian and Cicero were the acknowledged masters of rhetoric in the English grammar school: Ben Jonson remarked to Drummond that a thorough knowledge of Quintilian was all a poet needed in order to practise his craft.[27] Indeed, the sixteenth century's appropriation of and investment in rhetoric is one of the reasons the 'Renaissance' refers to a rebirth of the classical age, even as this rebirth and the direction it took would not have been possible without classical rhetoric's passage through the Middle Ages.[28]

So insistent is the Renaissance investment in rhetoric, however, that one critic claims a falling-off from the brilliant treatment of the subject in 1585 after the publication of Puttenham's *Arte of English Poesie*.[29] Whether or not the 'death of rhetoric' (like the 'birth of sexuality') can be traced in so precise a manner, most critics agree that the emphasis placed on rhetorical style during the Renaissance in England remains unparalleled.[30] Starting with Leonard Cox's *The Arte or Crafte of Rhetoryke* in 1529 and continuing to Puttenham's *Arte* in 1585, England saw the publication of several original handbooks and the translation of many continental and classical handbooks of rhetoric. Not only was there an overwhelming interest in rhetorical handbooks, but the study of rhetoric itself shifted from questions of 'content' to matters of 'style.' For Aristotle, *inventio*, the amassing of material, formed the largest part of his *Rhetoric*, while *elocutio* was only an adjunct to this high purpose. For Puttenham, on the other hand, the section 'On Ornament' is more than twice as long as the first two sections ('Of Poets and Poesie' and 'Of Proportion') put together; for authors in the next century, Francis Bacon among them,[31] this stylistic emphasis marked an unnatural and degenerate prioritizing of *verba* over *res*.[32] In the sixteenth century, however, the period often characterized as the 'era of imitation,' there was a growing awareness, not only of translation, but also of differences between and within languages, and the difference those differences make.[33] This consciousness about the translinguistic vicissitudes of rhetoric emerged as a result of increased emphasis on the *trans*, the carrying over of meaning that language enacts and that metaphor expresses in its Latin term of *translatio*. A consciousness about rhetoric, in other words, started also to seep into studies on the subject.

In England, this consciousness was encoded even at the formal level of rhetorical dissemination where the grammar schools followed Roger Ascham's method of teaching Latin by adapting the mode of the *double* translation.[34] This method involved translating a passage from Latin into English and then back into Latin in order to closely approximate the words and manner of the original. The gap between two languages implied in an exercise of translation was fundamental to grammar school teaching of rhetoric: Ascham's method tries to cover up this gap and stress the 'sameness' of two languages, but what his system really points to is the fact that 'purity' will never be free of *translatio*, or metaphor.

Another master seems to have taught a similar lesson. In his *De Copia Verborum ac Rerum*, Erasmus succumbs to the sheer copiousness of language; early on in the book he states: 'I think it is clear that copia is twofold' (15). While discussing the two parts of which *copia* consists (enlarging words and expanding ideas), he notes that 'these can be observed anywhere, so closely combined that you cannot tell them apart at all easily, so much does one serve the other' (16). The copiousness of language makes it impossible to extract meaning based on definable distinctions; Erasmus exemplifies this point in a section on 'Practice' in which he sets 'an experiment [to] try how far it is possible to have [a phrase] turn like Proteus into several forms' (38). He then goes on to render a simple Latin sentence – 'Tuae literae me magnopere delectarunt' (Your letter has delighted me very much) – into over a hundred different versions. In other words, one sentence can be variously *translated*, in Ascham's sense of the word. So much for fixity. So much for purity. So much for clarity. The twin properties of *copia*, at once copying and cornucopia, fit in well with the strain of doubleness and deceit that metaphor in general is said to enact. The title of Erasmus's work is often (questionably) rendered *De duplici copia verborum ac rerum*, 'On the *twofold* copiousness of words and subject matter,' pointing to the layering of possibilities that rhetoric enacts and the essential duplicity that metaphor engenders.[35]

In *The Arte of Rhetorique* (1560), Thomas Wilson presents his own ideas about copiousness in a narrative based on the 'first' appearance of tropes: '[w]hen learned and wisemen gan first to inlarge their tongue, and sought with great utterance of speech to commende causes: They founde full oft much want of words to set out their meaning. And therfore remembring thinges of like nature unto those wherof they speake: They used such words to expresse their mynde, as were most like unto each other' (170). The noble First Cause of tropes – to enable more copious verbal expression – is then followed by a definition of (among other things) metaphor, which is said to be 'an alteration of a worde, from the proper and naturall meaning, to that which is not proper, and yet agreeth thereunto by some likenesse, that appereth to be in it' (172). The escape clause, the 'and yet,' is a vital phrase for Wilson's definition because it enables impropriety to be naturalized under the rubric of rigorous academic endeavour. Even though both Wilson and Quintilian recognize the impropriety of the transfer that metaphor enacts ('from the proper and naturall meaning to that which is not proper'), propriety – the insistence that the 'wisemen' were right – still seems to be the only mode in which they can defend their use of metaphor in the first place.

There are two interesting moments at the beginning of Wilson's *Arte* that seem crucial to a reading of the text. The first, which serves as the preface to the text, sketches under the heading 'Eloqvence First Giuen by God, and After Lost by Man, and Last Repayred by God Againe,' the Fall of Man and all the woe that results therefrom, before proceeding to talk about rhetoric and eloquence as a means of *restoring* a lost perfection:

> And therefore (whereas through the wicked suggestion of our ghostly enemie, the ioyfull fruition of Gods glorie was altogether lost:) ... And therefore, whereas man through reason might have vsed order: man through folie fell into errour. *And thus for lacke of skill*, and for want of grace euill so preuailed, that the devil was most esteemed, and God either almost unknowne among them all ... God still tendering his own workmanshippe, stirring vp his faithfull and elect ... gaue his appointed ministers knowledge both to see the natures of man, *and also graunted them the gift of vtterance, that they might with ease win folke at their will* ... and such is the power of Eloquence and reason, that most men are forced, even to yeeld in that which most standeth against their will ... and among the eloquent, of all the most eloquent: him thinke I among all men, not onely to be taken for a singular man, but rather to be computed for halfe a God. (Preface, emphasis mine)

The Fall, this narrative seems to suggest, was caused because Man was rhetorically ill-equipped to face the onslaught of 'wicked suggestion' mounted by Satan. Even though the devil's role is contained within parentheses, his power of suggestion is seen as being powerful enough to ruin God's work. The postlapsarian *return* of this power, in the form of God's gifts to his ministers, is then hailed as the power of blessed utterance (as opposed to 'wicked suggestion') that will not only redeem Man from his fallen state, but also lift him (almost fully) back to the status of being 'halfe a God.' Man, now fully equipped with rhetorical ability, is a viable opponent to the rhetorically skilled devil. Rhetoric, in this instance, both causes the Fall by its satanic manipulation, *and* keeps subsequent evil at bay by its divine manifestation.

The 'gloz[ing]' tongue of the devil,[36] seen as the origin of human disrepute, is an organ that is peculiarly linked to rhetoric, and this association has always fascinated 'historians' of the Fall. In Book IX of *Paradise Lost*, Milton provides us with a more concrete image of what Wilson's scene of 'wicked suggestion' might have looked like:

> The Tempter, but with show of Zeal and Love
> To Man, and indignation at his wrong,
> New parts puts on, and as to passion mov'd,
> Fluctuates disturb'd, yet comely, and in act
> Rais'd, as of some great matter to begin.
> *As when of old some Orator renown'd*
> *In Athens or free Rome, where Eloquence*
> *Flourish'd*, since mute, to some great cause addrest,
> Stood in himself collected, while each part,
> Motion, *each act won audience ere the tongue,*
> *Sometimes in heighth began*, as no delay
> Of Preface brooking through his Zeal of Right.
> So standing, moving, or to heighth upgrown
> The Tempter all impassion'd thus began.   (IX.665–78, emphasis mine)

Satan, explicitly connected to Greek and Roman orators (or rhetors), uses his power of suggestion by mustering every rhetorical trick of the trade. He pauses for just the right length of time, paints a suitably sincere expression on his face, clears his throat, and then begins his persuasive pitch. The performance, to say the least, is dramatic. And this is the 'skill,' Wilson suggests, that is responsible for the Fall.

The second passage in Wilson's text that I want to point to is the epistle dedicatory to Lord John Dudley, which extols the *practical* power of rhetoric by narrating the anecdote of how King Pirrhus was in the habit of sending the orator Cineas to conquer by means of his eloquent tongue towns that were proving particularly hard to win by the sword. The *use* of rhetoric that had remained at the level of abstraction in Wilson's first narrative is here given a concrete function: rhetoric wins wars, and is therefore good.

If there is a causal link between (fallen) humankind and rhetoric, then that link both causes the Fall *and* redeems Man after the fact. Rhetoric both helps the devil to succeed *and* helps the king win his war. As Terence Cave points out, St Augustine, in a similarly structured approach to rhetoric, views the 'diseases of fallen language – plurality, ambiguity, obscurity – [as] themselves an antidote for the "sickness of human wills."'[37] The metaleptic confusion of cause and effect is the hallmark of a fallen rhetoric. Although it can be extolled as that which separates not only 'man' from beast, but also the good man from the bad, there is no escaping the fact that these distinctions are themselves necessitated by the use of rhetoric. The powerful effect of persuasion, notably seen in the instance of Cineas, may conquer both towns and the crippling effects of sin, but this victory is (always) only a Pyrrhic one. Even though Wilson is well aware of the rhetorical corruption he is disseminating, he nonetheless considers such dissemination a necessary evil.

In *The Arte of English Poesie* (1585), George Puttenham expresses a similar fascination with 'defect' when he writes that 'figurative speech is a noveltie of language evidently (and yet not absurdly) estranged from the ordinarie habite and manner of our dayly talke and writing ... giving [our speech] ornament or efficacie by many maner of alterations in shape ... sometime *by defect*, sometime *by disorder*, or *mutatio* ...' (159, emphasis mine). The beauty of language demands the price of (dis)figuration, and unlike the other rhetoricians, Puttenham is almost always willing to pay it. Even his enthusiasm, however, is tempered by the knowledge that rhetoric is the means that poetry uses to draw itself 'from plainnesse and simplicitie to a certaine doublenesse' (154).

Before giving us his definition of metaphor, Puttenham introduces us to the category of 'Sensible Figures':

> The eare hauing receiued his due satisfaction by the auricular figures, now must the minde also be serued, with his naturall delight by figures sensible such as by alteration of intendmentes affect the courage, and geue a good liking to the conceit. And first, single words haue their sence and vnderstanding altered and figured many wayes, to wit, by transport, abuse, crosse-naming, new naming, change of name. *This will seeme very darke to you, vnlesse it be otherwise explaned more particularly* ... (178, emphasis mine)

The material that introduces metaphor has to itself resort to a metaphorical explanation of its status. Far from being able to isolate the metaphoric 'noveltie' of language, Puttenham seems unable to write clearly without the help of these estranged cousins of clarity. Not only is Puttenham's explanation of figurative language charged with figurality, but he also implies that different parts of the body derive 'satisfaction' from different kinds of tropes: the mind must be 'served' by figural pleasure providers in order to satisfy its 'naturall delight.'[38]

Although (or perhaps because) metaphor is recognized as the dominant trope in relation to both language and the body, its power is never viewed as benign or even desirable. In his definition of metaphor, Puttenham characterizes its action as the '*wresting* of a single word from his owne right signification, to another not so naturall ...' (178, emphasis mine). The violence that metaphor wreaks on a natural language (thereby making it 'not so naturall') is in direct conflict with the 'beauty' that Quintilian associates with the trope. The eternal conflict between good and evil is played out on a metaphoric battlefield, and what is 'lost' in the encounter is precisely the precision that metaphor did not possess even to begin with.

The tendency to deviate from the straight and narrow is what highlights the role of metaphor (and of rhetoric in general) as the trope of textual corruption. In *Allegories of Reading*, Paul de Man states that 'rhetoric is a *text* in that it allows for two incompatible, mutually self-destructive points of view, and therefore puts an insurmountable obstacle in the way of any reading or understanding.'[39] To assume that metaphor is identifiable and controllable is to assume, as Puttenham does, that there is a realm of simplicity that exists *just outside* the metaphoric one. If acted upon, this assumption will only ignore the lessons that the handbooks, despite themselves, teach us.

Bawdy Bodies

While making the transition from the 'figures geometrical' of Book II to the 'Ornament' of Book III, Puttenham, like Quintilian and the author of the *Ad Herennium* before him, falls into confusion. In the anecdote about Polemon and Philino with which Book II concludes, Puttenham emphasises what will later become the subject of the book on 'Ornament,' interpretation.[40] Book III begins its introduction to tropes by justifying their necessity:

As no doubt the good proportion of any thing doth greatly adorne and

commend it and right so our late remembred proportions doe to our vulgar Poesie: so is there yet requisite to the perfection of this arte, another
maner of exornation, which resteth in the fashioning of our makers language and stile, to such purpose as it may delight and allure as well the
mynde as the eare of the hearers with a certaine noveltie and strange
maner of conveyance, disguising it no litle from the ordinary and accus-
tomed: neverthelesse making it nothing the more unseemely or misbe-
comming, but rather decenter and more agreable to any civill eare and
understanding. And as we see in these great Madames of honour, be they
for personage or otherwise never so comely and bewtifull, yet if they
want their courtly habillements or at leastwise such other apparell as cus-
tome and civilitie have ordained to cover their naked bodies, would be
halfe ashamed or greatly out of countenance to be seen in that sort, and
perchance do then thinke themselves more amiable in every mans eye,
when they be in their richest attire, suppose of silkes or tyffewes & costly
embroideries, then when they go in cloth or in any other plaine and simple apparell. Even so cannot our vulgar Poesie shew it selfe either gallant
or gorgious, if any lymme be left naked and bare and not clad in his
kindly clothes and colours ... (137)

The book 'On Ornament' acknowledges that proportion is not all, that
in order for poetry to be 'bewtifull,' it must move away from geometrical precision and acquire some beautiful clothes. The precise language
that Book II attempted to both embody and teach is abandoned here in
favour, unabashedly, of ornament. Even though Puttenham typically
equates rhetorical ornament with clothes covering a naked body, however, he clings to the notion of a (precise) body *beneath* the clothes, one
that will be left 'naked and bare' for lack of a gay exterior. Not unlike
certain critics in our own day, and in keeping with his earlier account
of poetry's movement from 'simplicitee' to 'doublenesse,' Puttenham
maintains the separation of 'true' inside and 'false' outside; even
though the outside is seen as necessary to the production of good
poetry, it is nonetheless viewed as something extraneous, an addition
that enhances, but does not posit, the body. The dichotomy of outside
and inside is meant to apply both to language and clothes: both are
assumed to have a core body that exists in its truest form without any
embellishment.

This opposition, what Paul de Man calls 'a binary polarity of classical banality in the history of metaphysics,'[41] is the same one that marks
Wilson's distinction between pre- and post-lapsarian rhetoric, and

with the same results. If there is a body *beneath* the clothes that is the repository of all that is good and true, then why do the handbooks spend so much time describing the clothes that *cover* this body? Why does the body need to be covered in the first place? If truth resides in placing the body beyond the effects of language, then why describe in detail the realm from which truth is ostensibly absent? I suggest that tropological language clothes, and therefore makes physical, a body that does not signify outside the realm of rhetorical interpellation. The existence of a body beneath the clothes, in other words, is a purely *hypothetical* (or metaphorical) assertion, conceived in order to provide a point of contrast to 'mere' ornament; the body makes ornament meaningful and real. Even as the causal link between the body and its cover is cast in the mode of truth and its vehicle, the handbooks nonetheless underscore the *primary* importance of ornament in bringing the body into focus; the body is the *projection* of ornament, rather than the other way round.[42]

But why the body? Why clothes? Why bright colours and gorgeous cuts? As we will see in the case of Quintilian, this is because the metaphor of the body and its garments is the one most *suited* to a description of tropological language. For Thomas Wilson, 'every translation is commonly, and for the most part referred to the senses of the bodie' (171). If metaphor is the 'most beautiful' of tropes, then that beauty is most persuasively explained by reference to a beautiful body. As with a beautiful language whose propriety can easily be perverted, however, the fear is that a beautiful body too can easily be transformed into a site of rank corruption. And so even as rhetoricians draw extensively on physical beauty and extol the magnificence of the human body, they also guard against the disease and corruption they fear is lurking in every fleshly and sartorial fold.

To Quintilian, for instance, tropes in general are like the 'tasteful and magnificent dress, [which] as the Greek poet tells us, lends added dignity to its wearer: but effeminate and luxurious apparel fails to adorn the body and merely reveals the foulness of the mind' (*Institutio Oratoria*, VIII.Pr.27). In addition to recording his own textual corruption of the Greek, Quintilian also introduces a new relation here, between opulent apparel and a corrupt mind. He is quick to note that not all magnificent dress is indicative of a foul mind; rather, only certain kinds of 'effeminate and luxurious apparel' point to mental corruption. The distinction between a proudly masculine rhetoric and a degenerate feminine one lines up with the distinction between Attic and

Asiatic rhetoric that fuelled a major rhetorical debate during Cicero's day. Attic rhetoric was meant to be plain and lucid. Asiatic rhetoric, on the other hand, was copious, ornamental, verbose, flowery, lingering, and more liable to linguistic corruption.[43]

According to Quintilian, one way of protecting against this 'foulness of mind' is by avoiding the use of 'obscene' metaphors. His examples of such obscenity are drawn from Cicero: 'The state was gelded by the death of Africanus,' and 'Glaucia, the excrement of the senate-house' (VIII.vi.16).[44] As the two examples indicate, the 'bad' metaphors deal either with castration or with shit, and the obscenity clearly refers to bodily functions and organs that are better off hidden than exposed, better off adorned than left bare. The images of a dismembered body and an excreting anus are interesting choices for what metaphor must avoid, since it is precisely their metaphoricity that is being responded to in the first place. Castration (that, too, of the state) as a loss of power and excrement as a loss of propriety are already metaphorical readings and renditions of what appear to be plain and simple anatomical details. Quintilian's desire to keep metaphor free from obscenity fails to read the metaphoric nature of obscenity itself. The dismembered body and excreting anus are anxiogenic, not only because they are 'obscene' organs, but also because they threaten the *integrity* of the body. They serve as the best examples of *translatio* because they carry over things that should, properly speaking, be fixed to and contained within the body. If the body is to be aligned with the truth, then dissecting it points to a loss of control that undermines Quintilian's epistemological project.[45] The body has to be both clothed and whole in order for metaphor to prevail, even as metaphor's action ensures that the body is both bare and fragmented.

This bare body gives rise to an interesting and seemingly impenetrable dilemma: bareness is to be avoided because it threatens both bodily and linguistic integrity, but bareness is also to be embraced because it provides the raw material for rhetorical embellishment. If bareness is to be both avoided and embraced, then where does that leave us as practitioners of rhetoric and students of Quintilian's text? If the body is denounced as being obscene, then how can it also house the 'beautiful' metaphor, which is allegedly the very antithesis of obscenity?

To be fair to Quintilian, he clearly (and consistently) warns against the use, not of metaphors to *hide* obscenity, but rather of obscene metaphors themselves. Nonetheless, the distinction between these categories is undermined by their very terms. He states, on the one hand, that metaphor is like a beautiful suit of clothes on a bare body, and on the other, that the bare body is too obscene for metaphor to interact with. The force of his own logic demands a close connection between metaphor and obscenity if rhetoric is to transform a bare language, but equally, the obscenity of that transformation does not go unnoticed. The obscenity of the body lies in the fact that it is itself subject to metaphoricity, or translation. Metaphor's attempt to ground itself in the body is a lost cause since the body is never able to stay whole. The persistent desire to ascribe a wholesome metaphor to a healthy body and the persistent *failure* of that desire is what makes the metaphoric endeavour obscene. Once metaphor is compared to a body, then nothing can stop the process of corruption from taking its inevitable toll; the option, which is to compare metaphor to something else, is not one that either Quintilian or his cohorts exercise since nothing else comes close to expressing the kind of rhetorical corruption that metaphor enacts. The handbooks seem to want both to describe corruption, and to keep it clean, but the impossibility of this project sees them returning, time and again, to the body as the most suitable dress for rhetoric, and vice versa.[46]

At some points more than others, Quintilian seems aware of the implications of his rhetorical project and the futility of trying to 'rescue' it from obscenity. In Book VIII, he states that 'an obscene meaning may be extracted from words which are as far removed from indecency as possible ... but if this point of view be accepted, *it will be risky to say anything at all*' (VIII.iii.48, emphasis mine).[47] The ubiquity of obscenity, the inherently obscene desire of language to approximate reality, is seen as a point of view that Quintilian cannot afford to accept if he is to continue classifying and legitimizing rhetoric. The transfer that metaphor is supposed to enact cannot be all beautiful if both its terms are capable of being misconstrued. But such clarity is only momentary (as is the case with all texts) and forgotten soon enough as Quintilian continues, with the horror of castration and shit in his mind, to say that 'ornament must, as I have already said, be bold, manly and chaste, free from all effeminate smoothness and the false hues derived from artificial dyes, and must glow with health and vigour' (VIII.iii.6).

While Quintilian's 'manly' metaphor would have a penis, it would (unfortunately) have to be hidden in a gunny sack. Unlike Puttenham, who demands that his ornaments be gorgeous, Quintilian wants to get rid of false colours and prides himself on the ability to wear coarse, homespun material. Even as he wants ornament, he wants it specifically to be *non-ornamental* and free of 'effeminacy.' A corrupt language is not only figured bodily, but it is also described in terms of textual deviancy and sexual corruption, opposed at every point by a rough simplicity that a properly tropological language would 'truly' aspire toward (the 'russet yeas and honest kersey noes' of *Love's Labour's Lost*). This is a far cry from acknowledging the inherent sinfulness of language, but the distance between the two statements is a necessary one since it enacts precisely the gap that metaphor both creates by transferring one word in order to explain another, and widens by pointing to the inadequacy of two words, even more than one, to approximate a 'truth' to which language has limited access.

The Sexual Text

As my opening epigraph from *Twelfth Night* makes clear, dallying with words can often make them wanton. This consequence is interesting not least because playing with language could easily result in a host of other effects: lack of clarity, long-windedness, circumlocution, and hyperbole, to name a few. The result of wantonness seems inevitable, however, in a play dealing with sexual turbulence, disguise, and disavowed desire. As with Puttenham's body, this wantonness of words results both from an operation conducted *on* language, and by an operation *of* language. The more 'nicely' or slowly, or delicately, or deliberately, one toys with words, the more quickly and steamily one makes them wanton, bringing out what is inherent to the functioning of language itself. Joel Fineman makes exactly this point when he notes that 'it is Shakespeare's historical achievement, in literature, to have derived desire from the "wantonness" of words, and to have done so in a way that precludes the possibility of putting things the other way around, i.e., as though the erotic charge of language might be derived from the experience of desire.'[48] The 'historical experience' that links desire and language is routed by Fineman specifically through literature; the 'history of sexuality' is thus redirected along a literary line, in which what we now term sexuality is shown to have a longer and more complex 'history,' a history specifically linked to an understanding of rhetoric.

Such an understanding, I argue, is to be found in the handbooks of rhetoric themselves, where rhetoric's pervasiveness and excessiveness is refracted by a desire that is the surest marker of its excess. Rather than being the external thing that a prolific language *refers* to, however, desire is more the ungraspable sediment that accumulates as a *result* of this multiplicity. Like metaphor, the desiring body, the body that always wants more, is a tropological function of language that in turn figures language's general tendency to perversion. The fertile associations of Erasmus's *copia*, Wilson and Puttenham's equation of 'arte' and cosmetics, Quintilian's 'manly' metaphors, the pseudo-Cicero's spirited (and futile) resistance to obscenity, are all instances from texts that have nothing whatsoever to do *with* the body, or even with sexual desire. They are all moments from rhetorical handbooks during which rhetoric comes face to face with the entity that it has created, and which it has to disavow in an attempt to maintain a semblance of 'purity.' During this journey, desire comes to stand in as the figure for a perverse figurality and as the trope emblematizing tropological language.[49] The corruptions of language are expressed as corruptions of the flesh, and the handbooks actively advocate the use of metaphor to transfer anxiety about rhetorical leakage onto a leaky body whose holes it can clearly not stop up.[50] To follow Thomas Wilson's advice on how to apply metaphor: '[f]irst ... alter a word from that which is in the mind, to that which is in the bodie' (173). In rhetoric, desire is not only *like* metaphor, it is also itself always metaphorical.

This transformative potential of metaphor and desire is encapsulated in the one word that crucially defines the activities of both terms: play. No wonder then that the potential subversion of play in general and plays in particular was picked up by enemies of the theatre in their fulminations against the stage. Writing his *Histrio-Mastix* in 1633, William Prynne laments that in the last two years, forty thousand play books have been printed, and have sold more than the stateliest volumes of choicest sermons; what else, he shrugs, can one expect from 'a Play-adoring Age' (306)? Even though Prynne is writing after both Marlowe and Shakespeare are dead, his comment, true enough as it was of the 1630s, was if anything, even more applicable to the decades immediately preceding it. If we take Prynne's comment as representative of the critics of play, then a few familiar features immediately stand out. Plays are prolific, ungodly, and idolatrous. These ideas, deriving originally from the Platonic idea that both poetry and eloquence are forms of witchcraft (or *goeteia*), defined the Renaissance resistance to play.[51] In *The Schoole of Abuse* (1579), Stephen Gosson attacks drama for being 'the cuppes of Circe, that turn reasonable creatures into brute beastes' (10); and Philip Stubbes, in his *Anatomy of the Abuses in England* (the nineteenth-century edition added 'in Shakespeare's Youth' to the title), calls theatres 'Venus' palace and Satan's synagogue' (143), after attending which people 'play the Sodomites, or worse' (145). This debate, first rehearsed between Plato and Aristotle as one argued for banishing and the other for retaining the poet in the polis, is not a new one, and had been levelled as an accusation several times against the transformative power of rhetorical 'persuasion.' If rhetorical style is viewed as being deceptive, then the theatre is the stage on which this deception gets enacted and its effects are considered even more malignant in the public sphere than in the relatively controllable environs of the grammar school. The idea of performative (or discursive) production not only links drama and desire, but also draws them both into the province of rhetoric. Drama provides the most sustained and rigorous look at a rhetorical 'fracture' (what later dramatists like Brecht were to term 'alienation') that language generally enacts. By making flesh the many possibilities that a clever use of language has at its disposal, Renaissance drama provides a sustained assault on a world of certainty and inaugurates instead the reign of irony. Even though other forms of literature (poetry, travel narratives, sermons) share drama's fascination with words and their fluidity,[52] only drama spawned a violent antitheatrical tradition that vociferously identified the theatre as a site of corruption. The energy that drama put into circulation was consistently read by its detractors as a *sexual* energy potentially disruptive of both Sex and State.[53] Stories abound of how people in the audience were moved into confessing crimes, but the frightening thought is that countless more were probably moved into committing them. Stubbes's characterization of people going directly from the theatre to sodomitical conclaves is the fear of an obscenity that has already been articulated (especially by Quintilian) in relation to rhetoric, but which now has a concrete *image* to cling to.[54] The potential that drama provides for taking on a different role and for acting a different part are merely extensions of the fear that metaphor will contaminate language by its free movement. The shape-changing ability of actors is seen not only as morally corrupt (and therefore ungodly), but also as sexually licentious. It is no coincidence that in Christian mythology Proteus, the god of changeable shapes, is reincarnated as Satan.[55]

The world as theatre is the chosen metaphor for those who both attack and defend the stage.[56] The totalizing scheme that blames the ills of the world on the theatre ironically achieves the purpose of collapsing the distinctions between drama and reality, so that the notion of a 'real' world disappears completely from the picture. With no remaining point of reference, the theatre looms large as the arbiter of a new world order in which (the antitheatricalists fear) anarchy reigns. The metaphor of the theatre, from Aristotle on, has been used to explain the way in which rhetoric 'sets the scene before our eyes' by depicting abstractions concretely. Metaphor seems indispensable while speaking of the theatre, and even two of the theatre's enemies, William Prynne and Stephen Gosson, found it most effective to (metaphorically) divide their antitheatrical tracts into acts and scenes.

Much work has already been done on the allegedly corrupting effects of Renaissance drama,[57] but what I am interested in here is the specifically *rhetorical* nature of this corruption, and once again, Philip Stubbes proves invaluable. Dividing plays into two categories, divine and profane, Stubbes states that divine plays (or plays which, like the medieval moralities, biblical plays, and saint's plays, deal with religious issues) are sacrilegious because they dare *to act out* the love of God, and profane plays (or those that deal with secular themes) abuse God by ignoring him, so however one looks at drama, one loses simply by virtue of having looked:

> All Stage-playes, Enterluds, and Commedies are either of diuyne or prophane matter: If they be of diuine matter, then they are most intollerable, or rather Sacrilegious; for that the blessed word of GOD is to be handled reuerently, grauely, and sagely ... and not scoffingly, flowtingly, & iybingly as it is vpon stages in Playes and Enterluds ... [W]e are taught that the word is GOD, and GOD is the word: Wherefore, who so euer abuseth this word of our GOD on stages in playes and enterluds, abuseth the Maiesty of GOD ...
> Vpon the other side, if their playes be of prophane matters, than tend they to *the* dishonor of God, and norishing of vice, both which are damnable. So that whither they be the one or the other, they are quite contrarie to the Word of grace, and sucked out of the Deuills teates to nourish us in ydolatorie, hethenrie, and sinne ... (*Anatomy of the Abuses*, 140–1)

Even as he identifies God with the Word, Stubbes is anxious to distance divinity from the corruptions of language: the 'Word of grace' cannot be reduced to a 'word' if it is to retain its purity. The very *act* of acting takes priority over *what* is being enacted, style is granted more importance than substance. This emphasis on style, however, is incompatible with the stress on purity, which demands that minimal attention be paid to ornamentation. The rhetorical stakes in the *Anatomy* ensure that Stubbes ends up granting style the importance he tries to deny it. Despite being blind to its own corruption, the text frames its discussion of linguistic sin in terms of sexual confusion. At the end of this section of his diatribe, Stubbes characterizes the devil as a *woman* whose teats are being sucked (which last word reads rather more pertinently in its early modern typography) for their yield of sin. In Stubbes's description the theatre is represented as a forum for scoffs, flouts, and jibes: these verbal abuses are seen as constitutive of plays, and they in turn nourish the vice that the text so eloquently rails against. The 'damn[ation]' that marks the theatre is a curse descended from an inability to fill a gap; for Stubbes this gap lies in apprehending the divine, since any *representation* of divinity is already prey to drama's peculiar curse. The gap that metaphor throws into relief is here embodied in the very process of acting, which depicts divinity as nothing more than drama.

The 'conversion' that horrifies the antitheatrical tracts so much is thus of the same *kind* that metaphor enacts. By turning 'reasonable creatures into beasts,' drama brings out the basest instincts in a human being and from there it is a small step to the sodomitical conclaves that Stubbes derives so much pleasure in describing. 'Thinkest thou,' he goes on to thunder,

> that thou canst make thy self fairer than God, who made us all? These must neede be their intentions, or els they would neuer go about to colour their faces with fibberfawces. And these being their inventions, what can derogate more from the maiejestie of God in his creation? For this dooing, they plainly conuince the Lord of untrueth in his word, who saith he made man glorious, after his own likenes, and the fayrest of all other terrestriall Creatures. If he be thus fayre, then what need they to make them fayrer? Therefore this their colouring of their faces importeth ... that they think them selues not faire enough, and then must GOD needs be untrue in his word. (64)

The fervour with which Stubbes rails against the use of make-up on and off the stage would suggest that if everyone has his own version of the devilish identifying 'mark,' then rouge is definitely his. It is, of course, quite another matter that Stubbes himself is not averse to a bit of (textual) rouge now and then, especially when he situates his 'abuses' in the country of Ailgna, an anagram of Anglia.

We can now begin to see what it was that exercised the antitheatricalists so much.[58] Not only does drama represent the 'popular' version of rhetoric, but it also enacts a metaphorical lack of boundaries that often gets expressed sexually. If desire, as Joel Fineman states, 'originates in and as the lack of structure,'[59] then drama (despite its five-act framework) symbolizes a breakdown of order by trying to represent desire (like God) on stage. This attempt, always made and always failing, is rendered ever more pathetic because desire can only be 'represented' by a language that is itself already wanton. The words necessary for the wanton to become visible are queer because *in themselves* they mean nothing. Dekker's cony-catching pamphlet makes clear that 'queer' signifies 'naught' and this naught assumes significance by its ability to signify prolifically. By signifying language's investment in tropology and variety, words appear wanton. As Quintilian discovered much to his horror, obscenity lurks at the very heart of beauty, and it surfaces precisely when beauty cannot sustain itself under scrutiny. The stage makes such scrutiny both public and inevitable; metaphor and drama both deprave 'natural' language by moving it into the realm of artificiality. The inevitable consequence is that we can never be sure if either natural language or reality exists outside this artifice.

If the twofold dream of drama is both to make 'play' equal 'truth,' *and* to keep them forever apart, then that impossible structure is expressed most eloquently by rhetoric, and grafted most glitteringly on the body. In the chapters that follow, I look mainly at what are called canonical plays in an attempt to see how their rhetorical makeup reflects certain sexual desires that in turn undermine their very canonicity. I do this not because I 'believe' in the supremacy and fixity of the canon, but rather because I believe in the necessity of *reading* it; the process of canon formation, I suggest, is a continually deconstructive enterprise. This study attempts to read the way in which a rhetorical trope reflects a sexual configuration, and sexuality becomes a horizon of textual possibility. I am less interested in the 'representations' of sodomitical, or homoerotic, or nonprocreative sexualities in Renaissance drama, and more inclined to look at the way in which a specific rhetorical trope brings into focus a mode of sexual desire with which it shares its outstanding features. The proliferation of rhetorical handbooks in the sixteenth century ensures a sharper focus on sexual desire as the site on which *rhetorical* battles are fought. This is not only to claim that sexuality is both created by and contained within the portals of rhetoric, but also to state that whenever a text deals with either rhetoric or sexuality, it will, despite itself, be talking about two things at once. Since sexuality is structured through and as rhetorical displacement, the choice of trope that a particular text makes will have immediate consequences on the kind of sexuality that it engages; a certain kind of textuality, to echo Joel Fineman, will 'predicate' a certain kind of sexuality.[60] In the case of rhetorical handbooks that deal with tropes in general, sexuality is spoken of in terms of general illicitness, but specific texts bring to light specific sexual configurations, and enable us to indulge our voyeurism with keener delight.

It would be ironic, and therefore rhetorically apt, if any of the tropes I detail are read as a master trope or key to 'understanding' a play. Rather, I am suggesting a way of reading that goes somewhat beyond the localizable 'application' of tropes, and emphasizes instead the continual imbrication of ways of reading texts with ways of reading bodily and sexual *desire*. This reading is not so much of two separate things as of doubleness itself, and this doubleness is figured by the handbooks as a doubling of figure and fetish, language and lust, rhetoric and rapaciousness. It is therefore not my contention that the pun (for instance) is the lens through which to read *Love's Labour's Lost*, but rather that our fascination with *Love's Labour's Lost* might be a response to its own fascination with words, and that its fascination with words is also a fascination with sex.

Each of the handbooks I look at orders its tropes differently, and even though most accord pride of place to metaphor, very often the extended metaphor – allegory – is put in a separate category entirely (as it is by Quintilian). The principle of organization is arbitrary at best, but the figures of speech in each text are laid out in an order justified by the author on his own terms. In this study those terms are dramatic; each trope is made to stand in for one particular stage of a dramatic ritual, and each is intended to be a dramatic unfolding of the ways in which we read, write, and think about language and sexuality. I have begun by looking at metaphor since it is given primary importance in all rhetorical handbooks. The substitution that metaphor enacts lays the ground for all other tropological functions, and the notion of *resemblance* – of the necessary distance between words and things – that metaphor embodies, is fundamental to the premise of this project. Closely related to metaphor (almost as closely related as metaphor is to itself) is metonymy, which is marked by the unremarked detail that nonetheless propels us in directions we might not have thought of taking. The lure of arbitrary contact that subtends metonymy threatens to throw into disarray the logic of necessity; metalepsis then takes over and tries to provide a credible link between two increasingly disparate worlds (inside and outside, private and public, early modern and modern, sex and gender), but always fails to do so. Once that failure sinks in irreversibly, the text tries to cover up its lack by furtively misnaming textual failure as *something else*, as that which perhaps could hitherto not have been spoken; the rhetorical term for that misnaming is catachresis. Once we reenter the realm of corrupt and mismatched names, metaphor takes over to such an extent that it becomes transmuted into an allegory or 'perpetuall' metaphor. Allegory mythologizes the realm of corruption and provides us with a narrative trajectory that promises to reveal the 'truth' as soon as the curtain rises. Even as we sit in the audience, riveted by that promise, metaphor stages a reentry to firmly reestablish its position as the most beautifully dangerous of tropes by undermining any notion of textual certainty.

Located between the loci of metaphor – 'that most beautiful of tropes' – and allegory – the 'perpetuall metaphore' – I plot the trajectories suggested by metonymy, which glosses over the heart of Richard's 'crime' in *Richard II* and tames Moll's 'canting' in *The Roaring Girl*; metalepsis, which ensures the tragedy of *Romeo and Juliet* even as it marks a Pyrrhic victory in *Sodom and Gomorrah*; and catachresis, which cleverly misnames *Othello's* profound unease of sexuality as racial miscegenation. Each of these tropes subtends a specific sexual configuration with which it shares its defining characteristics even as none of them provides an exhaustive account of any of the plays they read; rather, they help us with the process of reading itself. Classical and Renaissance handbooks of rhetoric offer us a paradigm of reading that has too often languished backstage, wilting under the footlights of 'history.' This reading I call, quite simply, reading excess. In the terms set forth in Jonathan Crewe's brilliant study of rhetoric in Thomas Nashe, this reading is an attempt to grapple with the phenomenon 'of a linguistic excess surpassing any functional explanation, any acceptable rationale, or any power of repression.'[61] It is also, to continue with Crewe's words, a reading that goes against the widespread understanding of reading as 'the attempted reduction of an offensive superfluity.' This superfluity, always present and always offensive, will not be explained away in the chapters that follow. Rather, I have attempted to locate the 'navel' (Freud's term) of this superfluity in relation to each of the texts that I read, a navel that then becomes the springboard for textual analysis. Rhetoric provides us with a *history* of sexuality that is not necessarily constrained by medico-juridical chronology. It nuances our understanding of history by presenting, as both inevitable and all-pervasive, a turn to the figure as it figures the workings of figurality itself. What this book seeks to do therefore, is not to shut down history or elevate 'theory,' but rather, at every turn, to *expand* our sense of both history and theory to include also a sense of superfluous and excessive *sexuality*. Reading Renaissance drama necessitates, not so much a reading of any *one* thing, but rather a reading of a seething cauldron that contains, apart from the 'eye of newt and toe of frog,' a huge serving of language, and a relatively new but already aggressively spicy discourse on what we now call with every degree of confidence and a singular lack of irony, *sexuality*.

2

Performance Anxiety: Metonymy, *Richard II, The Roaring Girl*

We debate about things that seem capable of admitting two possibilities.
Aristotle, *On Rhetoric*[1]

At the heart of rhetorical reality lies pleasure.
Richard Lanham, *The Motives of Eloquence*[2]

In John Donne's 'Sappho to Philaenis' – often considered the earliest 'lesbian' poem in English – Sappho dismisses her past affair with Phao in order to contemplate the beauty and symmetric perfection of two female bodies joining together:

> My two lips, eyes, thighs, differ from thy two,
>   But so, as thine from one another doe;
> And, oh, no more; the likenesse being such,
>   Why should they not alike in all parts touch?
> Hand to strange hand, lippe to lippe none denies;
>   Why should they brest to brest? Or thighs to thighs?
> Likenesse begets such strange selfe flatterie,
>   That touching my selfe, all seemes done to thee.
> My selfe I embrace, and mine own hands I kisse,
>   And amorously thanke my selfe for this,
> Me, in my glasse, I call thee; But alas,
>   When I would kisse, teares dimme mine *eyes*, and *glasse*.
> O cure this loving madnesse, and restore
> Me to mee; thee, my *halfe*, my *all*, my *more*.   (45–58)[3]

Sappho begins her blazon of Philaenis's body with a blazon of her own physical attributes: 'My two lips, eyes, [and] thighs' eventually leads to a consideration of her lover's body and the realization that its most erotic parts look different from her own. But this difference between the two bodies is quickly cast as the difference between parts of the same body: Sappho's thighs are different from Philaenis's in the same manner as Philaenis's left thigh is different from her right. Identifiably different bodies are replaced by a framework of identity based on the sameness within and between bodies. So far is Sappho willing to push this principle of erotic non inter-distinction that the prospect of physical contiguity ('brest to brest ... thighs to thighs') is enough to make her masturbate under the illusion of making love to another body; what seems to extend outward is actually turned inward into the body that acts. Making love to herself is as good as making love to Philaenis. The sensual chafing that pleasures indifferent bodies ('touching my selfe, all seemes done to thee') is Sappho's counterpart to the messiness of male-female coupling. Heterosexuality's visible trace (the poem's example is of footprints in the snow) is sublimated by Sappho into an invisible mark of beauty against which to measure perfection: 'to make blind men see / What things gods are, I say they are like to thee' (17–18). The only residue of Sappho and Philaenis's love is what 'fishes leave in streames, or Birds in aire.'

Sappho sets up a bodily paradigm for reading textual difference that characterizes the relationship between metaphor and metonymy. Her multiple blazons raise the question of the terrain for erotic desire: does it need to be mapped onto identifiably different bodies or can it exist within the crevices of an individual body and, by extension, in the crevices of bodies that might seem to be the 'same'? The first line of this section of the poem establishes the realm of visible difference between diverse anatomical markers only to collapse into the concept of sameness within and between unrelated bodies. The metaphoric cast of the first line notes and admires the similarity between two different objects, while the metonymic tinge of the second notes that differences exist (despite and) within apparent sameness. These two tropes would seem to align themselves with two different kinds of sexuality – visible desire based on the anatomy of different bodies suggests Sappho's heterosexual relationship with Phao, while the invisibility of desire related to 'sameness' characterizes her affair with Philaenis. However, this alignment is more complicated than might first appear. Sappho's relation to Philaenis seems entirely metonymic:

she revels in giving herself an orgasm inspired by the absent Philaenis. From within the depths of her metonymic delirium, Sappho asks to be restored *to* her self by 'thee, my halfe, my all, my more,' acknowledging the excessive nature of her desire, self-pleasured, other-motivated, and thriving greedily on 'more.' This excessive desire apparently eludes a metaphoric order that tries to contain bodies in relation to specific and present others, insisting instead that pleasure exists in excess of such containment. But despite its seductive appeal, Sappho's metonymy is never fully able to break free of metaphor since its excessive 'more' is always attached to a restrictive 'my.' Metonymy cannot exist on its own even as metaphor always exists in relation to metonymy. Sappho is free of Phao but her relationship with Philaenis seems destined to slide into the mode of discrete difference, forgetting its investment in discreet similarity.[4]

This moment has been anticipated at least once before in the poem. As part of her scornful dismissal of men, Sappho states:

> ... if we justly call each silly man
>   A little world, what shall we call thee then?
> Thou art not soft, and clear, and straight, and fair,
>   As down, as stars, cedars, and lillies are,
> But thy right hand, and cheek, and eye, only
>   Are like thy other hand, and cheek, and eye. (19–24)

This symmetrical perfection is also a moment of metaphoric negotiation. Sappho insists that Philaenis's body can only be described in a nonmetaphoric register: she is *not* as soft as down, clear as stars, straight as cedars, or fair as lilies; her eyes are also probably nothing like the sun. But despite being described in negative terms, Philaenis emerges from these noncomparisons only *through* the swirl of metaphor: after all, even negative judgments are based on visible comparisons. However, this implication in metaphor is strenuously disavowed in order to suggest that Philaenis's body acquires beauty only in reference to itself. Her hand, cheek, and eye, are like her other hand, cheek, and eye; she does not roam beyond her self in order to acquire meaning. Instead, she creates meaning by stroking her hands, fluttering her eyelashes, and performing the impossible feat of dancing cheek to (own) cheek. The body in question is therefore crucially defined both by what it is and is not; its field is delimited in advance so that the ostensible shutting down of metaphor can allow for closer and closer scrutiny until metaphor collapses into metonymy. Metaphor is apparently banished in order to make room for metonymic likeness, but this likeness can only come to light within a metaphoric universe based on explicit and specific comparisons: Philaenis is *like* herself even as Sappho's relationship with Philaenis is *un*like her affair with Phao.[5]

This tussle between two kinds of sexuality – male-female on the one hand and female-female on the other – is cast in this poem as a tussle between two kinds of rhetoric – metaphoric and metonymic. In a line that Yeats was later to make his own, Donne asks:

> Where is that holy fire, which verse is said
>   To have? Is that enchanting force decayed?
> Verse, that draws Nature's works, from Nature's law,
>   Thee, her best work, to her work cannot draw.
> Have my tears quenched my old poetic fire;
>   Why quenched they not as well, that of desire?   (1–6)

Poetry and desire, verse and fire, are the parameters within which this poem attempts to negotiate the often vexed relation between rhetoric and the erotic. In making this attempt, 'Sappho to Philaenis' sets up two modes of reading that bring different sexual desires into legibility. These desires are not only sexual; they turn out to be rhetorical as well. Sappho's relationship with Phao is dismissed scornfully in favour of her relationship with Philaenis, and this dismissal takes the form of valuing metonymic sex over metaphoric intercourse. However, as we have seen, metonymy is unable to extricate itself fully from a metaphoric register. The 'old poetic fire' continues to render Sappho's new desire, the only difference being that its rendition does not do justice to the magnificence of its subject. But even as the new love(r) is described as exceeding the limits of Sappho's poetic control, she also exists only within those denuded limits; the poem merely chooses (however falsely) to privilege one trope over another in the service of privileging Sappho's new love over her old. This chapter will examine the rhetorical stakes inherent in preferring one trope to another, and the sexual politics of that preference. Far from suggesting that metaphor and metonymy can be aligned along axes of hetero- and homosexuality, I will argue that metonymy always lurks in the folds of metaphor – Phao always haunts Philaenis, and vice versa – even though neither can stand the other's company.

The Unnecessary Mode

In handbooks of rhetoric, metonymy's most distinctive characteristic is its need to be distinguished from other tropes. Quintilian emphasizes the need to differentiate between metonymy and synecdoche (VIII.vi.23), the *Ad Herennium* between metonymy and metalepsis (IV.xxxi.43),[6] and Puttenham between metonymy and catachresis (181). Metonymy's constitutive tendency, it would seem, is to merge into other tropes so as to itself remain unmarked in the realm of signification. This in-significance is not the same thing as lacking significance, however, and despite their difficulty, the handbooks of rhetoric spend a substantial amount of time grappling with the trope. Metonymy's ability to pass undetected in tropological schematization and to be frequently misrecognized as something other than itself also bears a startling resemblance to understandings of early modern homosexuality. Alan Bray notes that in Renaissance England, there was 'an ordered conception of existence in relation to which homosexuality was defined – or rather from which it was excluded – as part of a universal potential for disorder which lay alongside an equally universal order. It was part, in a word, of its shadow.'[7] The shadowy nature of Renaissance (homo)sexuality and its potentially corrupting influence is distinctly reflected by the textual use of an indistinguishable metonymy, in which it is almost impossible to tell one trope and one sexuality from the partner that '[lies] alongside' it. After looking at what the rhetorical handbooks have to say about metonymy's dubious genealogy, I examine two plays, Shakespeare's *Richard II* and Middleton and Dekker's *The Roaring Girl*, to tease out the effect this masking has on the sexual drama these plays enact.

Quintilian states, in Book VIII of the *Institutio Oratoria*:

> It is but a short step from synecdoche to metonymy, which consists in the substitution of one name for another ... to indicate an invention by substituting the name of the inventor, or a possession by substituting the name of the possessor ... But it is important to enquire to what extent tropes of this kind should be employed by the orator. For though we often hear 'Vulcan' used for fire and ... while *Venus* is a more decent expression than coitus, it would be too bold for the severe style demanded in the courts to speak of *Liber* and *Ceres* when we mean bread and wine ... But to follow out these points is a task involving too much minute detail even for a work whose aim is not the training of an orator. (VIII.vi.23, 24, 28)

The 'short step' from one trope to the next turns out to be longer than Quintilian first anticipates. The essence of metonymy, for him, consists in the substitution of one name for another, which is in itself an unremarkable definition, since it could just as easily be the hallmark of metaphor. As he goes on to tease out the exact nature of this substitution, however, he gets bogged down in the many 'detail[s],' and decides to abandon the project altogether since it would take far too much time to complete.[8] But before arriving at this point, Quintilian attempts to ground metonymy by giving us some examples of its use. For instance, using 'Venus' in place of 'coitus' is lauded as an exemplary figure of speech, while using 'Ceres' for 'bread' is considered too flowery for the 'severe style demanded in the courts.' From these examples alone it would seem that metonymy has no place in the world of eating, drinking, and law-making, while it occupies a pre-eminent position in the realm where, for decency's sake, the act of coitus needs to be covered up. Since he cannot find a logical reason why these realms should be distinguished from each other, however, his argument stops at the threshold of metonymic *detail* which, he believes, leads to complexity rather than clarity.

The *Ad Herennium* draws a similar blank. It tries to define metonymy as 'the figure which draws from an object closely akin or associated an expression suggesting the object meant, but not called by its own name. This is accomplished by substituting the name of the greater thing for the lesser ... or the instrument for the possessor ... or effect for cause ... It is harder to distinguish all these metonymies in teaching the principle than to find them while searching for them, for the use of metonymies ... is abundant not only amongst the poets and orators but also in everyday speech' (IV.xxii.43). The author tries to distinguish both between metonymy and other tropes, and between different kinds of metonymy, but fails to live up to the extended scope of his disquisition. Like the *Institutio*, the *Ad Herennium* too blames its failure on the ubiquity of metonymy ('abundant not only amongst the poets and orators but also in everyday speech'), which makes the trope difficult to classify definitively.

Thomas Wilson's *Arte of Rhetorique* brings us closer to the *way* in which metonymy works by giving us examples of the necessarily arbitrary nature of metonymic association. After offering the usual definition of metonymy as the substitution of the container for the contained, Wilson instantiates with two examples: 'I pray you come to me' and 'This fellowe is good with a long Bowe.' He then glosses the metonymic chain set up by these statements and interprets the first one as an invitation to a house, and the second as pointing to the ability of shooting well. In these, as in his last example, 'The Sunne is vp, that is to say, it is day,' the text metonymically picks from among a mass of options (is the sun just rising? is it noon? is it evening?), each of which, by virtue of not being the complete truth, nudges us in the direction of other possibilities. The evocative power of metonymy is celebrated by Wilson as the hallmark of the trope.

But one man's evocation is another man's lie, as a comparison with Puttenham amply demonstrates. *The Arte of English Poesie* has this to say about metonymy:

> Now doth this understanding or secret conceyt reach many times to the only nomination of persons or things in their names, as of men, or mountains, seas, countries and such like, in which respect the wrong naming, or otherwise naming of them is due, carrieth not onely an alteration of sence but a necessitie of intendment figuratiuely, as when we cal loue by the name of *Venus*, fleshly lust by the name of *Cupid*, bicause they were supposed by the auncient poets to be authors and kindlers of loue and lust ... These and other such speaches, where ye take the name of the Author for the thing it selfe; or the thing conteining, for that which is contained, & in many other cases do as it were wrong name the person or the thing. So neuerthelesse as it may be understood, it is by the figure metonymia, or misnamer. (181)

Puttenham, whose greatest innovation over the rhetorical texts he inherited was to provide English names for the Greek and Latin, chooses to designate metonymy as 'the misnamer.' This trope misnames love as Venus and lust as Cupid because it 'confuses' the author of these desires with the desires themselves. For Puttenham, metonymy affects the very 'nomination of persons and things,' thereby attacking the integrity of the self and causing it to mutate into a misname. The *Arte of English Poesie* is wary of the associative chafing that Wilson's *Arte* recognizes as being key to the working of metonymy, and treats the trope with uncustomary caution.

However much these four texts might differ from each other in their dealings with metonymy, they all seem to agree on certain key features, which I will henceforth take to be the defining characteristics of the trope. Metonymy depends on an *affinity* between two things rather than an *innate* link between two terms. A table does not have to be *like* a chair in order to be suggested by it, and a man does not have to look like a woman in order to remind us of one. What ties metonymy to itself is a vaguely-defined affinity, rather than a physically determinable resemblance. One can metonymically substitute a shoe for the person one loves (because it is in contact with his/her body), but one cannot say the person one loves is *like* a shoe without inviting a certain amount of ridicule, since those two terms are not linked in the mode of necessity.[9] There is, therefore, a certain level of arbitrariness where metonymy is concerned, and this brings us to its second feature: the difficulty of distinguishing it clearly from either metaphor or synecdoche or catachresis or metalepsis, since it partakes in the transference of the first, the telescoping of the second, the misnaming of the third, and the causal confusion of the fourth. Metonymy is both arbitrary and tropologically indistinguishable, which makes it at once the most fitting rhetorical figure for sexuality, and the least identifiable.[10]

Caterpillars of the Commonwealth

Nature that hateth emptiness, / Allows of penetration less ...
Andrew Marvell, 'An Horatian Ode'[11]

The tension between identifiable and indistinguishable desires plays out with some intensity in Shakespeare's *Richard II*, a play that has always been read either *as* a metaphor – for kingship, Christianity, poetry – or else *through* its metaphors – of garden, mirror, and clock, among others. Such an emphasis on the metaphoric register has ensured that Richard is criticized whenever he strays from the ideals of metaphoric consistency. As early as 1899, he is described as a good poet and bad king,[12] a charge later echoed by Harold Bloom, who insists that Richard is 'an astonishing poet and a very bad king.'[13] In such a reading, Richard's 'inability to distinguish the external sign or symbol ... from what the symbol represents'[14] is the overwhelming reason for his deposition: the king is bad *because* his poetry is good. Since he attempts to straddle the unlike spheres of kingship and literature, action and words, Richard is judged by 'the efficacy of [those] words,'[15] the spectacular lack of which has meant a corresponding loss of metaphoric value.[16] Richard's impropriety in this regard is compounded by the fact that the man who deposes him, Bullingbrook, has an eminently 'sensible' attitude to language. When advised to think of happy times in an attempt to divert attention from his banishment, for instance, Bullingbrook states mockingly: 'O, who can hold a fire in his hand / By thinking of the frosty Caucasus? / Or cloy the hungry edge of appetite / By bare imagination of a feast?' (I.iii.294–7). Unlike Richard, the man who would be king does not wallow indolently in the luxuries of language. While Richard 'fondles words and tropes,'[17] Henry tests the keenness of his sword. Such an insistently *sensible* reading of the play – a reading in which words make sense to one royal candidate while remaining elusive in the speech of the other – lays out the rationale for Richard's deposition. However, this rationale makes sense only at the expense of those parts of the text that do *not* make sense, parts devoted almost exclusively to pronouncements by and about Richard. In traditional pairings of rhetoric, such textual details – aligned with yet ignored by metaphor – are often described as metonymy, and it is their import for *Richard II* that I propose to examine in this section.

In her discussion of the metaphorical plot Patricia Parker lays out the *locus classicus* of metaphor: the idea of a locus itself. 'One of the remarkable features of classical writing on metaphor,' she notes, 'is the dominance of the notion of "place" – of territory already staked out, of the tropological as inseparable from the topological – and thus also of "property," or of a place where a word properly belongs.'[18] *Richard II* deals with both these senses of place: it contains at its heart a discussion on the specificity of words, set in a specific 'place' in the kingdom of England: the garden.

The horticultural metaphor – Gaunt's 'other Eden, demi-paradise' – is in keeping with a traditional textual mode in which gardens and nature are used to indicate the extent of depravity in a land. Alan of Lille's twelfth-century *Grammar of Sex*, for instance, revolves around the narrative of Lady Nature, who blames the rents in her garments on Man's 'homosexual' activities.[19] Hamlet too, we remember, plucks at the garden metaphor in his first soliloquy of disgust: 'How [weary], stale, flat, and unprofitable / Seem to me all the uses of this world! / Fie on't, oh fie! 'tis an unweeded garden / That grows to seed, things rank and gross in nature / Possess it merely' (I.ii.133–6). The violation of the 'natural law' (whether by homosexuality or incest) is a tried and tested explanation of human depravity, and so the internal siege of the garden of England is metaphorically evoked in *Richard II* to explain the state of decay that Richard's rule has bred in his kingdom. The so-called garden scene – Act III sc. iv – is therefore often considered the emblematic 'heart' of the play. This is both a scene of doom (for King

Richard) and a scene of optimism (for King Henry).[20] The garden scene is able miraculously to produce these diagnostic readings because it is read as a metaphor for the state of the state. The garden equals England and the gardener who controls the garden stands in for the ideal king.

Such a reading of the garden is an offshoot of the assumption that Richard's words and actions do not correspond with one another. Hence the metaphoric 'centre' of the play is also the location of its rhetorical realignment, seeking to reassert a trope that has been abused by the king. There are two ways of reading this garden scene and its realignment of rhetorical values just as there are two ways of reading the play itself. Criticism of *Richard II* has traditionally picked only the one in which the gardener aligns himself with the king and the garden with the state. While such a reading has considerable textual evidence to back its claim, the metonymic reading – which cannot lay claim to any such backing – turns up the more interesting gloss on what the play presents as the 'difference' between Richard and Henry. Such a reading is crucial, not only in expanding traditional criticism of the play, but also in making such criticism less heteronormative. As an understanding of metaphor and metonymy makes clear, the choice of rhetorical trope also implies a choice of sexuality that in *this* play makes all the difference between the proper and improper king of England.

Some of *Richard*'s precursor texts provide clues about the king's relation to metaphoric 'impropriety,' clues that Shakespeare's text echoes but which then disappear in criticism on the play. The first is *The Mirror for Magistrates'* 'Howe kyng Richarde the seconde was for his euyll gouernance deposed from his seat, and miserably murdred in prison,' where the character of King Richard is made to lament his fate:

> I am a Kyng that ruled all by lust,
> That forced not of vertue, ryght, or lawe,
> But always put false Flatterers most in trust,
> Ensuing such as could my vices clawe:
> By faythful counsayle passing not a strawe.
> What pleasure pryckt, that thought I to be iust.
> I set my minde, to feede, to spoyle, to iust,
> Three meales a day could skarce content my mawe.
> And all to augment my lecherous minde that must
> To Venus pleasures always be in awe.   (p. 113, ll. 31–40)

King Richard 'admits' that his crime has been excessive lust and that his 'mawe' is in awe of Venus. His sense of justice has been dictated, not by consular advice, but by what is most pleasurable. His voracious appetite is insatiable and his mind has tended toward the 'spoiling' of customs and traditions. All the vices that Shakespeare's play attributes to its king – ignoring good counsel, favouring false flatterers, overriding the law of the land – are present in this speech. The notable absence in Shakespeare, of course, is the one the king seems most apologetic for in the *Mirror*: his voracious carnal appetite.[21] The 'pryck[ing]' of pleasure, and the 'lecherous minde' are both acknowledged here as holding the king in their sway. Admitting that he has been 'ruled all by lust,' Richard puts down lechery as the foremost reason for his deposition, the thing without which his deposition would not make sense, and which justifies his tragic fate. Strangely, this same justification seems to be absent in both Shakespeare's play and in our readings of it.

Another precursor to Shakespeare's *Richard II* is Holinshed's description of Richard's reign. True to its title, the *Chronicles* provide us with a detailed list of reasons urged by the commons against the king and in favour of Bullingbrook. Among these, that Richard 'caused his vncle the duke of Glocester to be arrested without law and sent him to Calis, and there without iudgement murthered him' (Item 2); that the king 'put out diuerse shiriffes lawfullie elected, and put in their roomes diuerse other of his owne, subuerting the law, contrarie to his oth and honor' (Item 11); and that he 'banished the bishop of Canturberie without cause or iudgement, and kept him in the parlement chamber with men of armes' (Item 27). Of the twenty-nine charges of murder, nepotism, and wilfulness, the one given pride of place, however, is Item 1, the very first accusation that 'king Richard wastfullie spent the treasure of the realme, and had giuen the possesions of the crowne to men unworthie' (359–61). This 'wastfull' expenditure has 'subuert[ed] the law,' and this subversion, broadly hinted at in Shakespeare's text, is given direct and indirect expression in the garden scene.

A metaphorical reading of the garden scene, however, is unable to account for Richard's admission of having given 'possession of the crowne to men unworthy.' Who are these unworthy men and how do they abuse Richard? In what does Richard's 'wastfull'ness consist? And in what ways is it fatal? Even though the answers to these questions do not lie in metaphor alone, the questions themselves have their roots firmly embedded in the gardener's whole(some) speech:

GARD: Go thou, and like an executioner
    Cut off the heads of [too] fast growing sprays,
    That look too lofty in our commonwealth:
    All must be even in our government.
    You thus employed, I will go root away
    The noisome weeds which without profit suck
    The soil's fertility from wholesome flowers.
[1.] MAN: Why should we in the compass of a pale
    Keep law and form and due proportion,
    Showing as in a model our firm estate,
    When our sea-walled garden, the whole land,
    Is full of weeds, her fairest flowers chok'd up,
    Her fruit-trees all unprun'd, her hedges ruin'd,
    Her knots disordered, and her wholesome herbs
    Swarming with caterpillars?
GARD.:   Hold thy peace.
    He that hath suffered this disordered spring
    Hath now himself met with the fall of leaf.
    The weeds which his broad-spreading leaves did shelter,
    That seem'd in eating him to hold him up,
    Are pluck'd up root and all by Bullingbrook,
    I mean the Earl of Wiltshire, Bushy, Green.
[1.] MAN: What, are they dead?
GARD.:   They are; and Bullingbrook
    Hath seiz'd the wasteful King. O, what pity is it
    That he had not so trimm'd and dress'd his land
    As we this garden! [We] at time of year
    Do wound the bark, the skin of our fruit-trees,
    Lest being over-proud in sap and blood,
    With too much riches it confound itself;
    Had he done so to great and growing men,
    They might have liv'd to bear and he to taste
    Their fruits of duty.   (III.iv.33–63)

This speech deliberately and repeatedly sets itself up as a metaphoric one – 'our sea-walled garden, the whole land,' 'what pity is it / That he had not so trimm'd and dress'd his land / As we this garden' – and provides ample textual justification for reading the garden scene as a metaphorical comment on Richard's reign in England.

As head gardener of the realm, Richard is accused of having failed to 'cut off the heads of too fast growing sprays,' and not sufficiently 'wound[ing] the bark' of trees. This negligence has led to too much power being concentrated in too few hands, and these hands are now raising the banner of rebellion against the gardener-king.[22] In this metaphor, the rebellious subjects are those who have had too much licence and too little restriction; those whose riches have thickened their sap to the point of seepage. If, as the gardener indicates, Richard had pruned and lopped in time, he would have lived to taste '[t]heir fruits of duty.' As it stands, however, the garden of England is decrepit because its head gardener has allowed rebellion to foster in the shade of spreading branches; as a result, blooming flowers have withered and luscious fruit has rotted. The 'wasteful King' – a formulation that clearly echoes Holinshed – has not only expended his spirit in vain, but has also exerted himself in an improper manner; the garden now has to bear the consequences of this unproductive indulgence.

The metaphoric reading thus blames the king for not having lopped off sufficiently swollen heads. In terms of the dramatic action prior to this scene, the insufficient lopping might refer to Bullingbrook; after all, Richard banishes him for ten years and then reduces that number to six, instead of having him killed, thereby insufficiently trimming Bullingbrook's ambition while simultaneously fanning his distemper. As the play unfolds, we see Bullingbrook cut short his sentence and return to England to reclaim his possessions, beginning with ancestral lands and ending with the throne. Thus read, the metaphor of the garden makes perfect sense as a gloss on the state of England: Richard has been a bad gardener and so the garden has gone to seed, enabling rebellion where order should have existed.

However, not all the trees can be classified under this explanation. If Richard's 'crime' is inept pruning, then how does one explain the fact that if anything, the king has pruned too much rather than too little? The play opens, after all, with Bullingbrook attempting to avenge the duke of Gloucester's death in whose end Richard was widely believed to have had a hand. The duke of Gloucester, part of the infamous 'Lords Appellant' who virtually ruled the kingdom when Richard was in his minority, was only one of the many heads the king had allegedly caused to be lopped. Other members of the junta, the earls of Warwick and Arundel, were arrested on charges of treason and while one was banished, the other was executed. Richard's pruning of powerful trees, it can be argued, was somewhat overzealous, and the play draws dramatic attention to that fact by beginning with Bullingbrook's attempt to settle old scores and bring the pruners to justice. If anything, Richard is a compulsive gardener since he tries to get rid of both his enemies and his friends: Mowbray is banished so he can no longer remind Richard of his crime and Bullingbrook so he cannot challenge him for it. In the play's dramatic structure, Richard's 'mistake,' far from being insufficiently bloody-minded, is to have been far too ruthless. Still, if we are to stay within the gardener's metaphoric universe, then Richard's shortcoming is that he did not have Bullingbrook killed, an act of mercy that has now come back to haunt the king. So even as Richard might be, in this metaphor, an impolitic king, Bullingbrook is the immediate villain of the piece, the one who has taken advantage of the king's sheltering branches to wreak havoc in the garden of England.

But far from being the villain in the eyes of the gardener, Bullingbrook is instead the *saviour* of England, the one who has 'pluck'd up root and all' the noxious weeds stifling his country's garden. Far from being the proud, over-sapped, rebellious tree unfairly sheltered by Richard, Henry is instead praised as a gardener par excellence, who has with great prudence, and in one fell swoop, rid the garden of all that was plaguing it. Even as Richard is blamed for not sufficiently suppressing rebellion, the rebel himself is praised as England's redeemer. Bullingbrook shores up the gardener's belief in a metaphoric reading of good governance by lopping and pruning plants that are hazardous to the garden's well-being.

This switch in roles causes some difficulty for the gardener's metaphor, which threatens to crumble under the weight of its own rhetorical complexity. How can Bullingbrook be both scoundrel and saint, villain and saviour? The only way this would be possible is if Bullingbrook's apparent villainy – rebelling against the king of England – were to be converted into a valiant effort to root out an even more noxious villainy. In other words, Bullingbrook's rebellion needs to be sanitized; for the gardener's metaphor to work, a different set of enemies needs to be found on whom to blame Richard's crimes and against whom to compare Bullingbrook's glory. Opposed to the heroic Bullingbrook in the passage, therefore, are the caterpillars and weeds of the commonwealth that destroy horticultural health. In an attempt to drive home the nature and extent of their villainy, the gardener's description of these caterpillars enters into a sexual register; their 'crimes' – in a tone later echoed by Hotspur in *1 Henry IV* – sound eerily like that of a rape: '... our sea-walled garden, the whole land, / Is full of weeds, her fairest flowers chok'd up, / Her fruit-trees all unprun'd, her hedges ruin'd, / Her knots disordered, and her whole-some herbs / Swarming with caterpillars' (III.iv.43–7). The sexually rapacious weeds prey on the beautifully virginal English flowers and untie their knots.

Who are these caterpillars and what exactly is their crime? Does this crime take place despite the king or does it include Richard in its ambit? In what way do the caterpillars *justify* Bullingbrook's rebellion? Who are they and what do they do? Of what is Bullingbrook ridding the realm? The gardener's speech raises questions that a metaphorical reading of the play – content with casting Richard in the role of villain and Bullingbrook as saviour – feels free to gloss over. Nonetheless, these are the questions we need to ask, not just of this passage but also of a text in which the murder of a king is cast in the mode of inevitability. Why does Richard *have* to be deposed? What role do the caterpillars – from Holinshed to Shakespeare – play in that deposition?

When Bullingbrook first returns to England, ostensibly to claim his ancestral lands after John of Gaunt's death, he wins over the duke of York to his side and then proposes to march to Bristol Castle, 'which they say is held / By Bushy, Bagot, and their complices, / The caterpillars of the commonwealth, / Which I have sworn to weed and pluck away' (II.iii.164–7). The metaphor of the weeds is echoed by the gardener when he clarifies the identity of the noxious elements in the garden: 'The weeds which his broad-spreading leaves did shelter, / That seem'd in eating him to hold him up, / Are pluck'd up root and all by Bullingbrook, / I mean the Earl of Wiltshire, Bushy and Green' (III.iv.50–3). Both Bullingbrook and the gardener spell out their metaphorical intent and tell us in no uncertain terms the identity of the caterpillars and weeds. Bushy, Bagot, Green, and the earl of Wiltshire, at least three of whose names metonymically evoke the verdure and profuseness of a garden, live nasty, brutish, and short lives in the state of nature. Their murder forms the prelude to the deposition and murder of the king, and is described as the *necessary* first step in Bullingbrook's grand scheme of justice.[23]

In addition to identifying these weeds, the gardener also gives us a sense of their operational strategy: they 'seem'd in eating him to hold him up.' Not only have the weeds pretended to be supportive, but they have also used that pretence to consume the king; what should have been a productive prop is turned into a damaging drain. Rhetorically, the emphasis is more on the crime of 'eating' than on the charge of 'seem[ing]'; the weeds are blamed for being parasitic and their behaviour becomes unacceptable to gardener and future king alike because the object upon which they feed is the king's *body*. At one level – in keeping with the metaphor of the body politic – the king's body would indicate the state of England: by feeding on the king's body, the caterpillars turn that body into England itself and deplete it of vital resources; we are told at the very start of the play that Richard's coffers cannot afford his campaigns against the Irish, but at another level – at an explicitly *un*-metaphorical level – the king's body is the king's body: it cannot be compared to anything outside itself – like the state – but rather circulates its energies in such a manner as to be indistinguishable from itself. The king's crime thus becomes not only that he has lavished too much care on the weedy Bushy, Bagot, and Green, who have consumed him while appearing to prop him up, and not even that he has allowed there to be a confusion about which body belongs in which metaphoric realm. Rather Richard's crime lies in the fact that he is not metaphoric enough and that he has allowed the caterpillars to feed on his *own* body, reducing the king from being an (active) gardener to a (passive) garden. Instead of battening on herbs, the favourites have been feeding on the *king's* body and depleting it of (fruitful) energies. The '[s]uperfluous branches' the gardener recommends lopping away 'that bearing boughs may live,' have clogged up Richard's productivity and have, so to speak, sucked him dry.

Such a belief is voiced quite clearly by Bullingbrook when he accuses Bushy and Green to their face. In terms that startlingly echo the gardener's, the usurper insists that he will

> ... unfold some causes of your deaths:
> You have misled a prince, a royal king,
> A happy gentleman in blood and lineaments,
> By you unhapped and *disfigured* clean;
> You have *in manner* with your sinful hours
> Made a divorce betwixt his queen and him,
> Broke the possession of a royal bed,
> And stain'd the beauty of a fair queen's cheeks
> With tears drawn from her eyes by your foul wrongs;
> Myself, a prince by fortune of my birth,
> Near to the King in blood, and near in love
> Till you did make him *misinterpret* me ...   (III.i.7–18; emphases mine)

In listing the accusations against Richard's courtiers, Bullingbrook asserts primarily that the *figure* of the king has been corrupted and that this corruption has caused a rift between Richard and his queen. Another word for 'figure,' of course, is 'body'; in such a reading, Bushy and Green are accused of having corrupted the king's *body*, of having cleanly corrupted (Bullingbrook is more a master of rhetoric than he lets on) the royal figure, and *thus* causing a divorce between Richard and Isabella. Bushy and Green's 'crime' is that the king has been more loyal to them than to his own wife. They stand accused of having broken 'the possession of a royal bed.' If Isabella has been dispossessed by them, might they have taken her place in bed instead?

Criticism has obliquely and productions have directly engaged such a possibility. Laurence Olivier allegedly identified Richard 'as an out-and-out pussy queer, with mincing gestures to match,'[24] while Harold Bloom suggests that a 'Freudian reading would find Richard an instance of "moral masochism," the collapse of the ego before the superego, sometimes related to strongly manifested bisexuality.'[25] In 'The "Parasitical" Counselors in Shakespeare's *Richard II*,' Paul Gaudet remarks that theatrical productions frequently portray the favourites as 'effete, homosexual peacocks,' and that this 'commonly accepted view marked the favorites as insinuating subverters of royal integrity on whom Richard has squandered what was not his to give.'[26] The idea of Richard's deviant sexuality is thus often alluded to – the frequent coupling of the play with Marlowe's *Edward II* makes this allusion obvious – but as an accusation against the king, it runs parallel to rather than merging with, the play's investment in language.

However, it is precisely this investment in the language of the play – this digging in the dirt of the gardener's speech – that turns up and makes explicit the crime lurking in the margins of greens and the depths of bushes. If theatrical productions are able to portray Richard as an 'effete' king, then that effeteness stems from the pervasive presence in the play of the trope of desire, metonymy. Richard's 'crime' of favouring his favourites is only brought into focus by the textual 'crime' of metonymy. After all, the other sense of figure – figure of *speech* – is equally important in the list of accusations against Richard and his courtiers. Bullingbrook suggests that the favourites have corrupted Richard's language, or rather, that they have corrupted the proper figure of kingship, owing to which Richard has been misled. Echoes of this figural corruption abound in the passage: the caterpillars are said to have made Richard 'misinterpret' Bullingbrook, to have acted on him in an unbecoming 'manner,' and to have sullied forever the king's 'lineaments,' which last can refer to both bodily and linguistic figures. In this figural sense, Bushy, Bagot, and Green stand accused of a crime that is never spelled out in the play but part of which routinely circulates in criticism on the play: the sense that Richard's fall has something to do with his relation to language. In such a reading, a disfigured language explicitly shares pride of place with a diseased sexuality; indeed in this passage, the former *figures* the latter. In such a reading, it almost does not matter what precisely the courtiers or Richard stand accused of since a lack of precision makes up the bulk of the accusations against them. Bullingbrook's outrage at being 'misrepresented' is an outrage that Richard has dared to corrupt his own body and that this corruption has the same source and uses the same factors as a corruption of the king's speech. Bullingbrook's outrage consists in the fact that the king speaks in corrupt figures rather than in pure metaphor, that he introduces dishonest (illegitimate?) figures into his bed rather than sleeping with his wife.

In Holinshed's account of the fall, the king's crime is expressed quite explicitly as the king's unnatural attachment to his courtiers: Richard's back is broken not so much by the news that Bullingbrook is planning to oust him, or even that he might be separated from his wife, as much as by the report that his favourites have been slaughtered: 'hearing how his trustie councellors had lost their heads at Bristow, he became so greatlie discomforted, that sorowfullie lamenting his miserable state, he vtterly despaired of his own safetie, and calling his armie together, which was not small, licenced euerie man to depart to his home' (*Chronicles*, 355). The courtiers' bodies have here literally replaced Isabella's, and concern for them takes precedence over concern for either her or the state.

Shakespeare reflects Holinshed quite faithfully in this respect; when his Richard receives several pieces of bad news while trying to muster together a force against Bullingbrook, he asks in desperation:

> ... Where is the Earl of Wiltshire? where is Bagot?
> What is become of Bushy? where is Green?
> That they have let the dangerous enemy
> Measure our confines with such peaceful steps?
> If we prevail, their heads shall pay for it:
> I warrant they have made peace with Bullingbrook.
> SCROOP: Peace have they made with him indeed, my lord.
> RICHARD: O villains, vipers, damn'd without redemption!
> Dogs, easily won to fawn on any man!

Snakes, in my heart-blood warm'd, that sting my heart!
Three Judases, each one thrice worse than Judas!
Would they make peace? terrible hell make war
Upon their spotted souls for this offence!
SCROOP: Sweet love, I see, changing his property,
Turns to the sourest and most deadly hate:
Again uncurse their souls; their peace is made
With heads, and not with hands; those whom you curse
Have felt the worst of death's destroying wound
And lie full low, graved in the hollow ground.   (III.ii.122–40)

After hearing of this turn of events, Richard loses all hope and begins reciting the first of several magnificent pieces of poetry that characterize him till his end. As in Holinshed, the death of Richard's 'friends' is the straw that breaks the camel's back; Scroop aptly describes Richard's condition when he says: 'Sweet love, I see, changing his property, / Turns to the sourest and most deadly hate.'[27] The extremities of Richard's emotions are reserved for Bushy, Bagot, Green, and the earl of Wiltshire.

Richard's crime, as this passage in conjunction with the gardener's speech seems to indicate, is that neither his language nor his sexuality is metaphoric enough, that he fails to realize both the *value* of words and the worth of heterosexuality. We might then begin to fathom how such a crime might be considered basis enough for murdering an anointed ruler. While criticism has seized eagerly on the failing of excessive verbosity, it has tended to ignore the echo of this excess in the king's sexuality, an echo that both brings Richard's love of words into focus *and* makes it unacceptable. The alternative reading of the garden scene suggests a metonymic corruption not immediately visible even as it is everywhere present; it feeds accusations that are made metaphorically but whose criminality lies in their metonymic detail. In *Richard II*, sexuality is not – cannot be – metaphorized *as* the garden or *as* the state: all such attempts fail to answer the questions to which they themselves give rise. Rather, sexuality, and the garden, and the state can metonymically be read as the workings of a(n) (in)different language, figures that can only be disfigured by turning the top soil over. A refusal to turn the soil is also a refusal to read the figurality of *Richard II*, a refusal that matches Bullingbrook's physical violence with the rhetorical violence of ignoring metonymy. Such a refusal – expressed as a compulsorily metaphoric reading of the garden scene – also ensures a compulsorily heterosexual reading of both the scene and the play.

To read the play metaphorically, then, is to ignore the text's met-onymic insistence on the sexual nature of Richard's state rather than the stately nature of England's garden.[28] Reading the garden as a meta-phor-for-the-state, in other words, provides an account of Richard's crimes that is both damning and insufficiently accusatory: it identifies the weeds and their protector as the criminals but can only locate their criminality in the knots of an ineffectively poetic language. An atten-tion to the garden's rich metonymic detail, on the other hand, makes clear the universe in which such language registers as criminal: a uni-verse in which weedy vice is screened by the flower of royal language. Metonymically, Richard's florid affect brings together the accusatory strains running through the play more effectively than the metaphori-cal denunciation of his insufficiently floral effect. Metaphor fails to describe Richard's crime except as a failure of metaphor, but this fail-ure of metaphor is ensured – and perhaps nowhere more so than in the profusion of the garden scene – by the presence of metonymy. Despite setting a discussion of Richard's crimes in the state of nature, then, nei-ther the gardener nor Bullingbrook is able to *spell out* the nature of the king's crime: in *Richard II*, metaphor fails 'in the supremely difficult task of providing a name for everything.' Northumberland prepares a detailed list of Richard's crimes to be read out before the commons, but the king refuses to comply and so his crimes remain – despite Bulling-brook's triumph – in the realm of *unread* textuality and horticultural innuendo. Criticism has been happy to accept this innuendo but not to interpret it, and these unread crimes have been read as an indulgence in language leading to inefficient rule.[29] A metonymic reading, on the other hand, has the virtue of mirroring the corruption of language – so horrific as to be publicly unreadable – with a corruption in sexuality, reinforcing both Freud and Lacan's analyses of the link between metonymy and desire. As the trope governing that which cannot be clearly and independently articulated, metonymy lurks in the shadows of this English garden threatening, like that other serpent, to cause the Fall of Man.[30]

Power-Dressing

Hic Mulier will shortly bee good latine, if this transmigration hold.
                                      Thomas Adams, *Mystical Bedlam*[31]

If the central problematic in *Richard II* is the nature of the king's crime, then the disconcerting fact in Middleton and Dekker's *Roaring Girl* is the softness of Moll's roar. Moll Cutpurse – the cross-dressing, man-hating, tobacco-smoking, bad-mouthing protagonist – is the surprisingly 'good' heroine of this play who comes into being as an entity separate from the tavern wench who 'beats the watch,' and the city wife who 'shakes her husband's state.' This sanitized roaring girl spreads sunshine and good cheer throughout the play and fights only the good fights. Moll is rescued from the gutters and given wings on which to soar to the highest point of decent behaviour leaving all her guttural tendencies behind. Why does Moll's 'sanitization' have to take place and what are the rhetorical stakes involved in this hygiene? Does Moll need to be rescued from the rhetorical traps that consumed Richard? If so, what repercussions does this rescue have on the sexual fabric of the play?

One way of addressing these questions is by looking at the fabric *in* the text since the play is, arguably, obsessed with clothing. In his note to the 'Comic Play-Readers,' Middleton admits that 'the fashion of play-making I can properly compare to nothing so naturally as the alteration in apparel,'[32] and then details the links between different kinds of clothes and plays. When we first see Moll (who, like Hamlet, enters rather late into her own text), she is going about the business of buying a shag-ruff. When Laxton waits for her in Gray's Inn Fields, for what he thinks is a sexual assignation, he keeps an eye out for a certain suit of clothes by which to identify Moll. Puns and jokes around clothing abound and form a vital source of dramatic humour; the link between this play and clothes is, we can safely say, essential. But what function do these clothes serve and is that function a necessary one? In other words, is the correlation that the play tries to draw between clothes and drama direct or inverted? To carry the mathematical metaphor a little further, does the play plot a graph whose coordinates are significantly different because of the clothes it wears?

The modern editor of *The Life and Death of Mrs. Mary Firth, Commonly Called Moll Cutpurse*, the so-called autobiography of Moll, suggests that 'Moll Cutpurse is a rich and enticing signifier – her garb must *mean* something – to whom each of her examiners attempts to attach a signified.'[33] Moll's greatest enemy in the play, Sir Alex Wengrave, for instance, states that 'this wench we speak of strays so from her kind, / Nature repents she made her; 'tis a mermaid / Has tolled my son to shipwreck / ... (they say, sometimes / She goes in breeches)' (I.ii.217–19, 229–30). Moll's breeches are here a definitive sign of her warped femininity, and Sir Alex objects to the idea of her marrying his son because he wants a 'proper' woman rather than a 'codpiece daughter.'

The man he hires to cause Moll's downfall, Trapdoor, displays a similarly dismissive attitude while plotting to trap the roaring girl:

TRAP: ... Mad Moll –
s. ALEX: Ah –
TRAP: Must be let in, without knocking, at your back gate.
s. ALEX: So.
TRAP: Your chamber will be made bawdy.
s. ALEX: Good.
TRAP: She comes in a shirt of mail.
s. ALEX: How? Shirt of mail?
TRAP: Yes, sir, or a male shirt; that's to say, in man's apparel.
s. ALEX: To my son?
TRAP: Close to your son; your son and her moon will be in conjunction, if all almanacs lie not; her black safeguard is turned into a deep slop, the holes of her upper body to buttonholes, her waistcoat to a doublet, her placket to the ancient seat of a codpiece, and you shall take 'em both with standing collars.   (III.iii.13–29)

The bawdy that enters Sir Alex's house is described in terms of the sodomitical masculinity of the female Moll's dress, a masculinity that outrages the patriarch's sense of propriety as it makes its entrance through the 'back gate.' The thought of Moll's 'standing collar' protruding from the 'ancient seat of [her] codpiece' is enough to send Sir Alex into paroxysms, both because of its inappropriateness and its (un)desirability. The stress on 'proper' relationships, which the play has insisted on right from its letter to the reader ('The fashion of play-making I can *properly* compare ...') is what Quintilian recognizes as the hallmark of metaphor, and clothes in this play are meant to secure the metaphoric propriety of persons and things. So if Moll dresses like a man, she is assumed to be 'untrue' to her feminine self since male clothes properly signify a male body. The corruption of the self as reflected by a corrupt suit of mail reiterates the metaphoric fabric of the play by stressing the *necessary* connection between the two poles.

But the rescue of Moll – from the Prologue on, where we are told that the roaring girl of the play will 'fl[y] / With wings more lofty' – seems to chart a different course, and the lofty curvature of Moll's flight takes place *despite* the impediment that her strange dress throws up. The rescue of Moll's 'good' name is undertaken by acknowledging, rather than ignoring, her metaphoric eccentricity. Thus, Sebastian Wengrave,

Moll's pretend-suitor, defends his 'fiancée' by projecting her as a pattern for womankind:

> Sh'as a bold spirit that mingles with mankind,
> But nothing else comes near it; and oftentimes
> Through her apparel somewhat shames her birth;
> But she is loose in nothing but in mirth.
> Would all Molls were no worse!   (II.iii.182–6)

Sebastian points to the disjunction between Moll's clothing and her 'self,' a disjunction that echoes her *Life*, where the preface states that 'she was the living description and portraiture of a schism and separation, her doublet and petticoat understanding one another no better than Presbytery and Independency.'[34] The defence of Moll takes her dress into account, but turns it from a liability into an asset. Even though Sebastian admits that she 'shames her birth' by her clothes, that shaming is in itself considered a venial sin; Moll's 'birth' has deemed her female no matter what clothes she wears. Her birth is not allowed to be like her suit, and her clothes are not allowed to taint the inner purity of her self. If the metaphoric collapse of clothing and selfhood indicates that Moll is a depraved person, then that collapse has to be disavowed in order to protect the protagonist. Therefore, while a metaphoric reading of the play insists that dress reflects self, the rescue of Moll insists that in *her* case, this metaphoric rigidity needs to be relaxed a little, and the 'clean-up' of the roaring girl is achieved by realigning metaphoric correspondence in order to maintain sexual purity. The text thus insists on rewriting metaphor by emphasising a *disjunction* between inside and outside, a rewriting that creates a rhetorical vacuum where metaphor once used to reign, and this vacuum is pressed into the service of rescuing Moll's reputation.[35]

One step in this rescue focuses on enforcing the distinction between clothes and the 'man' and disproving that Moll's masculine attire has tainted her feminine sensibility. Sebastian's defence of Moll belongs to this camp, and Moll herself is made the spokesperson for this conservative view on several occasions. After shaming Laxton for presuming to have had a sexual assignation with her, Moll muses aloud:

> If I could meet my enemies one by one thus,
> I might make pretty shift with 'em in time,
> And make 'em know she that has wit and spirit,

May scorn to live beholding to her body for meat;
Or for apparel, like your common dame,
That makes shame get her clothes to cover shame.
Base is that mind that kneels unto her body,
As if a husband stood in awe on's wife ...   (III.i.143–50)

By asserting that the mind occupies a superior position vis-à-vis the body, Moll pours scorn on people for whom bodily pleasures are paramount. She specifically renounces all love of apparel, deeming a love of clothes fit only for the province of the 'common dame' who allows society to parasitically feed on her 'body for meat.' In a telling analogy, Moll compares the evil influence of these common dames to the apocalyptic possibility of a husband being ruled by his wife. The threat of women on top is one that Moll disavows even as she flaunts her 'masculine' independence. While a moll's clothes are taken as proof of debased behaviour, Moll's own clothes supposedly do not enact any such corruption. The metaphoric link between outside and inside only applies in selective cases, and never to Moll herself, in whose case base clothes become a debased indicator of her (true) mind. A cross-dressed body, by this twist of logic, is made symbolic of a pure mind. Clothes become a free-floating signifier to be interpreted by people as they will, and Moll interprets hers as reinforcing, rather than questioning, virtuous and obedient femininity.

This virtue is made to spill over into the realm of sexuality, and Moll self-righteously condemns prostitutes and unfaithful wives for allowing their bodies to rule their minds. In fact, she is utterly disdainful of bodily desire altogether, and firmly believes it should be kept in check within the confines of marriage. This emphasis on chaste heterosexual coupling causes Moll to panic when she sees Sebastian kissing the cross-dressed Mary Fitzallard (whom Moll has herself dressed as a boy to facilitate an encounter between the two lovers). Startled by this unusual sight, Moll exclaims: 'How strange this shows, one man to kiss another!' (IV.i.47). Not only does this place Moll firmly in the conservative camp (where even Sebastian does not belong),[36] but it also takes her away from her earlier position that dressing like a man doesn't necessarily make one 'male.' Moll displays what de Man would call a 'constitutive tendency' to forget the disavowal of metaphor while passing judgment on the sexual actions of others.

This sexual conservatism is paralleled (and created) by the linguistic 'order' of the text. In the first scene of the final act, a scene that follows close on the heels of the male-male kiss, Moll, accompanied by her friends and Lord Noland, a peer of the realm, encounters Trapdoor and Tearcat, who are pretending to be poor soldiers and hoping to make a little money off Moll's entourage. What follows is an intense battle of wits between Moll and Trapdoor in the canting language of the underworld. Moll acts as the interpreter for an incredulous audience who cannot even begin to fathom the trappings of Trapdoor's language. This scene follows a set pattern in which Moll translates the language of the underworld much to everyone's delight and admiration:

ALL: Doxy, Moll? What's that?
MOLL: His wench.
...
L. NOLL: Nay, nay, Moll, why art thou angry? What was his gibberish?
MOLL: Marry, this, my lord, says he: 'Ben Mort.' Good wench, 'shall you and I have a booth, mill a ken, or nip a bung?' Shall you and I rob a house, or cut a purse?
OMNES: Very good.
...
MOLL: Pox on him, a gallant? Shadow me, I know him; 'tis one that cumbers the land indeed; if he swim near to the shore of any of your pockets, look to your purses.
OMNES: Is't possible?
MOLL: This brave fellow is no better than a foist.
OMNES: Foist! What's that?
MOLL: A diver with two fingers, a pickpocket ...   (V.i.163–4, 201–4, 286–91)

Moll, the professor of language, translates gibberish into meaning, much to the amazement of her simplistic audience. She banishes the bafflement generated by canting and quickly institutes sense where its lack had threatened to reign. Moll insists that language can and should be meaningful. Crucially, she creates this meaning for the representative of the law, thereby implying that her primary commitment is to spreading legality and curbing subversion. By allowing her access to the signification of language and by making her use that knowledge to prevent the spread of crime, the play completes its process of sanitizing Moll, the roaring girl.

Or does it? The text attempts, on the one hand, to clean up Moll's image by disavowing metaphor – her clothes do *not* make her a man – but on the other hand, it also reinstates metaphor by insisting on the singularly meaningful nature, and internal coherence, of both language and clothing. Even as the sanitization of Moll cannot take place without the repudiation of metaphor, the *means* of achieving that sanitization are themselves forced to fall back on the trope in order for Moll to make sense of a world filled with sexual and textual turmoil. The departure from metaphor is marked by its return.

But this return is not a direct one. As several of the play's names attest to, there is something in the play's nomenclature that resists the overwhelming triumph of metaphor. Both Laxton and Trapdoor, for instance, are intimately connected with Moll, but neither of their names quite fits their bodies. 'Laxton' suggests a lack of stones, or testicles, an implication seized upon by more than one character in the play ('furnish Master Laxton / With what he wants, a stone,' says Sir Alex in I.ii.58), while Trapdoor, a dangerous mercenary, is hired by Sir Alex to trap Moll. Far from lacking testicles, however, Laxton has an active sex drive and he tries to seduce, with varying degrees of success, both Moll and Mistress Gallipot. Trapdoor too fails to live up to his name and is instead trapped by Moll in a suit of her own clothes ('if you deserve, I cast off this, next week, and you may creep into't' III.i.210). This opposition between signifier and signified, between name and essence, points to a reversal of metaphor; that which is normally suggested by a word is at odds with the 'truth.' The name of Moll Cutpurse, for instance, suggests both that she is a thief, which role she is explicitly *distanced* from, and that her virginity has been broken into, leaving only a bleeding wound behind, which is repeatedly stated to be untrue. The suggestive rather than appropriate explosion of names in the play is directly at odds with the proper metaphoric desire of having an externality matching an inner being. The impotence of metaphoric propriety and the perverse suggestiveness of proper names provides some clue about the rhetorical mode in which the 'rescue' of Moll is undertaken. If metaphor is to be distanced from the roaring girl, can metonymy possibly take its place?

But the case for metonymy is weakened almost as soon as it is made since the cleansing of Moll specifically involves distancing her from desire, which therefore also involves a distancing from metonymy. And even though Moll's masturbatory skill in 'strok[ing]' herself has been much celebrated, these strokes keep time to a profoundly misogynistic and undesirable discourse.[37] In one of its more powerful evocations of metonymy, the play tries to *collapse* the distance between Moll and other women by enacting the seemingly seamless substitution of Moll Cutpurse and Mary Fitzallard. Sebastian pretends to be in love with Moll in order to take the sting out of his intended match with Mary, and the two women dress alike at crucial moments in the play. Mary assumes male attire in order to keep her assignation with Sebastian (when the 'male-male' kiss takes place, much to Moll's wonder), and Moll dresses like Mary in Sebastian's final trick on his father. But the women, both of whom are literally cross-dressed at points in the play, are not allowed to cross rhetorically since that would ruin the sanitization of Moll. Even as clothes are deemed the metaphoric 'thing' to which one can apply in case of sexual doubt – Mary's male clothes make her a man and make the sight of her kissing Sebastian a 'wondrous' one – they are also made to testify to the great worth of the masculinely attired Moll's *female* chastity. Clothes in this play become metonymic in their interpretive freedom; Moll's clothes do not make her a worse *woman*. Rather, they make her *as good as a man* since the status quo is safe in her keeping. Instead of metaphorically liberating her from gendered identity, Moll's 'masculinity' metonymically joins her to the misogynistic discourse that dominates the play. The metaphor of clothing is disavowed in favour of the metonymy of association, but this metonymy is then itself shunned in favour of metaphorically stable language and sexuality. *The Roaring Girl* tries, even more than readings of *Richard II*, to exclude metonymy from its fold by asserting that a seemingly radical woman, however she may dress, really *does* believe in the existence and justice of gender difference. Moll's exclusion at the end of the play from the comic circle of marriage is less an indicator of her uniqueness in being metonymically unstable and more a comment on her uselessness now that the metaphoric order she has championed has been reinstated.

Moll's 'rescue' only serves then, to reinscribe with a heightened conservatism, the metaphoric reading of the play's clothes. In order to make amends for slighting metaphor sexually, the text entrenches it even more deeply at a textual level by ignoring the metonymic possibilities opened up by the names and the clothes in the play. Much like the movement of sexuality in the text, we are carried from the realm of metaphor (clothes make the man) to the kingdom of metonymy (that man is a woman), only to be brought painfully back to metaphor (the woman was always a woman) by what we thought was the very figure of metonymic incomprehensibility. Just as she wears man's clothes but is always a 'woman,' so too can Moll both cant and translate into the King's English. The possibility of metonymy is shown to be a lie in order for metaphor to be reinstalled. In the canting scene, therefore,

Lord Noland and Sir Thomas Long express their shock at Moll's nick-name: 'L.NOLL: I wonder how thou camest to the knowledge of these nasty villains. / S.THO: And why do the foul mouths of the world call thee Moll Cutpurse? A name, methinks, damned and odious.' (V.i.324–7) Moll Cutpurse continues to be called by her name, but she is purged of all its unsavoury connotations. So much so, that Moll becomes the *victim* of an unbridled, metonymic, language system that takes no note of necessary connections:

> ... Must you have
> A black ill name, because ill things you know?
> Good troth, my lord, I'm made Moll Cutpurse so.
> How many whores in small ruffs and still looks!
> How many chaste whose names fill slander's books!
> Were all men cuckolds whom gallants in their scorns
> Call so, we should not walk for goring horns.   (V.i.356–62)

Moll hates being called a whore because she is none. She also hates the rhetorical system that allows for the possibility that women with ruffs can be whores and that men can grow horns (merely) by being slandered (we need think only of Othello). Moll hates the metonymic language system because it does not follow the causal logic by which she makes sense of the world and by which the play makes a saint of her.

Her reaction to being called a whore is therefore very different from the reaction of one of her counterparts, the 'White Devil,' Vittoria Corombona. Moll deals with the metonymic potential of language by trying to place herself beyond its reach, while Vittoria on the other hand, employs metonymy to beat her oppressor at his own game. In *The White Devil*,[38] Cardinal Monticelso, enraged at Vittoria's role in her husband's death, accuses her of being a whore:

> MONT: Who knows not how, when several night by night
>   Her gates were choked with coaches, and her rooms
>   Outbraved the stars with several kinds of lights,
>   When she did counterfeit a prince's court
>   In music, banquets, and most riotous surfeits?
>   This whore, forsooth, was holy.
> VIT. COR: Ha! Whore! What's that!
> MONT: Shall I expound whore to you? Sure, I shall;
>   I'll give you their perfect character ... What's a whore!

She's like the guilty counterfeited coin
Which, whosoe'er first stamps it, brings in trouble
All that receive it ...
VIT. COR: You are deceived.
                    ... For your names
Of whores and murderers, they proceed from you,
As if a man should spit against the wind;
The filth returns in's face.   (III.ii.72–9, 97–100, 143, 148–51)

Vittoria knows that like the counterfeit coin she is accused of being, language too is exchangeable. If one coin can be taken for another, so too can one word, and so she returns the compliment of 'whore' with interest, as it were. Later in the same scene, she accuses the cardinal of having 'raped' justice by forcing it to do his pleasure. Yoking together whoredom (she wants it) and rape (she asked for it) is a classic example of metonymy, and Vittoria knows that if the cardinal can pin her down by calling her a whore, she too can formulate him using the same method of arbitration. The interesting difference between Vittoria and Moll, of course, is that the former is guilty *within* the scope of the play: she instigates Brachiano to murder her husband and his wife. The fact of guilt seems to be less important in *The White Devil*, however, than does the issue of innocence in *The Roaring Girl*. The reversibility of language and the boomerang effect of phlegm are embraced by Vittoria as means by which to question the status quo even as such metonymic links are disavowed by Moll in a bid to uphold it. The 'character' of a whore that the cardinal tries to map is as intangible (he compares her to a sweetmeat, a poisoned perfume, a shipwreck, a Russian winter, the tune of a bell, and a cadaver, among other things) as the quality of 'whore-ness;' like sodomy, neither the crime nor the criminal *necessarily* names the other, and the transference of attributes (Abraham Fraunce's definition of metonymy includes using 'the names of virtues and vices ... for virtuous and vicious men'),[39] is endlessly reversible. Using metonymy, as Vittoria knows, can endlessly overturn the label of 'whore,' but admitting it, as Moll knows, can destabilize one's good and virtuous name.

   The Roaring Girl therefore insists that while Moll may dress like a man, she *is* none; that while two men might *seem* to be kissing, one of them will turn out to be a woman;[40] and that while language can be *transmuted* into nonsense, meaning will always be salvaged. The fluid nature of metonymy is put to rest by the irreversible metaphor of clothing even as the latter is made conveniently flexible in the case of Moll. Ironically, and fittingly, Moll misrecognizes the disruptive potential of the clothing metaphor even as she reinstalls it at the end. This wilful blindness is necessary in order for the play to reach a point at which Moll can gracefully retire, thinking she has forever laid to rest the seductive roar of desire.

Seduction remains on stage at the end, however, though not in the person of Moll. Even as the 'daring' protagonist turns out to be not so daring after all, the metaphoric ending is problematized as a closure for the text and the play produces an epilogue promising an appearance of the 'real' Moll Cutpurse in next week's performance. This promise of the 'real' Moll not only implicitly designates the play's (metaphoric) Moll as an unreal one, as a (metonymic) substitute for the real thing, but it also creates a residue of desire in the promise of the real Moll's appearance at a future date. The future date will always exist in futurity; instead of sexual and metaphoric completion, the epilogue leaves behind an audience full of lackstones who metonymically desire more than can satisfy their desire. As the dramatic Moll walks down her metaphoric way at the end of the play, the text pipes up one last time to announce that metonymy is not fully dead, after all.

Lies, Damned Lies, and Desire

Is not amorous a good word?

Middleton and Dekker, The Roaring Girl[41]

Richard II and *The Roaring Girl* both renounce metonymy for the comforting shelter of metaphor. The critical tradition of the one and the conservative heroine of the other display a profound unease with letting metonymy insinuate its way into the dramatic text, and prefer to let metaphoric certainty come out 'on top.' One reason for this unease, as de Man puts it, is that 'if metonymy is distinguished from metaphor in terms of necessity and contingency ... then metonymy is per definition unable to create genuine links.'[42] The fact that metaphor is also unable to create the genuine link (England's garden does not equal Richard's court, and Moll's dress equals neither her gender nor her sexuality), is selectively forgotten by both plays in order to keep metonymic contingency at bay. This, however, proves to be an impossible task, and the fabric of both texts bears the mark of its rhetorical violence.

Not all texts follow the same trajectory, however, and I want to end this chapter by looking briefly at a play that seems openly comfortable with the metonymic cast of (its) text. Towards the end of *As You Like It*, there is a highly stylized sequence during which 'Hymen' draws together the disparate genealogical and sexual threads that have been plaguing the play. Rosalind is united with both her father the duke and her lover Orlando, Celia is united with Oliver, Phebe with Silvius, and Audrey with Touchstone. However, not all these (re)unions are happy ones. Phebe, for instance, has been bullied into marrying Silvius even though her heart belongs to Ganymede,[43] and Audrey and Touchstone are joined with the same joy as 'winter to foul weather.' Nevertheless, this scene is the 'comic' denouement of the play where the text neatly details its heterosexual couples who then go on to dance happily ever after. Since metonymy lies in the details, an attention to the finer points of this coupling throws a somewhat less divine light on the (hetero)sexual happiness at the end of the play.

In the final scene, all the characters assemble at the express command of Ganymede who promises that all true lovers will be properly coupled by the end of the afternoon. She then goes away, changes into Rosalind, and rejoins the company accompanied by the unsatisfactorily unidentified 'Hymen,' who performs the wedding ceremonies. Interestingly enough, when Rosalind offers to unveil herself as the duke's daughter and as Orlando's lover, she sets off a chain of contingencies that threatens to undermine, or at least indefinitely postpone, the happy ending of the play:

> DUKE S: *If* there be truth in sight, you are my daughter.
> ORL: *If* there be truth in sight, you are my Rosalind.
> PHE: *If* sight and shape be true,
>   Why then my love adieu!
> ROS: I'll have no father, *if* you be not he;
>   I'll have no husband, *if* you be not he;
>   Nor ne'er wed woman, *if* you be not she.
> HYM: Peace ho! *I bar confusion,*
>   'Tis I must make conclusion
>   Of these most strange events.
>   Here's eight that must take hands
>   To join in Hymen's bands,
>   *If* truth holds true contents.   (V.iv.118–30; emphasis mine)[44]

If the anaphoric reiteration of contingency marks the entire wedding ritual, then Hymen rudely interrupts to *bar* the confusion even as he himself partakes of it. If truth be told, this seems to be a highly unsatisfactory conclusion to a tale of twisted love in which men have fallen in love with men (Orlando with Ganymede), and women with women (Phebe with Rosalind). Of course neither Orlando nor Phebe knows for certain if Ganymede/Rosalind is male or female, and this scene, by relying on 'sight and shape,' both of which are known to be mutable, does nothing to enlighten them. Even as Rosalind insists on keeping both possibilities open ('I'll have no husband, if you be not he; / Nor ne'er wed woman, if you be not she'), Hymen steps in to set the record straight. But like most records, this straightening proves immensely difficult textually, as a brief glance at two moments, one before and the other after Hymen's scene, demonstrate.

Since Rosalind needs time to change her clothes and effect the dramatic transformation from Ganymede to herself, the play buys time by giving us an extended exposition on how to sidestep duels at court. Touchstone tells his audience that most quarrels can be avoided by adhering to the strict protocol governing such situations, in which there are seven steps, each representing a moment at which either of the parties can bow out of the confrontation:

> TOUCH: O sir, we quarrel in print, by the book – as you have books for good manners. I will name you the degrees. The first, the Retort Courteous; the second, the Quip Modest; the third, the Reply Churlish; the fourth, the Reproof Valiant; the fift, the Countercheck Quarrelsome; the sixt, the Lie with Circumstance; the seventh, the Lie Direct. All these you may avoid but the Lie Direct; and you may avoid that too, with an If. I knew when seven justices could not take up a quarrel, but when the parties were met themselves, one of them thought but of an If, as, 'If you said so, then I said so'; and they shook hands and swore brothers. Your If is the only peacemaker; much virtue in If.   (V.iv.90–103)

The scene with Hymen that immediately follows picks up on the 'If' in order to settle its own sets of 'Lie[s] Direct.' The proximity between contingency and lying on the one hand parallels the proximity between faining and feigning on the other, resulting in the metonymic coupling of lies and desire. While wrapping the unsophisticated Audrey in reams of rhetoric, Touchstone touches on this Sidneyan problem of differentiating between poetry and truth and concludes that it is impossible to do so because 'the truest poetry is the most feigning' (III.iii.19). The pun on fain/feign, on desire and pretence, is one that runs through the text, and leads directly to the contingent acceptance of love with which the play ends.

But does this contingency imply that metonymy always tells tales of falsehood, and of false desire in particular? The play seems to offer an affirmative answer to this question, but since Touchstone has exposed us to a *range* of lies, we can also say that desire fits more into the category of the 'Lie with Circumstance,' than the 'Lie Direct.' The text seems to endorse this view when it has a newly married Rosalind come back as the epilogue to say: 'If I were a woman I would kiss as many of you as had beards that pleas'd me, complexions that lik'd me, and breaths that I defied not' (Epilogue, 18–20). The eternally teasing nature of desire does not reach a resting place even (or especially) in marriage, a point that both *The Roaring Girl* and *As You Like It* make in their epilogues. The metaphor of marriage – despite drawing legitimate connections between things hitherto unrelated, like one man and one woman – cannot contain the 'iffy' metonymy of illegitimately sliding desire; if 'amorous' is a good word for dandy Jack Dapper in *The Roaring Girl*, then it is only good *as* a word that can continually be exchanged, keeping the f(r)iction of desire alive. This continued friction then becomes the province of another trope and another chapter.

3

First Night: Metalepsis, *Romeo and Juliet*, *All's Well that Ends Well*

This The cannot be said.

Jacques Lacan, 'A Love Letter'[1]

We look upon all adornment, except that attached to the female body, as undesirable and forget that it may serve a purpose.

Robert O. Evans, *The Osier Cage*[2]

In or around 1680, the earl of Rochester wrote a closet drama in which graphic sexual encounters end with fire, brimstone, and the destruction of a kingdom. Perhaps unsurprisingly, Rochester called his play *Sodom and Gomorrah*.[3] The play's trajectory moves from presenting sodomy as a 'natural' force to ferociously clamping down on it as the Vice beyond redemption. This curious split in the narrative results in a sexual morality that develops near the end of the play and defines sodomitical debauchery as the perverted opposite of procreative sexuality. Despite its remarkable beginning in sodomy's unremarkableness, then, *Sodom* enacts the process of investing sodomy with disease and procreative heterosexuality with health; the play ends with a character called Nature descending into the world of corruption in order to cleanse it of its sins. The entire play is an exercise in yoking together two disparate worlds, but when they do finally come together, the sodomitical world is completely destroyed, and the 'Natural' realm transformed for life. Metalepsis is the rhetorical term designated to bridge the gap between two worlds even as it is the trope that undermines any absolute opposition between the two. Indeed, metalepsis insists that every claim to absolute identity (whether sodomitical or natural) is differentially constituted in relation to the other. Metalepsis might be described as the trope that inhibits the formation of lasting bonds; as such, it often needs to be hidden away from the light of day.

Bolloximian, the king of Sodom, flouts the law of nature by preferring male courtiers to his wife, Cuntigratia; his courtier of choice is Pockenello. The king appoints a Buggermaster-general, Borastus, to 'proclaim, that buggery may be used / O'er all the land, so cunt be not abused' (I.i.69–70).[4] Meanwhile, Queen Cuntigratia, celibate since the king left her bed, is yearning to have sex. The queen consults her maids of honour, Fuckadilla, Cunticula, and Clitoris, all of whom suggest that she seduce the army general, Buggeranthus, and that in the meantime she masturbate 'to ease [the] pain' (I.ii.64). The dildos they provide, however, fall short by a yard and the queen and her ladies-in-waiting are left gasping for more. In a state of desperation, the queen finally manages to seduce General Buggeranthus and have her desire (temporarily) satiated. Not to be outdone by his parents fucking Pockenello and Buggeranthus respectively, the heir-apparent, Prince Prickett, loses his virginity under the expert guidance of his sister, Princess Swivia. The entire kingdom participates in this 'quintessence of debauchery': from the king who prefers arse to cunt, to the queen who cheats on her husband, to the royal offspring who commit incest.

All these scenes of graphic sexual activity are brought together under the rubric of 'waste.' The play is filled with images of women who cannot masturbate and men who prematurely ejaculate. Prickett 'spends' himself before providing any pleasure to Cunticula, and Virtuoso the dildo-maker comes too soon, much to Fuckadilla's dismay: 'That bliss for which my cunt so long did stay, / He gave to fancy, and 'tis thrown away.' Sexually unused seed permeates the kingdom across divisions of sexual proclivity, and the play proceeds along a course that remarkably does not distinguish between sexualities in terms of debauchery and chastity. Bolloximian and Buggeranthus, Cuntigratia and Clitoris are knit together in an orgy of pornography that seems unmindful of details like perversion and prudery. However, these unremarkable encounters come to a head in and as the end of the play when 'Nature' intervenes to destroy a kingdom and people so thoroughly steeped in sin.[5]

In this first and final attempt to restore order to the wayward kingdom, Nature (designated female in the text) begins by singling out the people who most need to be punished for their sexual 'crimes.' Compiling this list involves distinguishing between homo- and heterosexuality even though Nature's seed has been 'wasted' by all in equal proportion. Thus it is that the ruler of Sodom, King Bolloximian, comes in for particular fire under the new dispensation. The king refuses to comply with Nature's urgings to renounce his sexual proclivities, and questions both her mandate and the basis for her judgment. But Flux, a former courtier and current representative of Nature's edict, urges the king to accede:

> BOLLOXIMIAN: What act does Love and Nature contradict?
> FLUX: That for which Heaven does these pains inflict.
>> Nor do the beauties of thy throne escape –
>> The Queen is damned, Prince Prickett has a clap.
>> Raving and mad the Princess is become,
>> With pains and ulcerations in her womb.
> BOLLOXIMIAN: Curse upon Fate to punish us for nought.
>> Can no redress, no punishment be sought?
> FLUX: To Love and Nature all their rights restore,
>> Fuck no men, and let buggery be no more.
>> It does the propagable end destroy,
>> Which Nature gave with pleasure to enjoy.
>> Please her, and she'll be kind; if you displease,
>> *She turns into corruption and disease.*
> BOLLOXIMIAN: How can I leave my own beloved sin,
>> That has so long my dear companion been?
> FLUX: Sir, it will prove the shortening of your life.
> BOLLOXIMIAN: Then must I go to the old whore, my wife?
>> Why did the Gods, that gave me leave to be
>> A king, not grant me immortality?
>> To be *a substitute* for heaven at will –
>> I scorn the gift – I'll reign and bugger still.   (V.i.36–57; emphases mine)

Bolloximian is outraged by the fact that the gods insist on his returning to Cuntigratia rather than continuing to enjoy the charms of Pockenello. By claiming that he should be able to 'substitute' his own nature for whatever set of codes Nature has dictated, the king asserts his divine right in the face of inhuman wrath. Bolloximian seeks to emphasise the exchangeability of apparently discrete natures – human and divine, corrupt and natural. Despite being absolutely opposed to Bolloximian, this substitutability is also emphasised by Nature herself; indeed it provides the basis for her punitive behaviour even though the very prospect of substitution (or change) implies a corruption from which Nature recoils.

As Nature's protean representative, 'Flux' signifies the changeability of nature even as he tries to insist on its fixity. Threatening Bolloximian with dire consequences for non-compliance with his punishment, Flux states that when Nature is pleased, she is kind, but when things do not go her way, she 'turns' into corruption and disease. This 'turning' is also a troping (in Greek, 'to turn') as Bolloximian's sodomy makes Nature *turn* corrupt and modifies the idea of the 'natural' to include what has hitherto been thought of as diseased. Such a turning is anticipated by Bolloximian's opening question: 'What act does Love and Nature contradict?' For him, sodomy is simply (and literally) the law of the land. As such, it is the most 'natural' thing of all. So even as Nature seeks to distance its purity from the depravity of sodomitical nature, the two terms (Nature/nature) threaten to taint one another rhetorically. Nature tries to distance the natural from its sodomitical self in order to retain some semblance of moral superiority. Bolloximian, on the other hand, is invested in making precisely the kind of collapse between purity and impurity with which he has ruled his kingdom and for which he is now being punished. For the king, this collapse is enacted by elevating sodomy as the defining principle of nature under which all sexuality is equally creative. For Nature, however, sexuality has to be stamped with the mark of productivity in order to justify its role in the proper propagation of the species.

Therefore, the punishment meted out to the prime actors – the queen's damnation, the princess's sick womb, and the prince's clap – are all diseases that obstruct the 'propagable end[s]' of Nature. These diseases are specifically described as perversions that need to be distanced from kind Nature in order to make the natural order Natural. Bolloximian's crime is that he openly brings together concepts that should be kept apart; in retaliation, Nature represses 'diseased' sex both by sickening individual members of Sodom and attempting to banish its king. Bolloximian's embrace of sodomy and Nature's repression of it, I will suggest, partake of a move known to the rhetoricians as metalepsis, in which one trope has the power to bring to visibility the link between two hitherto unrelated or oppositional terms even as it is itself rendered invisible. For both Bolloximian and Nature, this metaleptic term is 'sodomy' since it threatens to bring together Nature with what passes for natural in Sodom. When Bolloximian's sodomy threatens to reduce Nature to a mere tropological fiction, Nature responds with the end of the world.

Nature and the king thus jointly partake of the metaleptic urge to enact a change around the figure of sodomy: the one to elevate it and the other to repress it. In doing so, they highlight the rhetorical force of sodomy and its figural ability to infect what passes for the sanctum of holiness. The sodomy of troping infects the natural order to such an extent that Nature has to tropologically distance itself from rhetoric in order to maintain her own ineffable status. As Leonard Barkan points out, metalepsis lends itself 'so directly to troping that [it] become[s] the means whereby a culture thinks in figural terms.'[6] Nature achieves this production of cultural meaning by metaleptically collapsing disease and sodomy and ignoring the 'nature' of sodomy altogether, while Bolloximian insists on the sodomitical markers of Nature herself. As the text makes clear, the equation between Nature and Sodomy is one that the natural order cannot afford to acknowledge even as it is everywhere marked by it. In an otherwise vapid play, this fact stands out with a clarity not easily found in other texts.

Sodom plots for us the inevitable connection between desire and rhetoric that this chapter will explore: from the tragedy of *Romeo and Juliet*, where desire is unable to express itself as anything but death, to the 'problem play' of *All's Well that Ends Well*, where desire is suppressed until it signifies *properly*. In itself, however, Rochester's play stands as an excellent instance of metalepsis. By granting sodomy the rhetorical power of linking nature with Nature, *Sodom and Gomorrah*, like Donne's Sappho, situates rhetoric in the realm of the erotic excessive. This excess, however, has to be made invisible – has to be destroyed – in order for Nature to triumph. The mark of failure thus has to be inscribed on the trope whose success ensures its defeat: Nature can only emerge victorious if it manages to erase its own tropology, repress its own rhetorical underpinnings, and devalue its own sodomy. But this desire to banish sodomy also clearly exposes Nature's sodomitical proclivities. Punishing sodomitical nature brings Nature's sodomitical trappings into focus, and sodomy can only point to its pervasive presence by accepting its own rhetorical repression.

Repression and Its Discontents

Metalepsis is rhetoric's repressed term, a trope whose most eloquent expression is silence.[7] The Latin *transumptio* is defined as a rhetorical device that must be subsumed by two terms between which it provides a link, and so every textual transaction involving metalepsis is perforce a bracketed one. This subsuming sometimes takes place to such an extent that rhetoricians prefer not to speak of metalepsis at all; the author of the *Ad Herennium*, for instance, does not list *transumptio* among his figures of speech.[8] Metalepsis lurks in textual shadows, invisibly working its rhetorical effects and unable to assert its own tropological identity. As such, it has neither a clearly defined ontological status nor a sharply delineated physical form; its existence is purely relational.

Classical, Renaissance, and contemporary studies of rhetoric align themselves with the caution that Terence Hawkes expresses: 'Something in the mind withers at the prospect of unfolding the mysteries of ... Metalepsis.'[9] The mysteries of metalepsis are rarely exhumed and are often subsumed under the larger figures of metaphor or metonymy or catachresis. But even though many rhetorical handbooks ignore or scant a discussion of metalepsis, not all of them suppress it altogether. Unlike the author of the *Ad Herennium*, Quintilian deals with *transumptio* in some detail, and provides us with an extremely powerful instance of its use. He begins, however, with uncharacteristic dismissiveness:

> There is but one of the tropes involving change of meaning which remains to be discussed, namely, *metalepsis* or *transumption*, which provides a transition from one trope to another. It is (if we except comedy) but rarely used in Latin, and is by no means to be commended, though it is not infrequently employed by the Greeks ... It is the nature of metalepsis to form a kind of intermediate step between the term transferred and the thing to which it is transferred, having no meaning in itself, but merely providing a transition. It is a trope with which to claim acquaintance, rather than one which we are ever likely to require to use. The commonest example is the following: *cano* is a synonym for *canto* and *canto* for *dico*, therefore *cano* is a synonym for *dico*, the intermediate step being provided by *canto*. We need not waste any more time over it. (*Institutio*, VIII.vi.37)

Even in the process of defining metalepsis, Quintilian cannot resist disowning it as a 'Greek' corruption that no upstanding Roman should emulate. The 'foreignness' of metalepsis is also reflective of a (tropological) corruption that Quintilian wants to distance himself from, and so he defines metalepsis as an 'intermediate step ... having no meaning in itself.' The trope merely provides a bridge between two terms and its role is not necessarily acknowledged in the credits. Nonetheless, it remains a trope that involves a 'change of meaning,' and this change is further complicated by the fact that the two terms between which the transition takes place are themselves *tropes*, rather than just words.

The example Quintilian gives is helpful, but more in reinforcing than in clarifying confusion. For him, metalepsis is at work in the transition between *cano* and *dico*, with the intermediate term being provided by *canto*. In Latin, *cano* means 'to sing, sound, play; to rehearse and recite; to prophesy and predict'; and is here linked with *dico*, 'to proclaim, make known; to describe, relate, sing, celebrate; a prediction, a prophecy'; with the linking term being provided by *canto*: 'to sound, sing, play; to reiterate, to make known, say.'[10] Singing is thus connected to speaking by suppressing reiteration. *Cano* shares similarities with *canto*, and *canto* shares a set of assumptions with *dico*. Much like a venn diagram, *cano* and *dico* get linked by the common area provided by *canto*, but in Quintilian's sketch, this site of overlap is then erased to make the link between *cano* and *dico* appear unmediated. Metalepsis thus confers the cloak of respectability on two terms that might not, in its absence, be linked at all. The cloak also inevitably hides its owner, and masks the trope that creates commonality between two seemingly disparate circles. This is probably why we can only ever 'claim acquaintance' with the trope, since a lasting bond would require a presence that metalepsis is unable to provide for itself.

The problem, or at least one of them, that arises from a consideration of Quintilian's example is the location of metalepsis: is *canto* the metaleptic term, or does the *cano-dico* relation embody the trope of metalepsis? In terms of *Sodom and Gomorrah*, is sodomy the metaleptic term, or does the Nature-nature link lay the metaleptic ground? If *canto* is the metalepsis in this example, then we no longer have an immediately identifiable trope, since *canto* is precisely that which cannot be pointed to, and is unearthed as a linking term only in a *retrospective* analysis of the connection between singing and speaking. This belatedness of metalepsis is picked up by later commentators as the defining feature of the trope, and so it is entirely apposite that *canto* (or sodomy) be nominated the metaleptic term only after the fact. If we consider the second option – that metalepsis is the link forged between *cano* and *dico* or between Nature and nature – then the trope can never be an entity fully present unto itself. Is metalepsis that which suppresses or that which is suppressed? The impossibility of answering that question is one of the reasons that metalepsis is a difficult trope to explicate. By figuring the *relation between words*, metalepsis both denies us a face that we can recognize, and provides us with a form that continually changes shape. It is the figure of figurality and, in a sense, the essence of rhetoric.

In his description of metalepsis, Thomas Wilson uses a famous example from Virgil to signify his meaning: 'Transumption is, when by degrees wee goe to that, which is to be shewed. As thus. Such a one lieth in a dark Dungeon: now in speaking of darknesse, we understand closenesse, by closenesse, we gather blacknesse, & by blacknesse, we judge deepnesse' (*Arte of Rhetorique*, 175). Taking the linguistic route from Quintilian via Erasmus, Wilson describes metalepsis as the process by which we arrive at a conclusion of depth from the detail of darkness.[11] This example not only provides a clear ontological structure – metalepsis is a trope that takes us from X to Z, noting and then ignoring Y along the way – but it also clearly emphasizes the idea of repression, moving from darkness to depth and repressing closeness and blackness en route. Wilson's metalepsis ends up sounding suspiciously like metonymy since he claims there is an associative chafing between words that leads from one concept to another, in this case, from darkness to depth. This slippage between metalepsis and metonymy highlights one of the ways in which *transumptio* is able to escape detection while still fulfilling its function.

Many definitions of metalepsis deem it a second-degree metonymy in which metonymy's associative tendency is exponentially raised to the nth degree. The *Random House Dictionary*, for instance, defines metalepsis as 'the use of metonymy to replace a word already used figuratively.' The *OED*, after echoing the same sentiment, adds the following caution within parentheses: '(In many English examples the use appears to be vague or incorrect).' Unlike metonymy, in which the word that starts the associative chain is considered unproblematic and nontropological, metalepsis, as Quintilian and these dictionary definitions insist, links two *tropes*; in other words (a good description of the metaleptic inability to exist as itself), it links two terms that have already had their meaning 'turned' from their pristine state. Wilson's link between darkness and depth implies a vector, a direction, that metalepsis can never ensure because its starting point (and therefore its end point) is itself uncertain. The darkness of the metaleptic conceit is the darkness of figurality itself, a darkness that is perforce the antithesis of hermeneutic light.

Yet the greater the gap between two spheres, the more urgent the need for metalepsis. George Puttenham picks up on this sense of distance in his definition of transumption:

> The sence is much altered & the hearers conceit strangely entangled by the figure Metalepsis, which I call the *farfet*, as when we had rather fetch a word a great way off than to vse one nerer hand to expresse the matter aswel & plainer. And it seemeth the deuiser of this figure, has a desire to please women rather than men: for we vse to say by manner of Prouerbe: things farrefet and deare bought are good for Ladies: so in this manner of speech we vse it, leaping over the heads of a great many words, we take one that is furdest off, to vtter our matter by: as Medea cursing her first acquaintance with prince Iason, who had very vnkindly forsaken her, said:
>
> > *Woe worth the mountaine that the maste bare*
> > *Which was the first causer of all my care.*
>
> Where she might aswell haue said, woe worth our first meeting ...
>
> (*Arte*, 183)

Puttenham's sense of rhetorical distance opens onto distances of all kinds: proverbial, spatial, and gendered. He forsakes the usual distinctions between generic types (Quintilian does not, designating metalepsis as the province of comedy alone), and focuses instead on a gendered division of experience to nominate his metaleptic field. The 'deuiser of this figure,' according to Puttenham, was obviously a ladies' man since he wrought this trope peculiarly for the women of the world to beautify their language with. The 'adornment' of the female body that my epigraph from Evans clearly approves echoes Puttenham's description of metalepsis, which is allowed only as a womanly ornament.

In keeping with this metaleptic tendency, Puttenham instantiates his rhetorical point with Medea. Instead of simply cursing her first meeting with Jason, Medea curses the mountain that grew the tree that built the mast that steadied the ship that first bore Jason to her shores. This journey is intended as an example of a trope close to Puttenham's heart, but far from summoning up the indulgence with which he treats this trope of the 'fairer sex,' the example of Medea summons up a picture of fearful femininity. After all, Medea is associated with exploits of sinister sinfulness ranging from filial betrayal and murder to the 'unnatural' killing of her children. She is said to have sent Glauce, her competitor for Jason's affections, a poisoned robe, and is alleged to have thwarted attempts by men (Jason, Aegeus, Perseus) to control her. Like sexual desire in relation to rhetoric, Medea too is a figure that exceeds the powers that attempt to curb her. This is evidenced in no surer way than by the fact that Puttenham himself has to import a *farfet* figure with which to instantiate the far-fetchedness of this figure.

Puttenham's *Arte* seems to have hit on some hidden sexual concern associated with metalepsis, a far-fetched concern that has to do with the monstrosity of femininity itself. Such a conclusion seems to be supported by Quintilian's example of the link between *cano* and *dico*. According to the *Lewis and Short Latin Dictionary*, *cano* denotes 'the *faulty* delivery of an orator ... speak[ing] in a sing-song tone' (emphasis mine). The gloss on *canto* describes it as 'the singing pronunciation of an orator ... declaim[ing] in a singing tone,' while with *dico*, the equivalent definition reads: 'to assert, affirm ... to call, to name.' Quintilian's example, moving as it does from *cano* to *canto* to *dico*, moves also from the 'faulty' sing-song delivery of the orator (via *canto*'s 'singing pronunciation') to *dico*'s manly assertion. These definitions plot the transformational curve from effeminate oration to manly affirmation that is *exemplary* of metaleptic transumption. Puttenham's 'womanly' trope, figured as it is by Medea's erotic transgressions, thus takes on a whole new meaning of sexual perversion. By ensuring the transition is from weakly effeminate to proudly masculine, Quintilian's metaleptic term serves its civic purpose of maintaining the status quo.[12]

Metalepsis might thus be provisionally characterized by the following features:

1. It provides a link between two tropes, and is very clearly an in-between term.
2. These tropes are themselves twisted versions of plainness, and so metalepsis is perforce a doubly complicated trope since it acts *on* tropes.
3. Metalepsis can only be successful as its own death. This death is figured in both *Romeo and Juliet* and *All's Well that Ends Well* as an absent sex scene. In both plays, sexual consummation is discussed before and after the fact but sex is never presented as a visual spectacle; in fact, sex is actively represented in the form of (dramatic) repression. In *Romeo and Juliet*, this repression has fatal consequences while in *All's Well that Ends Well*, metaleptic absence is forced to comply with what Puttenham terms in a different context,

a 'pleasanter construction.' In both cases, however, the unrepresented and/or unacted sex scene creates a textual scar by its metaleptic absence.

Death and the Maiden

Romeo is coming.

Romeo and Juliet, III.iii.158

In *Romeo and Juliet*, this scar results in a tragedy. But what makes *The Tragedy of Romeo and Juliet* tragic? Or rather, how does one recognize *Romeo and Juliet* as a tragedy? This is not necessarily a generic question so much as a rhetorical one, by which I mean, of course, that it is a constitutive one. What constitutes the tragedy of *Romeo and Juliet*? The answer might lie in the fact that the two lovers are dead at the end of the play, but this fact does not require any labour of recognition since it is announced within seconds of the text's opening. Rather, I will suggest that what makes this play a tragedy is not the *fact* of death but the way in which that death is *figured* in the text. The play only begins to unfold after the death of the lovers has already been announced, and the rest of the text is a rhetorical mapping out of this fact of death. This is not to spell out an alternative definition of tragedy but rather to suggest that the *marker* of tragedy might lie in a place somewhat different from where we usually look. And even as *Romeo and Juliet* has been endlessly recycled as the tragedy of true love and of lovers marred by a malign fate, it is more interestingly the tragedy of *rhetoric*, in which a malign fate and crossed stars are but the external manifestations of a rhetoric gone awry.[13]

This failed and tragic rhetoric is most intriguingly expressed, not in the famous balcony scene,[14] but in Act III sc v, Romeo and Juliet's nightingale and lark scene. Act III sc v is the scene of love's consummation – or rather, it is the scene that stands in for what should have been the scene of love's consummation. The specular economy of the play does not allow us to peep into Juliet's bedroom, and we only have an earlier description about what the act *will* look like as Juliet imagines having sex with Romeo:

Spread thy close curtain, love-performing night,
That [th'] runaway's eyes may wink, and Romeo
Leap to these arms untalk'd and unseen!

Love can see to do their amorous rites
By their own beauties, or, if love be blind,
It best agrees with night. Come, civil night,
Thou sober-suited matron all in black,
And learn me how to lose a winning match,
Play'd for a pair of stainless maidenhoods ....
O, I have bought the mansion of a love,
But not possess'd it, and though I am sold,
Not yet enjoy'd.   (III.ii.5–13, 26–8)

Not only does Juliet feel the need to cloak her sexual escapades with the darkness of night, but she also wants her escapades to be *silent* affairs, or at least affairs devoid of language. She hopes Romeo will leap into her (arms) both 'untalk'd and unseen.' The 'amorous rites' of love are best performed in the darkness characteristic of Wilson's definition of metalepsis, and these rites are made even more curious by the fact that they are represented as games without consequences, as matches in which victory is the same as loss. Similarly, Juliet becomes both the buyer of the 'mansion of love' and the thing that is sold, both the penetrator and the penetrated in the sexual act. The rhetorical confusion around the discussion of sex explicitly ignores Juliet's injunction to silence even as the later *act* of sex is by its very absence reduced to absolute silence. The importance of this silence is as yet unclear, and when we see the lovers three scenes later (after Juliet's fantasies, we imagine, have borne fruit), the question becomes 'what role did silence play in your act of love making' rather than 'was it good for you?' Why is silence crucial to sex and what are the consequences of the fact that the all-important sex scene in this play is presented as an absence?

When the lovers finally register their presence and start to speak, the sun is rising and they sing their traditional aubade before parting from one another.[15] This aubade serves as the *representation* of a sex act that is otherwise never seen. Unlike Juliet's earlier speech, this conversation takes place after sexual consummation and dwells on the relationship between language and sex from a vantage point of intimate sexual knowledge. Juliet's earlier insistence on sexual silence is here both maintained and disrupted as the lovers talk *after* having sex, relying as they do on a time-tested textual tradition:

Enter Romeo *and* Juliet *aloft* [*at the window*].
JUL: Wilt thou be gone? it is not yet near day.

It was the nightingale, and not the lark,
That pierc'd the fearful hollow of thine ear;
Nightly she sings on yond pomegranate tree.
Believe me, love, it was the nightingale.
ROM: It was the lark, the herald of the morn,
No nightingale. Look, love, what envious streaks
Do lace the severing clouds in yonder east.
Night's candles are burnt out, and jocund day
Stands tiptoe on the misty mountain tops.
I must be gone and live, or stay and die.
JUL: Yond light is not day-light, I know it, I;
It is some meteor that the sun [exhal'd]
To be to thee this night a torch-bearer
And light thee on thy way to Mantua.   (III.v.1–15)

This conversation is arguably not about sex at all. It is also sandwiched between Tybalt's death and Romeo's banishment on the one hand, and Juliet's wedding feast and Romeo's departure on the other; it appears, therefore, between two scenes crucial to the tragedy of the play. In addition to never referring explicitly to sex, this scene – squeezed in between two scenes of blood and death and loss – is almost lyrical in its peacefulness. I will argue, however, that this seemingly peaceful and lyrically eloquent scene enacts the most constitutive violence of all and precisely *because* it is lyrical. Act III sc v enacts a violence that Juliet fears in her pre-sex speech and from which there is no escape by either death or banishment, since its violence is a violence of rhetoric that marks the play as a tragedy for all time.

Romeo and Juliet's conversation begins with Juliet insisting that it is night and the bird they have heard is the nightingale. If that is the case, then Romeo need not leave just yet for Mantua. Romeo, on the other hand, insists that the bird is a lark whose cry presages the onset of day, which means he needs to leave immediately or he will be put to death. The issue at hand is the identity of the bird whose song signals either life or death. Juliet's equation – it is the nightingale therefore it is night therefore Romeo need not leave – is directly opposed to Romeo's conclusion: it is the lark therefore it is day therefore he must 'be gone and live, or stay and die.' By the end of the speech, both lovers have changed their minds – Juliet now insists it is the lark and Romeo insists it is the nightingale – but they continue to oppose one another.

The burden is proof. Romeo and Juliet need proof, not so much for themselves, but to make the *world* believe they have had sex. This is clearly an impossibility, not only because of Romeo's immediate situation in the play, but also because of the feud choking both families. Perhaps it is best to step back for a moment and briefly dwell on the phenomenon of the First Night, in which bloody sheets are displayed as proof of both consummation and of the bride's virginity.[16] This practice usually takes place on the morning after the wedding, following the couple's first night together. The privacy of sexual intercourse needs to fulfill *public* specifications in order to signify properly, and the first night thus acquires importance as that without which a couple, despite being married, cannot rise to the status of a married couple.

Romeo and Juliet's conversation about birdsong is thus what the text presents both *in place of* the act of sex and as testimony that consummation has taken place. The debate about the name of the bird is a metaphoric rendition of what has just passed between the lovers. It is the expression of an act that has necessarily to be covered up even as the expression is itself proof that the act – piercing the 'fearful hollow' – has taken place. In the absence of any proof of consummation, the play presents us with a conversation that both represses sex and represents it, and this conversation gives us an indicator of what the sex was like and what the sex implies. Romeo and Juliet try to enact the metaleptic impulse of linking the lark and the nightingale but are unable to agree on any one explanation or ornithological identity. This failure to arrive at a decision is reflected by the continuing presence of doom: 'Look love,' Romeo says to Juliet, 'What envious streaks do lace the *severing* clouds in yonder east' (emphasis mine). Juliet attempts to reconcile this severance by asserting that even if it *is* light, then it is only a meteor rather than the sun itself; but metalepsis is unsuccessful in this speech, and Romeo must depart.

The positioning of the nightingale and lark speech between Tybalt's death and Romeo's banishment gives it a centrality that, as I have been suggesting, sheds more than a little light on the specifically *tragic* nature of the play. This tragedy, so nakedly portrayed in this scene, is a tragedy of rhetoric in which the text and the lovers are unable to fix a determinate label on an otherwise simple phenomenon. After all, one might say that Romeo and Juliet are faced with a fairly straightforward situation: it is light outside and so the bird *has* to be a lark; but despite the arguably simple solution to their predicament, the lovers and their text are unable to allow *fact* to seep into the unconscious of their fiction and instead endlessly grapple with rhetorical debate. What Quintilian remarked as the metaleptic ability to 'change' meaning, is here remarked as the metaleptic inability to fix meaning and therefore, to fix life.

The surest indicator of that inability is, of course, the postcoital chatter that is unable to attach a determinate label to the bird intruding on its privacy: 'It was the nightingale, and not the lark,' 'It was the lark, No nightingale.' Once we read/hear that conversation between Romeo and Juliet, we know with some certainty that things are not going to end well for them. Local problems of interpretation (lark or nightingale? day or night? life or death?) ensure that sexual consummation is consumed in, by, and as, death since sex fails to metaleptically translate into a life lived together. The failure of their sexuality in this play is created and figured by the failure of rhetoric, which is also a success since failure is the hallmark of metalepsis. This success operates also at the level of delaying the departure of Romeo for the duration of the conversation, which is Juliet's minimal desired aim. But *Romeo and Juliet*'s chatter cannot get beyond its own rhetoricity in order to ensure lasting victory; rather, the conversation's 'success' makes even more apparent the chain of arbitrary associations that eventually guarantees its failure. The lovers try and fix language soon after having sex, but their inability to agree on any one meaning is our surest rhetorical indicator that their relationship is a doomed one.

The two feuding families, Tybalt's death, Romeo's banishment, and Juliet's impending marriage to Paris are therefore all objective correlatives of a rhetorical mode that is unable to make love overcome its own obstacles. As though to highlight this inability, Lady Capulet enters to announce her daughter's wedding to Paris immediately after Romeo leaves Juliet's bedroom. The imminent and legitimate marriage thus highlights the marriage that must be denied, and the consummated first night does not have the power to countermand an assault on its chastity. In other words, the act of sex is not only unrepresented in this text but is also impotent when it comes to making Romeo and Juliet an acceptable item. The lovers try to link their disparate worlds metaleptically by having sex but sex is too bound up in its own tropological conceit to be of any use to them. The failure of love in this play is thus figured in terms of a failed rhetoric, most clearly embodied in the debate over the nightingale and the lark.

This failure of sex, represented as a failed rhetoric, is also what ensures the tragedy of the play. In other words, metaleptic sex marks the play as a tragedy. Each of the lovers tries to gather 'evidence' to support claims that cannot ultimately be proved. Romeo relies on visual proof – 'Look love' – while Juliet relies on epistemological certainty – 'I know it.' The First Night, which is usually nominated as the event that allows the act of sex to take on the legitimacy sanctioned by the public realm, is here doubly endangered. Not only does Romeo and Juliet's first night serve to highlight the perverse nature of a desire that refuses to guarantee any permanence, but it also emphasizes how insignificant sex can be. By virtue of its suppression, a metaleptic marriage will always end in public divorce, and this divorce is signalled by the night the lovers spend together, and which is represented by a conversation on the nature of objective reality and the difficulty of arriving at a singular answer.

In Shakespeare's text, sexuality is not an acceptable signifier of legitimacy because it both figures and is figured by an illegitimate rhetoric. This rhetoric is unable to sort out the tropological implications of sexuality and assert that signification is non-tropological. In fact, the world of sexuality is here emphatically not the world of significance since the latter requires a uniformity that desire is simply not equipped to provide. When Juliet says, 'Yond light is not day-light, I know it, I,' that assertion of knowledge shocks us by its deeply ironic, dare I say pathetic, nature. The text tries to link the two worlds of private romance and public bloodshed and goes to great lengths and through many ploys in order to make that link hold. We need not wait for the Friar's message to Romeo to go astray, we need not wait for Romeo to mistake Juliet's death as the real thing, we need not wait for Juliet to stab herself, we need not wait for the awful doom that finally ends the enmity between the two feuding families, we need not wait for the play's final renunciation of rhetoric in the two golden, unspeaking statues to which Romeo and Juliet are reduced, we need not wait for any of these moments to figure out the tragic potential of this play; as soon as we read Romeo and Juliet's nightingale-and-lark / nightingale-or-lark speech, we know that this play is a tragedy because its rhetoric cannot overcome its own machinations.

After all, it need not necessarily have been thus. We can conceive of a *practical* scenario in which Romeo and Juliet, with the prince's help, work on reconciling the feuding families, who then accept their marriage. What this play violently demonstrates though is that desire has no bearing on and is not borne by, practicality. Instead, desire is definitionally that which is unable to obliterate its *textual* trace, which is why all possible 'solutions' to the predicament of Romeo and Juliet end up only complicating the problem further since they reckon without the rhetoric of the text. The status of 'truth' is denied to the lovers because truth is a term that has to contend with its own rhetoricity before it can be linked with another trope. Like desire itself, the rhetorical *canto* both links two terms and refuses to provide any stability to that link, and so the most forceful and poignant representations in this text are of the excess of desire and the insufficiency of truth. Moving against metaphor, meaning refuses to be transferred: 'Let's talk, it is not day. / It is, it is'.

If metalepsis collapses under the weight of its own burden in *Romeo and Juliet*, then that is because, like the two tropes it tries to link, it is 'too flattering-sweet to be substantial.' The story of *Romeo and Juliet* is tragic because one trope is unable to provide the solution to the text's tropological problem. It is a tragedy that hinges on the very constitution of meaning and of a signification that goes on *as though* sex has not happened. It is, of course, classically ironic that sexual desire is nonetheless the thing that a 'social reality' is most obsessed with as it plots and plans its marriages and their consummations. Like marriage in society, metalepsis is meant to act as a dam that channels desire toward its proper signification, but when that dam does not hold, the end of the world is nigh ('the sun, for sorrow, will not show his head'). The figural nature of sexuality in *Romeo and Juliet* ensures that it can only transition to the meaningful world if it ignores the contingencies of language, but desire is unable to perform without rhetoric and even if Romeo hopes to 'come,' as the epigraph promises, he never arrives; as for Juliet, she makes no such claim at all. The abortive nature of this attempt to over'come' is made amply clear within the postconsummation scene itself when language suddenly fails to make sense. Juliet starts speaking at cross purposes with her parents in order to escape marriage with Paris, the Friar's letters to Romeo are waylaid, and Romeo hears only partial news about Juliet's death, which leads immediately to the bloodbath at the end.

Sexuality is thus placed in the position of the metaleptic term in the play as the lovers try and push their way into a socially significant space. The text, however, rejects this process of transumption, the plot banishes its hero, and rhetoric insists that the tropes of sexuality and meaning cannot be bridged unless simplified, and cannot be simplified unless destroyed. The impasse that Romeo and Juliet find themselves in is a rhetorical impasse that rhetoric is then unable to bridge, and in the process of dying, metalepsis tragically takes the world's most famous lovers with it.

Limitless Means, Limited Ends

This is the monstruosity in love, lady: that the will is infinite, and the execution confined; that the desire is boundless, and the act a slave to limit.

Troilus and Cressida, III.ii.81–3

In his brilliant and exhaustive analysis of metalepsis, John Hollander identifies three components of the trope:

1. There is a transition from one trope to another.
2. The tropes in question are in some way anterior and posterior.
3. There will be one or more unstated, but associated or understood figures, transumed by the trope, but which are to be reconstructed by interpretation.[17]

This definition seems to suggest that 'interpretation' and 'transumption' are linked terms, so that the presence of the one is most fruitfully discovered by the employment of the other. By virtue of relying on the terms provided by an 'original' text, interpretation always appears more remote in time than the rhetorical terms it is trying to link. The temporal emphasis in Hollander's definition is echoed in a gendered register by Puttenham's example of Medea, in which at least one of the reasons for the absurdity of her anger at the mountain is because of its remoteness in time. If she had instead cursed her first meeting with Jason, that would have seemed less far-fetched since it is temporally closer to her current predicament. The 'far-fetched' nature of metalepsis telescopes time so that the far appears near, and vice versa.[18] This temporal inversion also leads to a *logical* inversion in which anterior and posterior are somehow jumbled up. The 'understood' figures that (literally) stand under a metaleptic link, are, for Hollander, to be reconstructed by interpretation. Such a reconstruction would then (one presumes) be used to restore, or at least understand, the order that metalepsis necessarily disrupts. This *second* understanding would not negate the first, but would rather throw into relief the *means* by which an end has been achieved. It is in the service of this very knowledge that *All's Well That Ends Well* employs the trope of transumption.

The central dilemma in *All's Well* is that Bertram despises Helena, the wife he is supposed to love, thereby manifestly disproving the first half of the play's title. The title also has a latter half, however, and the play turns its steps in that direction right from the outset, trying to bridge ends and means, to make sure things end well so that they can always have *been* well. For this to happen, Bertram has to fall in love with Helena, a position he is far from willing to occupy. In fact, so scornful is he of such a possibility that he repeatedly asserts its impossibility: 'When thou canst get the ring upon my finger, which never shall come off, and show me a child begotten of thy body that I am father to, then call me husband; but in such a "then" I write a "never"' (III.ii.57–60). The 'when ... then' clause is qualified by a never that marks the very redundancy of the condition; the conditions are not conditions of possibility since they can 'never' be met. But even though we despair for Helena, Bertram's terms ensure that the text embarks on a rhetorical *tour de force* during which it attempts to reconcile Helena's happiness with Bertram's, and vice versa. Even though Bertram's conditions contain their own impossibility, they nonetheless allow for an exploration of possibility precisely by marking the possible as impossible. For Hollander, metalepsis 'involves an ellipsis, rather than a relentless pursuit of further figuration,'[19] and so the impossibility of Bertram's letter becomes the very condition for the possibility of metalepsis, a word that (almost) contains ellipsis within itself.

The elliptical (and metaleptical) letter corresponds closely to, and figures, the issue of virginity that the play is arguably obsessed with. From Helena ('Bless our poor virginity from underminers and blowers-up') to Parolles ('Virginity, like an old courtier, wears her cap out of fashion, richly suited, but unsuitable'), people in this play know the high value of virginity. Helena is continually referred to as a virgin ('queen of virgins,' 'poor unlearned virgin'), and thus it is particularly appropriate that Bertram should rely on her virginity to ensure the impossibility of their marriage.[20] The play's emphasis on virginity points to the fact that this is far less a 'love story' and far more a tale about the markers of sexual possibility and the conditions under which sexuality can result in a 'meaningful' end. Helena and Bertram both know that a successful consummation will lead to a marital condition even more binding than the exchange of vows. *All's Well* knows that if it is, in fact, to end well, then it needs its marriage to be consummated. But consummation, as we saw in the case of Romeo and Juliet, is a rhetorically tricky affair and Bertram is convinced that in order for things to end well for *him*, the marriage must remain unconsummated. In fact, so loathsome is the thought of having sex with Helena that Bertram makes sure he leaves the country before the all-important ritual can be enacted, and sends Parolles to make his excuses:

Madam, my lord will go away to-night,
A very serious business calls on him.
The great prerogative and rite of love,
Which, as your due, time claims, he does acknowledge,
But puts off to a compell'd restraint;
Whose want, and whose delay, is strew'd with sweets,
Which they distill now in the curbed time,
To make the coming hour o'erflow with joy,
And pleasure drown the brim.   (II.iv.39–47)

Like a good diplomat, Parolles assures Helena that what might seem at present to be a defeat is really only a victory postponed. The 'very serious business' that beckons to Bertram displaces seriousness from the act of sex and sublimates it into the act of war. Timing seems to be of the essence as Bertram is 'compell'd' to put Helena off and don the garb of a warrior on the very night when he should be removing her garb. But, Parolles hastens to add, delay will enhance the pleasure of sexual consummation and make it 'drown the brim.' There is, in other words, virtue in waiting. Helena responds to this speech with: 'In every thing I wait upon his will,' a waiting that is both in concordance with and the opposite of a (sexual) will; Helena has to wait for her will to be satisfied, but that satisfaction has to take note of Bertram's delayed will. Parolles speaks hyperbolically of the 'great prerogative and rite of love' which, as he and everyone else in the play realizes, is the only rite of passage that will rhetorically bind Bertram to making good on his conditions. Bertram is, of course, well aware of this fact and times his departure from France to coincide with the exact moment that should have marked the First Night: 'to-night, / When I should take possession of the bride, / [End] ere I do begin' (II.v.25–7), and then writes a letter to his mother, clarifying that 'I have wedded her, not bedded her, and [have] sworn to make the "not" eternal' (III.ii.21).

The 'wedding' thus has no validity in the absence of the First Night, and so the act of consummation acquires particular importance in this text, where it functions both as a signifier of independence for Bertram and as a marker of marriage for Helena. There is, therefore, at the heart of *All's Well that Ends Well*, a scene similar to III.v in *Romeo and Juliet*, except here it is both unwritten and unrepresented. Unlike

Romeo and Juliet, we are not even given a postcoital conversation by which to synecdochally judge the sex; nonetheless, the act of sex is all-important, not only in resolving the play's plot, but also in justifying its title and ensuring that no matter what the problem, a 'happy' solution can be forced onto a tricky sexual situation. The dramatic space between Act IV sc iii and Act IV sc iv is the space inhabited by the missing night in this text, the night that, as we will see, finally manages to bridge the gap between sex and its signification.

Determined to make her husband fulfil his sexual duties, Helena follows him abroad and coopts his paramour in a plan to trick the Count. Bertram's flame, Diana Capilet, agrees to go up in smoke in order to help the legitimate wife and carry out the latter's plan. This plan involves both getting the Count's ring and letting Helena substitute for Diana on the First Night of their sexual interaction. In an interesting confluence of names (so important in the feudal and feuding context of *Romeo and Juliet*),[21] Helena's original in Boccaccio's tale is called Giletta, whose name could easily have been anglicized (as Bertram's was from Beltramo) to Juliet. And Juliet, yoked together with Diana Capilet, produces the heroine of the earlier tragedy: Juliet Cap(u)let.[22] Helena thus seems to be a composite of Juliet and Diana; even though both Juliet and Diana miss out on the fruits of sex, Helena is determined to make love bloom for herself. The missing 'i' that would conflate Diana's last name with Juliet's is, of course, entirely appropriate in a drama where Helena has to hide herself precisely in order to find it, where the 'i' has to turn to a 'u' in order to find (i)tself, and where the metaleptic term has to be bracketed in order to connect with a good end.

This secrecy is translated as the unspoken consummation scene in the play. Even as virginity is the structuring presence in the text, its loss is the structuring absence which ensures both the 'utility' and presence of consummation. As Barbara Hodgdon notes, 'in this text, avoiding access to sexuality constitutes a mode of paying heightened attention to it.'[23] By not representing the consummation of love, the romance remains, at one level, purely 'theoretical,' and Helena needs the theory to translate into 'practice' before Bertram can be trapped by his words into owning her as his legitimate wife. The silence in the text has to *speak* before the deed can be pronounced consummated, or, in the terms of the play's title, before the tale can be ended. At another level, however, the trouble with Helena's predicament is that it is not theoretical enough. In the manner of the *theorein* in Greek drama who testified to the performance of an action, Helena needs to provide a theoretical account of having had sex in order to legitimize her marriage; she needs visible testimony that will speak *for* her. But Helena's problem, of course, is that she is unable to access public acknowledgment immediately after her sexual consummation; this failure threatens to undermine all her plans and is the most urgent loophole to be overcome if Bertram is to be hoist on his own rhetorical petard. (Helena's) sex has to be made to speak in a play where it remains unspoken. But equally, this speech has itself to be disguised in order to set the stage for Helena's dramatic revelation. Appropriately enough, then, when sex speaks in this play, it takes the form of a riddle.

As part of Helena's grand scheme, Diana and her widowed mother come to the French court to expose Bertram as a faithless wretch. Diana's 'problem,' as we know, is the opposite of Helena's. In one case, Bertram has not slept with the woman he married, and in the other, he has not married the woman with whom he has slept. Diana comes armed with Bertram's ring as 'proof' of her sexual encounter with Bertram and this token is yet another proof of the warped causality of the text. The ring, in Western culture, is the marker of marriage rather than of sex, and Diana's presenting the ring as proof of an act that should *properly* have occurred after marriage, in an attempt to force a marriage, is a move that reeks of the metaleptic reversal of both chronology and causality.[24] The ring is itself a physical marker of metalepsis since its hole or absence is meant to ensure the presence of the whole. To further the confusion in the French court, Diana refuses to provide any straightforward answers to the questions addressed to her. Instead, she asserts that Bertram should be punished

> Because he's guilty, and he is not guilty.
> He knows I am no maid, and he'll swear to't;
> I'll swear I am a maid, and he knows not.
> Great king, I am no strumpet, by my life;
> I am either maid, or else this old man's wife.
> [*Pointing to Lafew*]   (V.iii.289–93)

This speech sets up an antagonistic relation between Bertram and Diana in which the one swears to her lack of virginity and the other swears to its presence. Bertram both 'knows ... and ... knows not' and Diana's 'not' picks up on Bertram's 'not' to reinforce the play's stress on the knot of virginity and the disastrous consequences of not untying it. Her exposé of Bertram is structured in the same terms as Bertram's conditions to Helena – a negation structuring and infecting a positive possibility – leading us to believe that if the logical hurdles to the one can be overcome, then the other too will start to make sense. Diana's virginity summons up the ghost of the virginal Helena and makes clear that the path to logic is strewn with its lack. In an attempt to pull itself out of a rhetorical quagmire, the text has to resort to speaking in tongues, and these tongues explore the crevices of every possible female state from strumpet to maid to wife. Diana thus comes up with another riddle whose solution will unravel the knot in the play:

> ... this lord,
> Who hath abus'd me, as he knows himself,
> Though yet he never harm'd me, here I quit him.
> He knows himself my bed he hath defil'd,
> *And at that time he got his wife with child.*
> Dead though she be, she feels her young one kick.
> So here's my riddle: one that's dead is quick –
>
> (V.iii.297–303; emphasis mine)[25]

The riddle begins by muddling the source of (its) knowledge since Diana claims that Bertram both does and does not know the answer. He knows the truth 'as he knows himself': given the sexual freighting of the verb, could this mean that like Berowne in *Love's Labour's Lost*, Bertram too is only capable of making love to himself? If so, then this proclivity needs to be curbed in order to ensure a fruitful sexual relation between Bertram and his wife. It is to this end that the remainder of the riddle tends. Diana insists on the absolute conflation of two events: Bertram's alleged 'taking' of her chastity, and his alleged impregnation of Helena. Clearly, only one of these can be true unless there is a rhetorical sleight of hand by which two seemingly unconnected events (shall we call them tropes?) can be connected without any visible *sign* of connection or contact. Diana's riddle – the key to the play and the key to Helena's happiness – flirts dangerously with solutions of metaleptic proportions. We are presented with two 'realities' and challenged to pick the only one that can possibly be true. What makes this choice difficult is that these two events, seamlessly linked in logic and time, name neither participant nor consequence and hide the fact that the sexual transgression may not have been conventionally transgressive at all. By successfully veiling crucial facts, Diana's chaste riddle is able to link a consummation and an impregnation without any hint of wrongdoing. If the temporal and causal sequence has been collapsed to such a degree that it can then *guarantee* one version of the 'truth' and guarantee that there is no impropriety in this truth, then metalepsis has done its job. By linking consummation with the proper version of reality, Diana becomes the embodiment of metalepsis in this play and provides Helena with access to Bertram's seed, quashing her own desire in the process. Helena is able to join Bertram because Diana gracefully opts out of the equation even as her cooperation is essential to forging their relationship in the first place. Helena successfully negotiates a metaleptic link by nipping illegitimate desire in the bud and replacing it with chaste, marital sex. Once that has been done, the consummated marriage is allowed to bloom, literally, as it turns out, with Helena's pregnancy.

David McCandless points us in the direction of Helena's mastery in the play by noting that '[a]n often overlooked marker of Helena's control is her curious postcoital detention of Bertram ... What, one must ask, is the point of this detention? What takes place during that hour?'[26] While teaching Diana how to beguile Bertram, Helena makes sure the Count is asked to stay on for an hour after the consummation, without speaking a word ('When you have conquer'd my yet maiden bed, / Remain there but an hour, nor speak to me. / My reasons are most strong ...'). What 'happens' in this one hour, I suggest, is that Bertram rolls over on his side and falls asleep while Helena eagerly searches for the bloody 'proof' that her marriage has, finally, been consummated. In the absence of a socially structured search party, Helena has to do the dirty work herself and ensure that the knot of marriage has been fastened by the dissolution of another (k)not. Bertram's 'not,' by insisting on conception *before* (and outside) consummation, reverses the logic of cause and effect, and this reversal is itself the hallmark of metaleptic far-fetchedness. His riddle dares to be answered and Helena rises to the challenge by means of another riddle. These riddles are the literal (and literary) embodiments of tropological systems that the trope of metalepsis then tries to connect. If Bertram requires proof of consummation *before* he will bed his wife, if he wants Helena to be deflowered by him before he will deflower her, then this sexual impasse can only be answered by a rhetorical debacle. Bertram's riddle is solved by the riddle of one who is both 'dead [and] quick.' This interplay of riddles ensures stable meaning rather than its opposite, as one might suspect. Each of the riddles comes complete with an answer that can be pointed to as 'proof' of its solution, and as it turns out, both Bertram's and Diana's riddles can be solved by pointing to a pregnant Helena.

Helena's metaleptic pregnancy is the only event that can force Bertram to accept her as his wife in 'name, and ... thing.' His refusal to 'blow up' her virginity blows up in his face, and he is now bound to accept that something has translated his marriage from word to deed.[27] That 'something,' of course, turns out to be *two* things: the *fact* of sexual consummation that Bertram cannot now deny since the ring (the zero, the 'naught') is part of the irrevocable proof against him, and a *rhetoric* that has solved his own riddle in the form of a riddle that brings his promise to light by keeping sexual details in the dark. If metalepsis is only able to fulfill this rhetorical function by suppressing itself, then the 'pitchy night' in which Bertram and Helena consummate their marriage is the site of that suppression. Unlike in *Romeo and Juliet*, where words fall into a state of confusion after intercourse, sex in *All's Well* does its metaleptic work of solving the riddles that rhetoric has set up. While secret sex thwarts (and enables) metaleptic suppression in *Romeo and Juliet*, purloined passion ensures a metaleptic twisting of cause and effect in *All's Well That Ends Well*. It is not surprising then that the latter text ends more happily than the former, but neither should it be surprising that *All's Well* is designated one of Shakespeare's 'problem' plays.

The problematic nature of this play, for most critics, lies in its ending, which is unconvincing in its assurance of future happiness for Bertram and Helena. Bertram's inadequate transformation and Helena's reduction to wife and future mother strike a false note at the end of a play that has been obsessed with sexual manipulation. But the problematic nature of the ending lies not (only) in Bertram's inadequate transformation from cad to dad, but also in the fact that the text is well aware of the tenuous nature of its rhetorical solution. If the metaleptic term in this text is sex, then there can never be any guarantee that it will continue to produce the (beneficial) effects it has been forced into producing in a single instance. The ambiguous nature of the happiness at the end owes to the fact that metalepsis is, as Quintilian knows, an unstable term that can at any moment thwart all the good it may earlier have wrought. *Romeo and Juliet* is a tragedy because this undoing takes place within the text and the possibility of a logical reversal of cause and effect – the golden statues signify the greatness of a love that went unacknowledged during its lifetime – occurs only after permanent damage has been inflicted. Sexuality's relation to signification is a vexed one in the tragedy and Romeo and Juliet's consummation is unable to make itself signify properly. *All's Well That Ends Well*, in contrast, arbitrarily terminates rhetoric's logical end in illogic, and forces sex into meaning instead; as such, it is problematic rather than fatal since it temporarily bypasses the tragic by twisting causal necessity. Sex in this latter play suppresses the impropriety that lies at the heart of desire and allows it to take fruit as a legitimate and stable entity.

Far from belonging in the province of comedy, then, metalepsis is most at home in texts where the circle at the end requires proof of consummation before it can be tied into a lasting knot. The First Night syndrome casts these two Shakespearean plays in the metaleptic mode, where the far-fetched becomes the surest guarantor of the here and (not) now. That such a guarantee can never be permanent since it requires ever further theoretical proof to keep it going (the round ring, the bloody consummation, the round belly, the bloody afterbirth, and so on) is borne out tragically by Romeo and Juliet, and problematically by Bertram and Helena. Metalepsis can only guarantee the efficacy of sex by withholding its signification. Such a withholding is necessarily a rhetorical trope that can either destroy the desired meaningfulness of sex, as Romeo and Juliet discover, or twist sex into meaning, as Bertram realizes. Either way, sex needs to have a rhetorical witness that can testify to its occurrence, even when that occurrence can only be presented as lack of one kind or another.

4

Cast in Order of Appearance: Catachresis, *Othello*, *King John*

Signs are now purely vacuous, dead letters emptied of all constraining content and so free to couple promiscuously with each other in an orgy of inbreeding ... A sign can be roughly defined as anything which can be used for the purpose of lying.

Terry Eagleton, *William Shakespeare*[1]

Have you eyes?
Could you on this fair mountain leave to feed,
And batten on this moor? ha, have you eyes?

William Shakespeare, *Hamlet*, III.iv.65–7[2]

Even though a masque of blackness was not a uniquely 'bright idea' in 1605,[3] Ben Jonson's *Masques of Blacknesse and Beavtie* were specifically commissioned by Queen Anne to be performed at court.[4] The story of *Blacknesse* features a band of princesses who are convinced that dark skin renders them physically unattractive. After reading in a book of English verse that darkness is a consequence of being too much in the sun, Niger's daughters hope to escape the source of their discomfort but are unable to plot a path away from the sun's rays.[5] The princesses wilt in the heat of their seemingly irresolvable dilemma until miraculously, a countenance emerges from a lake to give them the following advice: 'That they a Land must forthwith seeke, / Whose termination (of the Greeke) / Sounds TANIA ...' (188–90).[6] In the land that fits this verbal clue, they will be removed from the harmful rays of the sun and regain the beauty for which they were once renowned. After several wrong turns in this treasure hunt – 'Blacke Mauritania first; and secondly, / Swarth Lusitania; next /... / Rich Aquitania' (198–200) – they finally alight on the shores of 'Britania,' which both answers to the constraints of their verbal clue by ending in 'tania,' and is nicknamed 'Albion the faire' to reinforce its nominative whiteness. This whiteness also signals coolness;[7] after all, having fled their native land because of its proximity to the burning rays of the sun, the princesses presume they will avoid the sun's rays entirely in the magical land of 'Britania.'

But this presumption turns out to be presumptuous. Far from escaping the heat, the Nigerian princesses are immediately ushered into the presence of a sun '[w]hose beames shine day, and night, and are of force / To blanch an Aethiope, and reuiue a Cor's' (254–5). This sun turns out to be the blazing James whose rays shine benevolently on his subjects. But rather than burning them with the force of his splendour, they only 'blanch' (or bleach) onlookers into beautiful whiteness. The king's benevolence is stressed repeatedly: 'This sunne is temperate, and refines / All things, on which his radiance shines' (264–5). Far from escaping the sun then, Niger's princesses are exposed in England to a more intense, albeit metaphorical, sun that achieves its benevolent splendour by enacting a violence far greater than the damage done by the Nigerian sun. By chiastically crossing people and objects so that the 'Aethiop' is equated with the 'Cor's,' the text suggests that bleaching (the Aethiops white) is the only way of keeping them alive: James renews life by bleaching darkness. In light of this logic, as long as they are black, the princesses are as good as dead. If self-esteem is the psychological point at which *Blacknesse* commences its narrative, then the rhetorical violence generated by a metaphorical sun arguably does more damage than the burning rays of its Nigerian counterpart. This damage is posited only to be ignored, however, and the masque proceeds to celebrate the ability of kindly kingly beams to overcome the drawbacks of burning Nigerian rays.

The situation in which the Nigerian princesses find themselves is thus a uniquely textual one, marked early on by the Greek riddle that leads them to England in pursuit of fairness, and then riddled by a brand of Jacobean violence that insists on its own stainlessness. However, despite the continued rhetorical violence, the text acts as though there were no physical impediment to renewing the 'beavtie' of the princesses. The first step in this process of beautification is spelled out for Niger by the moon:

Call forth thy honor'd Daughters, then;
And let them, 'fore the Brit[t]aine men,
Indent the Land, with those pure traces
They flow with, in their natiue graces.   (258–61)

Rather than closeting themselves in a shady grove out of reach of the sun, the princesses are told to dance before the sun's gaze in order to 'indent' the land with the 'flow' of their native graces. Coupling in the sun is thus prescribed as the first step toward shedding blackness and gaining beauty; the native graces are clearly expected to squeeze the native juices out of the royal system. At this point in the masque, the Nigerian nymphs (played by Queen Anne and her ladies-in-waiting) dance their measure of purification before King James.

After the dance, the moon sends Niger home and spells out the second stage in the process of en-lightenment to the princesses and their dancing partners alone. This second stage involves performing a set of rites 'thirteene times thrise, on thirteene nights.' These rites are never spelled out for the audience, thus appearing on paper (and on stage) as unspoken and perhaps unspeakable; they are merely referred to as 'these rites.' After performing these rites, the nymphs are instructed to wash themselves thoroughly in the Ocean's foam, described specifically as the element that gave birth to Venus. Thirteen complete immersions in the element that produced Aphrodite is thus posited as a cure for the nymphs' blackness: 'You shall your gentler limmes ore-laue, / And for your paines, perfection haue' (345–6).[8] Here the masque ends with a promise that soon all will be well and dark complexions will be a thing of the past; the princesses' whiteness is predicated on and guaranteed by an absolute engagement with Venus's 'foam.'

Aphrodite's birth element, we remember, was itself born of the castrated genitals of Uranus. In addition to Cronos taking over as king of the sky after this violent event, Uranus's defeat also ensured that the phallus became a free-floating signifier unattached to any body; castration marked the estrangement of the phallus from its source of power. Paradoxically, this lack of sexual prowess gives birth to a Goddess of Love who is well endowed with an erotic drive, especially as it mythologically manifests itself in her pursuit of Adonis. The Nigerian nymphs thus immerse themselves in a foam that is both castrated and sexual, in a whiteness that both debilitates and enables. The masque works out its 'colour question' by resorting to the sexual one, and the text forges a mutually rewarding, if somewhat circular, association between the two: the blacker you are, the more sexually active you need to be since the more sexually active you are, the whiter you get. However, as soon as one gets to the white end of the spectrum, which is the point at which one is presumably the most sexually active, one is already marked as sexually deficient and castrated. What starts out as a relationship between blackness and emasculation ends up being a connection between castration and whiteness, and there seems to be no easy way out of this rhetorical mess. It was another three years after the *Masque of Blacknesse* before Ben Jonson attempted to solve these contradictions in *Beavtie*.[9]

The *Masque of Blacknesse* presents us with complicated combinations of sexuality and colour, and the text can never quite decide if blackness is too sexual or not sexual enough, if whiteness is the end of sex or merely its absence. The masque presents blackness as a cover (literally, since for the first time in the court of James, black paint substituted for hand-held masks) behind which the princesses can get to matters of the body; blackness is the intricately wrought veil that the Nigerian princesses don as a pre-text to introduce and colour the text of sexuality. The tension between text and pretext stems not so much from the opposition of blackness and sexuality as from their mutual imbrication. *The Masque of Blacknesse* suggests a dramatic engagement between darkness and Aphrodite, between, for lack of better terms, 'race' and 'sexuality,' that a play like *Othello* takes to a tragic extreme, and that threatens to undermine the framework of royal legitimacy in *King John*. Before we get to the plays, however, we need to find a more technical term with which to describe this relationship that *Blacknesse* so clearly urges us to see.

Textual Abuse

The text in itself ... gives indications, as it were, *for its own use*, directions indispensable to the appropriate reception of its specific mode of textuality.
                    Alessandro Serpieri, 'Reading the Signs'[10]

Usually placed in close proximity to metaphor, catachresis (in Latin, *abusio*), is another trope that enacts a change in meaning. The *Ad Herennium*, which lists catachresis between synecdoche and metaphor, says that the 'ten Figures of Diction ... indeed all have this in common, that the language departs from the ordinary meaning of the words and is, with a certain grace, applied in another sense' (4.30.42). The particular grace with which catachresis acts is then spelled out:

> Catachresis is the inexact use of a like and kindred word in place of the precise and proper one, as follows: 'The power of man is short,' or 'small height,' or ... 'a mighty speech' ... It is easy to understand that words of kindred, but not identical, meaning have been transferred on the principle of inexact use. (IV.xxxiv.45)

The most interesting feature in this definition, one that recurs in Quintilian and Puttenham, is the *absence* of any disapprobation while describing the 'abuse' that catachresis enacts. In fact, catachrestic abuse is elevated to an accepted and acceptable axiom: 'the principle of inexact use.' Unlike metaphor, in which a word is rudely wrenched from its proper signification, in catachresis, the 'misnaming' takes place as a gracious service to enhance the quality of life of other not-so-fortunate phrases. The fraternal glow that these 'kindred' words bask in contains none of the animosity with which metaphor is sometimes treated. Catachresis is merely considered a fact of a beautiful, benevolent life; much like the Jamesian sun, it warms without scorching.

Quintilian spells out the catachrestic mode even more explicitly:

> By this term is meant the practice of adapting the nearest available term to describe something for which no actual term exists ... We must be careful to distinguish between abuse and metaphor, since the former is employed where no proper term is available, and the latter when there is another term available. As for poets, they indulge in the abuse of words even in cases where proper terms do exist, and substitute words of somewhat similar meaning. But this is rare in prose. Some, indeed, would give the name of *catachresis* even to cases such as where we call temerity valour or prodigality liberality. I, however, cannot agree with them; for in these instances word is not substituted for word, but thing for thing, since no one regards prodigality and liberality as meaning the same, but one man calls certain actions liberal and another prodigal, although neither for a moment doubts the difference between the two qualities. (*Institutio Oratoria*, VIII.vi.34–6)

There are, as always, several key moments in Quintilian's disquisition, not least of which is the chiastic crossing of catachrestic naming and metaphoric misnaming. Both tropes enact a necessary task (in an earlier passage, Quintilian has praised metaphor for 'providing a name for everything' and adding to the 'copiousness of language' [VIII.vi.5]), but catachresis, despite being etymologically 'abusive,' is nonetheless viewed as the kinder trope, and unlike metaphor, it is not open or prone to abuse. Apart from poets who use substitutions even when none is required, catachresis is generally not an abused trope at all. Even in those cases where abuse might be suspected – for instance, those who regard prodigality and liberality as meaning the same –[11] what is being abused is not really catachresis, since catachresis involves a substitution of words rather than things, and for Quintilian, prodigality and liberality are, clearly, *things*, and so their chiastic crossing is specifically deemed *not* catachrestic, and catachresis remains *abusio* without an example of abuse.

Quintilian's definition differs significantly from the pseudo-Ciceronian one which, after all, outlines catachrestic activity as that which provides a 'kindred' word to denote an object. In Quintilian catachresis actually brings an object into being by bestowing a name on it and by granting it a signifier by which it can identify itself to other signifiers. While pseudo-Cicero speaks of catachresis as the 'use of a like and kindred word in place of the precise and proper one,' Quintilian describes it as that which 'adapt[s] the nearest available term to describe something for which no actual term exists.' The *Ad Herennium* espouses the notion that there is a proper word that the catachrestic term replaces, while the *Institutio Oratoria* insists that catachresis supplies a word where none existed before. While the crossing of liberality and prodigality would be catachrestic for the pseudo-Cicero, it is specifically not so for Quintilian. The Renaissance inherited these competing versions of catachresis and, I will argue, *Othello* adopts the *Institutio*'s definition over the *Ad Herennium*'s and focuses on what 'the nearest available term' could be for a concept that is as yet unnamed. This confusion at the heart of catachresis is, of course, central to the logic of the trope, and gets worked out in interesting ways in both *Othello*, where the 'nearest available term' is not itself always available for use, and in *King John*, where this term is susceptible to continual replacement.

Quintilian and the pseudo-Cicero, however, both agree on the mildness and *necessity* of catachresis. The kindness of catachrestic abuse, hinted at in the *Ad Herennium*, is made explicit in the *Insitutio Oratoria* as a benevolence serving those less fortunate phenomena that do not have a name by which to designate themselves. Erasmus too echoes this approval of catachresis in his definition of *abusio* as a trope which 'use[s] a word to express a meaning related to its own for which no proper word already exists, [while] metaphor [is used] when such a word already exists. Just as when we call one who has killed his brother a parricide, because fratricide is not used' (*Copia* 30). But what, we may ask, is the catachrestic word 'related' to if the phenomenon being described does not have its own descriptive word? Is the comparison made between what one *expects* an object to signify, and another word that signifies a similar thing? How close is this relation, and what should the grounds of similarity be? By whom, for instance, is 'fratricide' not used? And why, when it has certainly been used here by Erasmus? Such loopholes in definitions of catachresis are conveniently glossed over by rhetoricians who are evidently keen on recuperating its 'turn' on meaning as being pure and unfettered. In fact, Quintilian seeks to remove catachresis from the realm of tropes altogether by asserting that it is in no way abusive; he goes out of his way to provide us with instances that pass for catachrestic abuse, but which really are not. Catachresis is the place holder for a morally appropriate rather than a rhetorically twisted trope. So in the Erasmian example, killing one's brother, while heinous in itself, serves primarily to highlight a situation in which catachresis provides a name for a thing; the trope is pointedly not involved in the murder. Even in as bizarre an instance as *not* using a name that has already been used, the glory nonetheless redounds to catachrestic credit, leaving a bloodied brother lying unheeded in the dust.

The English rhetoricians provide useful examples with which to flesh out the Latin theory. Thomas Wilson, who sandwiches catachresis between synecdoche and metonymy in his *Arte of Rhetorique*, borrows his example from Erasmus: '[Catachresis is] when for a certaine proper worde, we vse that which is most nigh vnto it: as in calling some water, a Fish Pond, though there be no Fish in it at all' (174).[12] Wilson associates catachresis with fishy business, but in his universe, like in the pseudo-Ciceronian one, such fishing is legal since it is 'most nigh' to the thing it seeks to denote. No mention is made of whether the fry is big or small, or of whether a whale can be fitted within the fish pond; definitions of catachresis across rhetoricians consistently ignore these finer points and remain vague, as though to expand the freedom with which this 'nigh-ness' can be ascertained.

Puttenham too, in keeping with the long rhetorical tradition he inherits, adopts a mixed tone while describing catachresis in the *Arte of English Poesie*: 'But if for lacke of a naturall and proper terme or worde we take another, neither naturall nor proper and do vntruly applie it to the thing which we would seeme to expresse, and without any iust inconuenience, it is ... plain abuse' (180). 'Plain abuse,' Puttenham insists, exists in the *absence* of the natural term, and is an untrue application of a second-best phrase. However, even as he uses the familiar language of disapproval – 'neither naturall nor proper' – for catachresis, he uses it *approvingly*, and as we will later see, applauds instances of catachrestic use. Such approval perhaps best instantiates the misnaming that catachresis is supposed to enact. For the rhetoricians, *abusio* is not abusive at all since it enacts a necessary turning, without which our language would be much diminished. In fact, Erasmus confers the supreme compliment of considering catachresis and other tropes linked with it (*similitudio, collatio*) as leading to copiousness of *thought* as well as words.

The emphasis that these rhetoricians lay on the legality of catachresis is echoed in Sidney's *Apology*, in which he tries to ward off the accusations of deceit and abuse that poetry faces:

That they [poets] should be the principal liars, I answer paradoxically, but truly, I think truly, that of all writers under the sun the poet is the least liar, and, though he would, as a poet can scarcely be a liar ... for the poet, he nothing affirms, and therefore, never lieth ... [G]rant, I say, whatsoever they will have granted, that not only love, but lust, but vanity, but (if they list) scurrility, possesseth many leaves of the poets' books; yet think I, when this is granted, they will find their sentence may with good manners put the last words foremost, and not say that Poetry abuseth man's wit, but that man's wit abuseth Poetry. (123–4, 125)

The concerns that animate the rhetoricians vis-à-vis catachresis – the 'truth' of the name, the abuse of the word, and the propriety of naming – also animate Sidney's defence of poetry. His conclusion that poetry cannot be blamed for performing a function (and an affirmation) that human beings retrospectively tack onto it, is only partially convincing, but what is significant is that he tries to separate the abused (poetry) from the term(s) of the abuse, and claims that the one has nothing to do with the other. In other words, if we cast Sidney's text in a rhetorical light, we might say that his defence of poetry is made in a mode similar to the one employed by the rhetoricians in defining catachresis: it uses the same terms of judgment and merely switches their values around, so that what starts out as being a negative (lying) is now cast as a positive (not affirming, therefore never lying). Chiasmus ('when the first element and the fourth, and the second and the third are conjoined giving a scissor formation' [Sonnino, *Handbook*, 199]) is once again invoked, as Sidney crosses the abused and abuser and neatly places poetry in the seat of the abused, rather than in the chair of the abuser. The recurrence of chiasmus in close proximity to catachresis is indicative of the hypertropological nature of the latter. By allowing, indeed encouraging, the crossing of words and phrases and thoughts, catachresis highlights language's atavistic urge to be on the move, footloose and fancy-free, not tied down to any one signification. In its pairing with chiasmus, catachresis not only provides a name where none is immediately available, but it also crosses names so as to produce altogether different meanings. It is, therefore, a remarkable feat that catachresis, whose *literal* translation is abuse, is termed the least abusive of all the tropes in the rhetorical handbooks.

Puttenham provides us with another instance of catachresis at work (one slightly more believable than the fratricide/parricide link), and this time, the example narrates the abuse of love: 'I lent my love to losse, and gaged my life in vaine' (180). The text then glosses this example:

> Whereas this worde *lent* is properly of mony or some such other thing, as men do commonly borrow, for vse to be repayed againe, and being applied to loue is vtterly abused, and yet very commendably spoken by vertue of this figure. For he that loueth and is not beloued againe, hath no lesse wrong, than he that lendeth and is never repayde. (*Arte of English Poesie*, 180)

The by-now familiar mixture of disapproval ('vtterly abused') and approval ('very commendably spoken') permeates Puttenham's example of unrequited love. The *justness* of the catachrestic application – 'hath no lesse wrong' – implies Hamlet's edict: 'There is nothing either good or bad, but thinking makes it so,' and recalls the Sidneyan defence of poetry. The rightness of troping lies in the eye and ear of the beholder/hearer, and in the case of catachresis, all its official propounders are unanimous in their approval of its action. For Puttenham, the eccentric course of love is the perfect instance of a catachrestic arena since all is 'fair' in its many turns. Before we get to the fair vicissitudes of love, and how they are played out in *Othello*, however, it might be best to summarize the main thrust of catachresis as this chapter will henceforth employ the term. I will take Quintilian's definition of *abusio* as central, but there will also be a trace of the pseudo-Ciceronian text:

1. Catachresis *brings into being* objects and phenomena that have not yet been registered in language. It names the unnamable, and therefore (in Erasmus's terms) also thinks the unthinkable. In Puttenham's terms, catachresis lends love to loss only to gain a world for language; it turns the no name into a big star.
2. The question of right and wrong naming is given a curious twist since catachresis is termed abusive but the abuse itself is seen as good. The 'wrong' name thus becomes right and proper.
3. Catachresis adopts a *related* term to describe an object, even though what this term might be related to, since the object being named has not yet been named and therefore has no characteristics of its own, remains a mystery.

Is Black Beautiful and Sex Natural?

If it [*Othello*] did not begin as a play about race, then its history has made it one.

Ben Okri, 'Meditations on Othello'[13]

BRABANTIO: Thou art a villain.
IAGO: You are a senator.

William Shakespeare, *Othello*, I.i.117–18

This mystery of catachresis pales in comparison to the tragedy of Othello, or rather, the paleness of catachresis *is* the tragedy of *Othello*. I want to begin this section with the suggestion implicit in the first part of Ben Okri's statement: that *Othello* is not a play about race. This is not to say that the play does not have a black protagonist,[14] but merely to wonder whether that necessarily translates into its being a play about race and racism. This might seem counterintuitive; certainly, when the film version of *Othello*, with Laurence Fishburne in the lead and Kenneth Branagh as Iago, was released in 1996, most reviews commented on its relevance to the rampant racism in the United States. Hollywood's 'take' on *Othello*'s racism is, more or less, an echo of the academic discourse that has focused in various ways on the play's play on 'blackness,'[15] which has also been linked, in a manner eerily reminiscent of the O.J. Simpson case, with Desdemona's murder.[16] That there is, in *Othello*, a link between the 'racial' and the 'sexual' realms, I think, is clear. What is less clear, however, is the manner in which this link is forged, and the consequences of the text's rhetoric on its politics.

The problem with *Othello*, of course, is that at one level, attention to the text's rhetoric is extremely unsatisfying in its obviousness. The ensnaring of Othello by Iago, for instance, in the famous Act III sc. iii, where the villain traps the hero in his dizzying vortex of rhetoric, is excruciating to read and the pain is almost entirely due to the nakedness with which the power of rhetoric is presented; it is a scene unparalleled for its intensity in the Shakespearean canon. Nevertheless, there remains something that stubbornly holds out against Hollywood's essentializing label of 'a play about racism'; the way to work through the quagmire of 'race,' I suggest, is, in fact, by an even closer attention to the rhetorical skein of the text. *Othello* has often been the site of readings centring on textual anomalies, and Patricia Parker's meditation on 'dilation/delation' is the most famous of such studies.[17] Even as the textual conflict she focuses on involves a characterization *of* Iago, I would like to look at another strange usage, this time in an utterance *by* Iago, that might alert us to the widespread use of rhetorical abuse in connection with the play's arch-villain.

In the very first scene, arguably the most 'racist' scene in the play, Iago sets Roderigo on to wake Brabantio and alert him to the fact of Desdemona's elopement with Othello. After having kindled the senator's wrath, Iago prepares to slink away from the primary and primal scene of the play, a scene that bears the mark of what Arthur Little calls in a different context the 'primal scene of racism.'[18] The 'primal' scene, in the Freudian sense of the term, implies a scene of sexual identification and differentiation which, as I will suggest, is of primary interest in this play. 'Racial' prejudice acquires voice as sexual angst, and Iago suggests this complex interplay of signs early on in the text when he says to Roderigo:

> Farewell, for I must leave you.
> It seems not meet, nor wholesome to my place,
> To be producted (as, if I stay, I shall)
> Against the Moor ...
> I must show out a flag and sign of love,
> Which is indeed but sign.   (I.i.144–7, 156–7)

Emphasizing the fact that his presence is neither 'meet' nor 'whole-some,' Iago introduces us to a word that, in the context of the Shake-spearean canon, is not particularly meet or wholesome either; we are introduced to 'producted,' the only recorded use of the word in Shakespeare.[19] The *OED* records its use as a 'rare' one, and states that its meaning is the same as 'produced,' derived from the participial form of the Latin *producere*: to conduct, deduct, induct, etc. While the 'meaning' might be the same, the form (or 'sign') is certainly different, and given that Iago stresses the importance of the 'flag' that is visible, we may assume that 'producted' is one of those flags that the text sends out as a sign for its own use.

As another instance of 'producted' used in the period, the *OED* lists, as its first example, an occurrence from Nicholas Harpsfield's *Treatise on the Pretended Divorce Between Henry VIII and Catherine of Aragon*, a voluminous work written in 1555 during the reign of the Catholic Queen Mary. The controversy over Henry's divorce from Katherine pivoted on the legality of nomination. Katherine was labelled a virgin and thus 'allowed' to marry her brother-in-law, the future Henry VIII, after her husband died, but when Henry wanted desperately to get rid of her and marry Anne Boleyn, Katherine's having been his sister-in-law and the 'consummated' wife of his brother Arthur (legal consummation involved the deposit of semen rather than penetration) was one of the primary reasons that Henry cited. In Harpsfield's version, which is critical not so much of Henry as of his advisers, the text dismisses the arguments of the universities against the pope, and states:

> And thus much may now serve for the universities. You will perchance say that the said censures may the better be borne withal, and the divorce also in case there were any carnal copulation in the former marriage, whereupon as well the said [former] book of dialogue as the statute grounded itself. *For the proof of which copulation many reasons are producted in the said dialogue,* with mention of the Pope's brief made for the confirmation of the bull ... Wherefore, least any scruple or doubt before moved touching either the said bull and brief, or the said carnal copulation, may cause the reader to misdeem and mislike the said dispensation, we will now repulse and remove all such objections. (212–13; emphasis mine)

The link between 'proving' carnal copulation and 'product[ing]' reasons for whether or not this copulation, in fact, took place, hinges on the connection between rhetoric and sexuality. In a polemical intervention that deals with matters as important as religion and kingship, Harpsfield inserts his textual variant of 'producted' in a discussion of whether or not Arthur and Katherine had consummated their marriage – a discussion that was pivotal not only to Henry's reputation but also, later, to Elizabeth's legitimacy. The production of legitimacy is strongly tied to the interpretation of sexual relations and the two are irrevocably linked to the productions of rhetoric, by the universities and Henry on the one hand, and by Katherine and the pope on the other.

To be a 'producter,' therefore, is to perform an extremely important task, perhaps even to swing the balance of an entire country's beliefs (from Catholicism to Protestantism, for instance, under Henry VIII). Iago seems well aware of the gravity of the situation, even though *his* immediate task has only been to convince a senator of his daughter's treachery. But this task is also a 'flag' for what is yet to come, a sign of the times, and is enough to set off an inquiry into what precisely Iago's 'reasons' could be for wanting to 'product' the kind of catastrophe that is the subject of the play. Coleridge's famous characterization of Iago as being spurred by a 'motiveless malignity' is merely an indicator of what remains to be unravelled in Iago's text, which is always a 'product[ion]' achieved by a specific deployment of rhetoric. In other words, the psychological 'motive' that Coleridge was looking for, I will argue, is the consequence of the machinery of language, and Iago's 'malignity' is nothing more (or less) than the evil generated by that apparatus.

Before delving deeper into Iago's fear of being 'producted' and the fear he 'products,' we need to go back to the *Institutio Oratoria* and to the passage that immediately precedes its description of catachresis. This passage consists (in both the Latin and English versions) of a series of asterisks because, as a note informs us, it 'is too corrupt to admit of emendation or translation' (321). However, the text goes on to give us the gist of what the missing lines say: 'There seem to be references to *vio* for *eo* and to *arquitollens*, for which cp. *arquitenens*. *Septemtriones* can hardly be selected for censure, as it is not uncommon' (320); the last sentence is an exact translation of Quintilian's Latin original.

The next paragraph starts: 'These facts make catachresis (of which *abuse* is a correct translation) all the more necessary' (VIII.vi.34). However, since we don't know what the facts are (they are, after all, represented only as asterisks), the 'necessity' of catachresis is built on an absence, or corruption, of facts. The text quite literally enacts this in the English translation by basing catachrestic 'necessity' on a series of asterisks whose untranslatable significance lies elsewhere. In the Latin version, this 'necessity' is presented as a series of verbal corruptions that lead to no conclusion, except to urge the need for further catachresis. Iago's 'production,' I suggest, must be read in light of this cumulative abuse: what he produc[t]s is suspicious because it always bears the mark of the asterisk, of the parenthesis, and ultimately, of catachresis. In order to avoid 'be[ing] producted ... / Against the Moor,' Iago carefully and relentlessly produces both himself *and* the Moor. A glance at a couple of other 'strange' words in the text will, in effect, tell us how he manages to pull off his production.[20]

One of these words, strangely enough, is 'jealious' which, the *Riverside* assures us, is merely a variant spelling of 'jealous.' Of course 'jealous' itself did not connote sexual jealousy alone, but also hinted at an inclination to overreach, linking the term to both hermeneutics and rhetoric. Twenty instances of 'jealious' exist in the Shakespearean canon, and of these, thirteen belong to *Othello*,[21] more than exist in either of the other two 'jealousy' plays, *The Winter's Tale*, and *Much Ado About Nothing*. Iago, I suggest, spins his web of 'jealious' deceit with the help of another strange word, one that characterizes his main accomplishment in the play. The art of coining 'epithites,' a variation that occurs twice in the Shakespearean canon, at once places Iago's machinations firmly in the realm of rhetoric and insists that the names of jealousy are what Iago produces in and as and for the play.

To link these uncharacteristic textual occurrences is not to claim to have cracked the secret 'code' behind the text, but it is an exploration of textual *clues* that the play provides, and which seem constitutive of the tragedy of Othello. The plurality of these 'epithites' points to the fact that Iago comes up with multiple names/versions/reasons to stoke Othello's jealousy; he has many terms with which to designate the loathsome 'thing' that he grapples with throughout the text. The epithet *he* invests with the most stability, however, is 'black.'

As several critics have pointed out, 'race,' like 'sexuality,' was not a term that the Renaissance understood as an identificatory category. There will be more to say about this aspect of race in relation to *King John*, but with *Othello*, it is important to remember that the protagonist's colour did not automatically mark him as 'different.' In her brilliant essay on '*Othello* and Africa,' Emily Bartels has noted that 'race' in the Renaissance signified such diverse concepts as lineage, clan, and species, rather than only skin colour. In fact, as Bartels points out, 'the defamation of the Moor [is shown] as a serious threat to Venice's defense and safety';[22] racism explicitly does *not* pay in this play, and, as Martin Orkin has noted, this was probably one of the reasons the apartheid regime in South Africa frowned upon teaching *Othello* at the secondary level, where 'students [were] exposed to little more than the text itself,' without any accompanying propaganda.[23]

Yet, if the racial politics of the play have caused disagreement and debate, the sexual tension has been relatively clear to all. Iago fills Othello's mind with images of Desdemona's infidelity, which leads to a jealousy so overpowering that the hero murders the heroine in a fit of passion before killing himself in self-hatred and remorse. Sexual intrigue and licence are, in fact, *intrinsic* to the play since both places that serve as its settings – Venice and Cyprus – were widely known as places of sexual licence (Venice as the home of 'super-subtle' courtesans, and Cyprus as the birthplace of Venus).[24] Yet this intrigue and licence cannot be clearly separated from issues of race. Indeed, the extent to which race is an issue of sex can be seen in the Old Testament myth, popularized in the sixteenth and seventeeth centuries by George Best's *Discourse*, of Ham copulating with his wife in the Ark against the express command of God, and incurring the divine curse of blackness on his son Chus, and all his descendants.[25] But this is not a story that is actually *in* the Bible; the biblical tale, in Genesis 9.20–7, emphasizes sex even more forcefully:

> Noah, a man of the soil, was the first to plant a vineyard. He drank some of the wine and became drunk, and he lay uncovered in his tent. And Ham, the father of Canaan, saw the nakedness of his father, and told his two brothers outside. Then Shem and Japheth took a garment, laid it on both their shoulders, and walked backward and covered the nakedness of their father; their faces were turned away, and they did not see their father's nakedness. When Noah awoke from his wine *and knew what his youngest son had done to him*, he said, 'Cursed be Canaan; lowest of slaves shall he be to his brothers.' He also said, 'Blessed by the LORD my God be Shem; and let Canaan be his slave. May God make space for Japheth, and let him live in the tents of Shem; and let Canaan be his slave.'[26] (Emphasis mine)

Even more dramatic than the mythological Ham story is the biblical one, where Ham's viewing of his father's nakedness is heinous enough to incur the latter's wrath, and call down the curse of slavery on Canaan's head. The two good sons, Shem and Japheth, do not look upon their father's body as they cover him and are blessed by Noah and given Canaan as their collective slave. The descendants of Canaan, the Jebusites, the Amorites, and the Hivites, among others, settled in Asia Minor, and what are now the lands around Jerusalem and Palestine. The 'territory of the Canaanites,' we are told, 'extended from Sidon, in the direction of Gerar, as far as Gaza, and in the direction of Sodom, Gomorrah, Admah, and Zeboiim, as far as Lasha' (Gen.10.19). The connection between sexual depravity (surely it is no coincidence that the descendants of Canaan occupy areas around Sodom and Gomorrah) and slavery is made explicit in the Old Testament, and even though the tale is colour neutral (unlike the myth circulated by George Best), it is certainly not value neutral inasmuch as it creates a tension that has nudity and slavery as its two poles. Noah's rage at being 'seen' naked calls forth his curse of slavery and sets up a link that *should* seem completely arbitrary, but which is given the full backing of scriptural authority; it has since been used not only to link rampant sexuality with (black) slavery, but also to justify the 'White Man's Burden' of subjugating black people as an inevitable and valuable operation.

The inevitability of this tragic subjugation is also, I argue, tied to the inevitable deployment of sexuality.[27] Every derogatory mention of blackness in this play is either dismissed in the text or else eagerly embraced by the characters. Moreover, while the circumstances for dismissal are varied – an imminent war, an unreliable witness – in every instance in which racial prejudice is taken seriously, blackness is coupled with some form of sexual deviance. Brabantio accuses Othello of making 'the beast with two backs,' Roderigo dwells jealously on the Moor's 'thick lips,' Emilia accuses the general of being 'the blacker devil' after Othello has accused Desdemona of being a whore; indeed Othello himself inscribes his otherness at the site of his genitals when he describes himself as 'the circumcised dog.'[28] Like everyone else, Othello too begins to believe in the inferiority of his 'begrim'd and black' face when the sexual element becomes inextricably involved with the difference of colour.

In a representative essay, Jonathan Dollimore states that 'the implicit confrontation in *Othello* [is] between civilization and barbarism, and Othello's blackness becomes crucial in just this respect.'[29] But things in this play are rarely so simple as that and 'blackness' is not a term that can easily be pinned down in the debate between 'barbarism and civilization.' In fact, the difficulty of precise terminology is precisely the difficulty of this play. As though to demonstrate this, Iago drives home his advantage against Othello in IV.i by unfolding to him that Cassio has 'confessed' to being illicitly involved with Desdemona:

> OTH.   What hath he said?
> IAGO. [Faith], that he did—I know not what he did.
> OTH. What? What?
> IAGO. Lie—
> OTH.   With her?
> IAGO. With her? On her; what you will.   (IV.i.31–5)

Mary Beth Rose has pointed out that 'the power to create reality through language has increasingly become identified in the play with lying.'[30] The pun on 'lie' – as both untruth and sex[31] – captures the catachrestic cast not only of Iago's pronouncements, but also of the play that he produces. Cassio's (and Iago's) lie immediately becomes proof of *Desdemona's* sexual infidelity. It is supremely ironic that Othello, in the fit of epilepsy brought on by Iago's words, then disavows the power of rhetoric: 'It is not words that shakes me thus.' 'Epilepsy,' of course, is Iago's catachrestic name for Othello's fit which, rather than fitting into an identifiable category, is a series of asterisks that Iago seizes upon to press home his advantage. Iago uses these asterisks not only to name, but also to *misname* Desdemona's crime. Despite Othello's protestations to the contrary, Iago's words are crucial to understanding the webs of racism that he weaves and the manner in which he weaves them. In an attempt to get at the *truth* of blackness, I suggest, we need to go off on the tangent that catachresis etymologically enjoins us to explore.

This tangent, for Iago, the 'master and main exercise' of his metaphorical world, is a discomfort with sexuality. When called upon by Othello to explain the brawl in the streets of Cyprus, for instance, Iago states: 'Friends all, but now, even now; / In quarter, and in terms like bride and groom / Devesting them for bed; and then, but now / (As if some planet had unwitted men), / Swords out and tilting one at other's [breast]' (II.iii.179–83). Even the people on the street are described as brides and grooms who start behaving like brutes born under a malefic star while on the brink of sexual consummation. The very *imminence* of sex is sufficient to make men mad.

The text revels in not only the imminence, but also the excess, of sex. From the inn called the 'Sagittary' which, by its association with the figure of the centaur, denotes a voracious and unnatural sexual appetite, to Iago's characterization of Cassio's fingers as 'clyster pipes,' to his misogynistic outburst against Emilia ('you are pictures out [a' doors], / Bells in your parlors, wild-cats in your kitchens, / Saints in your injuries, devils being offended, / Players in your huswifery, and huswives in your beds' [II.i.109–12]), the text highlights the excessive nature of sexual desire and the concomitant loathing that accompanies it. Iago's sentiments and sentences are marked by a sexual obsession that both repels and fascinates him (and us). From Desdemona as deceptive, 'super-subtle' Venetian, to Emilia as 'villainous whore,' to Cassio as a 'knave ... with most hidden loose affection,' to Othello as a 'Barbary horse,' to his own villainous plans as a thing 'engender'd' that must be brought to 'monstrous birth,' Iago is obsessed with sexuality as diseased, depraved, and most significantly, as a lie. 'She did deceive her father, marrying you,' he tells Othello, 'And when she seem'd to shake and fear your looks, / She lov'd them most' (III.iii.206–8). In fact, Desdemona, the indirect object of Iago's hatred, is always depicted as being in love with lies and liars: she is supposed to have cheated her father, fooled Othello, and dallied with that gentleman of surfaces, Cassio. Iago assures Othello that he 'will make [Cassio] tell the tale anew: / Where, how, how oft, how long ago, and when / He hath, and is again to cope your wife' (IV.i.84–6). Telling 'the tale' of sexuality anew, Iago chooses a name that is 'most nigh unto it,' and alights on the story of racial colouring.

Othello, I suggest, teaches us two lessons about race and sexuality that have a profound impact on the way in which we read these subjects today. The first, emerging from among the folds of Iago's 'motiveless' malignity, is about a discourse on 'race' that provides a *substitutive* idiom for something that cannot *properly* be registered in language. This 'something' can range from dirty sexuality to smelly food to loud music, but in this text, the arch-enemy's potency in naming is reduced to a 'most lame and impotent conclusion' in the face of a multiplicity of *sexual* configurations: Othello and Emilia, Desdemona and Othello, Iago and Cassio, Iago and Desdemona, Cassio and Desdemona, Bianca and Cassio, Emilia and Cassio, Desdemona and Lodovico. There is no *one* name (and no single accusation) that Iago can find to describe a phenomenon that he sees existing everywhere, and since 'sexuality' quickly becomes a meaningless (because potently and potentially pro- liferating) phrase in its denotative power, Iago turns to skin tone (which, after all, is 'there' for all to see), and nominates that as the scapegoat for his hatred. The nonvisual, nonrepresentative nature of sexuality makes it impossible to fix, while colour, for Iago, can easily formulate a man, especially if there is only one man of that colour in the text. Unlike gender and colour, both of which can, with relative ease, be mapped on to a physical body, sexuality is always only an *assumption* that one makes on the basis of the body, and so it is always a name that cannot be verified publicly. And even though sexuality is not something that can be seen, it is that which *enables* sight. So, for instance, in the image of the black ram tupping the white ewe, it is the *tupping* that makes us see (ably guided by Iago) the blackness and whiteness of the people involved.

Despite or perhaps because of this inability to ever directly name his malady, Iago is obsessed with the *desire* to name the reason for, the cause, and the object of, his hatred. Joel Fineman's characterization of the play as the 'tragedy of desire' picks up on this obsession and aligns Iago with Othello as someone who is consumed by an overwhelming need to *know*. As Alessandro Serpieri has pointed out, Othello continu- ally asks for explanations and explications, asks for the names of things that continually elude naming. For instance, 'Othello, who asks [Iago] whether Cassio was not the person who crept away at their arrival – [asks] something that he already *knows*, but which has been *transformed* from a fortuitous event into *a sign of something else*.'[32] This transformation from unseen to seen, from known to knowing, from namelessly innocent to designatedly guilty, is what catachresis effects.

At the end of Act I, Iago announces that he is ready to give 'birth' to something 'monstrous.' The lines preceding this assertion state:

> I hate the Moor,
> And it is thought abroad that 'twixt my sheets
> [H'as] done my office. I know not if't be true,
> But I, for mere suspicion in that kind,
> Will do as if for surety. He holds me well,
> The better shall my purpose work on him.
> Cassio's a proper man. Let me see now:
> To get his place and to plume up my will

In double knavery – How? how? – Let's see –
After some time, to abuse Othello's [ear]
That he is too familiar with his wife.
He hath a person and a smooth dispose
To be suspected – fram'd to make women false.   (I.iii.386–98)

The 'wrongs' that Iago perceives are clearly sexual in nature and the remedy for those wrongs is also cast in a sexual light: Iago will make Othello jealous by insinuating a liaison between Cassio and Desdemona. However, as the play progresses, what is 'delivered' by Iago is not solely a discourse of sexuality, but a discourse of sexuality that pivots around colour difference. The idea of sexuality, 'engend'red' in Iago's fertile imagination, can only be born as blackness. Here, and elsewhere, the discourse of race always has a constitutive relation to the unspeakable nature of sexuality, which is marked by a lack of proper signification. Even as sexuality gives off odious vapours, it itself remains nonpresent both to the sight and to the tongue, and 'race' is produced as precisely that which is both *visible* and can be *apprehended* as disgustingly different. Blackness is used as a tool to fill up a discursive void created by sexuality, and as such, never functions as itself since its self is referenced by a discourse on sexuality that does not exist in this play as an accessible category. To a lesser extent, the text also produces gender (Desdemona, Emilia, and Bianca as unfaithful *because* they are women), and class (Cassio as the educated snob, schooled in 'bookish theoric') as similar covers for sexuality (Desdemona's figural, and Bianca's literal, 'whoredom'; Cassio's 'clyster pipes' of kissing fingers), but 'race' is worked on in the most sustained and relentless manner and is 'producted' as the most potent 'epithite' by which to work on Othello's powerful 'jealiousy.' Not only does Iago designate race as the primary *external* marker of the self, but he also designates it as the primary route by which to approach an *interior* essence. The name for an internal, sexual 'self' in *Othello* becomes the external and publicly verifiable 'race.'

In this, the second lesson the play teaches us about the vexed imbrication of race and sexuality, race is made to signify as the external marker of an internal self that has no stable name, and the 'difference' of colour is valorized as the guide to a self that would otherwise defy definition. Even though the accusations that fill the play – what is presented by Iago to be imagined by Othello – obsessively deal with images of a depraved sexuality, the *name* for these images is that of blackness. Sexuality remains, relative to race, in the realm of the invisible, but visions of its horrific nature are both presented and publicly responded to, as blackness. Iago makes this point explicitly in his verbal dalliance with Desdemona, where he equates fairness with wit and blackness with a sexual 'hit.' Race is seen as the identificatory mark that can never be eluded while the intensely secretive nature of sexuality makes it continually allusive. But what *Othello* shows us is that the discourse of race as 'knowable' is posited as an overcompensation for not being able to similarly 'know' sexuality, and Iago, who always needs to be in control of the action, *creates* the category of the known and knowable in a desperate bid to (con)figure the abstract and aberrant.[33] And so Iago uses Othello's colour as a mode of *sexual* violence, as a way in which to make his own sexual loathing *speak*; to give it, not only a face, but also a tongue.[34] 'Race' becomes for Iago what Quintilian terms the 'nearest available term to describe something for which no actual term exists.' Ultimately, it is this face that kills both Othello and Desdemona, sight unseen.

In *Othello*, racial 'identity' is used by Iago to catachrestically name a sexual malaise, but since 'race' signifies only obscurely, as the *Masque of Blacknesse* makes amply evident, it fails to successfully complete the catachrestic process. Not unlike many critics in our own time, Iago assumes that what one can see on the body can be used as a base from which to spin out 'immutable' truths. By calling sexuality 'black,' Iago hopes to focus attention on what is easier to see, but he fails because 'race' in this play is as fluid a term as 'sexuality.' A 'Turk' can be, as Othello himself so tragically demonstrates, both self and other, Christian and Muslim, 'white' and 'black,' *at the same time*. With the death of Othello and Desdemona, and the unravelling of his plot, Iago finally comes face-to-face with the terror of nonsignification. He stops speaking at the end because he cannot come up with any word to aptly contain his antipathy. Iago's 'motiveless malignity' is devoid of language at the end of the play because words, as my epigraph from Eagleton points out and as Iago always knew, are engaged in an 'orgy' of inbreeding. The act of 'naming,' an act that Iago prides himself on being master of, is always only an act of 'misnaming,' or rather, of unfixed naming. Iago's rhetoric tries to bring sexuality into being by giving it the catachrestic name of blackness, but the project fails because blackness is itself too elusive a concept to answer to any one name. Iago's attempts to racially colour racy sexuality are eventually rendered speechless since he is unable to rely on the fixity of either term; as such, what should have been the reliable nature of race and the unreliable nature of sexuality turn out to be unstable, both in themselves and in relation to each other.

And so catachresis turns out to be rather more sinister in *Othello* than the handbooks of rhetoric envisaged its action could ever be. In fact, the extent of catachrestic abuse is eerily reflected by the play's frequent use of the word 'abuse' which, in conjunction with 'abused,' occurs fourteen times in the play, more than in any other Shakespearean text. 'I am no strumpet, but of life as honest / As you that thus abuse me' (V.i.123–4), claims Bianca when Iago attempts to establish Cassio's relationship with her as indicative of corruption in other realms. Bianca's alleged harlotry is abusive because it names her as something she claims not to be. And even though it is Emilia who actually calls her a strumpet, this scene is yet another production in which 'abuse' is made to name a sexuality that Iago then uses as proof of incompetence elsewhere. At the same time as Brabantio characterizes Othello's (sexually charged) wooing of Desdemona as proof that his daughter has been 'abus'd, stol'n from me, and corrupted' (I.iii.60), Othello himself seizes on Iago's suggestion of Desdemona's infidelity by asserting that he has been 'abus'd, and my relief / Must be to loathe her' (III.iii.267–8). 'Abuse' as both a synonym for and an instance of, catachresis, abounds in this play that catachrestically names sexual desire as racial deviance. The trope both brings blackness into being as a term that can substitute for sexuality, and insists that this blackness gives us access to an inner essence of identity. The approval of 'unnatural' naming that rhetoricians from Quintilian to Puttenham bestowed on the trope here lives up to its literal name of *abusio*, sprinkled liberally through the text in its English translation. If catachresis confers a name upon the nameless, then it does so by presuming on the stability of the racial sign and the invisibility of the sexual signifier. By labelling *Othello* a play about race and racism, we too enact the erasure of sexuality and run the risk of perpetuating catachrestic abuse.

Bastard Wills

If I should tell my history, it would seem
Like lies disdain'd in the reporting.

William Shakespeare, Pericles[35]

According to the *OED*, the word 'race' is 'of obscure origin.' This definition, of course, is classically ironic since 'origins' are primarily what race is about. Whether it traces these origins on the basis of skin colour or patrilineage, 'race' insists on throwing down roots (in fact, one of its meanings is 'a root'), and forging an identity based on those roots. In *King John*, the question of patrilineage becomes crucial to the idea of royal legitimacy as two opposing factions lay claim to the throne of England. So concerned is the play with this question of factionalism and legitimacy that the tension between the two is embodied in the person of the Bastard, who looms large in the fabric of the play. Born out of wedlock, the Bastard figures an illegitimate sexuality that the text uses also to comment on political and lineal illegitimacy. Even as *Othello* adopts racial colouring to tropologically represent sexuality, *King John* figures racial impurity through the marker of brazen sexuality. In this way, despite its narrative obsession with legitimate rule, *King John* is a meditation on the inevitability of catachresis in the project of naming legitimately.[36]

The protagonist of this play about the royal ancestry of England is a Bastard. Despite being named and brought up as Philip Faulconbridge by his adoptive father, and rechristened Richard after his real, but illegitimate father, Richard Coeur-de-Lion – King John's elder brother – Philip is referred to only as the 'Bastard' for the duration of the play. When Philip first appears in court, it is to settle the status of his father's will in which he has been disinherited despite being the first-born. The king decides in the Bastard's favour but nonetheless urges Philip to give up his inheritance and join the royal household, which the Bastard willingly does. The play's treatment of the Bastard focuses attention on the question of legitimacy, a question crucial to a play named for a king. Although King John's easy acceptance of the Bastard might suggest the strength of royal legitimacy to withstand the taint of illegitimacy, the Bastard in fact infects royal purity in a manner unique among Shakespearean history plays.[37]

Despite this comparison with the other history plays, however, the Bastard himself would plot his plans far from the historical fictions of Hotspur and Bullingbrook, and closer to the rhetorical webs of Iago. Even as the Bastard seems to oppose Iago's investment in catachresis – where Iago claims 'I am not what I am,' the Bastard asserts, 'I am I, howe'er I was begot' (I.i.175) – he nonetheless achieves Iago-like effects in this play, stemming from a similar investment in the power of rhetoric. Although positioning himself as Iago's ostensible antithesis – the good bastard instead of the bad one – the Bastard also identifies himself most with Iago as the (en)sign who is only as good as the sign. The play is thus dominated by the mark of the Bastard and its continual remarking on bastardy; loyalty to the throne notwithstanding (and this is the Bastard's most significant difference from Iago), the Bastard undermines the very ground on which England's monarchy is built. The play's emphasis on bastardy is thus daring because it overtly introduces the notion of illegitimacy into a play about the King of England. Even though the Bastard's presence in the text is politically benign, his bastardy is rhetorically violent as it insists on exposing the futility of any legitimacy to be legitimate.

Early in the play, both England under King John and France (nominally) under Prince Arthur, lay siege to Angiers. There ensues a rather comic and protracted bargaining scene with 'Hubert and Other Citizens' on the walls of the city, in which both kings try to stake their claim to Angiers:

> [HUB:] In brief, we are the King of England's subjects:
>   For him, and in his right, we hold this town.
> K. JOHN: Acknowledge then the King, and let me in.
> [HUB:] That can we not; but he that proves the King,
>   To him will we prove loyal ...
> K. JOHN: *Doth not the crown of England prove the King?*
>   And if not that, I bring you witnesses,
>   Twice fifteen thousand hearts of England's breed—
> BAST: Bastards, and else ...
> K. JOHN: Whose party do the townsmen yet admit?
> K. PHI: Speak, citizens, for England. Who's your king?
> HUB: The King of England, when we know the King.
>   (II.i.267–71, 273–6, 361–3, emphasis mine)

And so on and so forth, until the kings finally and jointly decide to wage war against the town. This scene is striking in its ability to generate a sense of tautological claustrophobia: the city belongs to the king of England, whoever the king of England might be. Most astounding of all is the fact that the kings seem to recognize the tautological nature of their predicament. Thus, King John is perfectly willing to accept the fact that his possession of the crown might, in the end, *not mean as much as it should*. To legitimate his claim, therefore, he offers the bodies of fifteen thousand English men as 'proof' of his authority over England. The Bastard points out, however, that some of those fifteen thousand men might be bastards whose bastardy would immediately taint the king's claim to royal purity. John wants the crown to stand as metonymic witness to his legitimacy but the Bastard insists that metonymy can easily be converted to catachresis, especially if its guarantors are bastards. And so the king quickly tries to convert sexual illegitimacy into its opposite – royal marriage – and agrees to the wedding of his niece with the dauphin in order to consolidate the English and French powers.

Eleanor, the king's ambitious and strong-willed mother, urges the marriage in the hope that it will secure the English crown: 'For by this knot thou shalt so surely tie / Thy now unsur'd assurance to the crown' (II.i.470–1); but marriage here, as in *Othello*, is never able to secure anything since it only catachrestically harnesses an issue (sexuality, power, knowledge) that is unstable at best. The assurance that the Crown seeks from the knot of marriage turns out to be the very opposite of a guarantee. Soon after the nuptials have been performed, a legate of the pope appears to announce John's excommunication for daring to defy the papal appointment of the archbishop of Canterbury and urges the king of France (newly related to the king of England) to wage a holy war against John. The knot of the marriage is speedily voided, France returns to his original position of supporting John's rival to the throne, and the two kings resume enmities, once again trying to ascertain the *true* king of England.

The rival claimant to the throne is a young lad named Arthur, who would rather not be the centre of such attention, but who has been successfully coopted by both his mother and the king of France. Arthur's mother Constance actively encourages what she sees as a rightful war to reinstate the rightful king on the throne of England. However, even as King John's claim to England is rhetorically tainted by his association with bastardy, so too is Arthur's as his grandmother swiftly accuses his mother of having been unfaithful to her husband's bed. This is probably not a claim we are meant to take seriously since it is never mentioned again, but the very possibility that it might be true makes the war for legitimacy more even in its choice of illegitimacies. Like *Othello*, *King John* starkly demonstrates that accusations of illegitimacy acquire most credibility when accompanied by proof of sexual inconstancy. Whether this illegitimacy is racial or racial, its guarantor is always sexual. John might have usurped the title that 'properly' belongs to Arthur, and Arthur might be attempting to ascend to a title not properly his, but in both instances, the contenders for royal legitimacy are undone by the taint of sexual illegitimacy, hoist on the petard of propriety. Royal illegitimacy is figured by a sexual illegitimacy that the court of England accepts into its fold in the form of the Bastard. This illegitimacy is embraced when the Bastard enters the court, and is compounded as he continues to live there.

If the bastard serves as the Folly-like underminer of this royal drama, then his unlikely allies are the two people most invested in legitimacy: the mothers of the contenders for the throne of England. Despite being in opposite camps, Eleanor and Constance join rhetorical forces with the Bastard in proclaiming the mutually reinforcing instability of racial and sexual legitimacy. In fact, the mothers of the two men who would be king know that legitimacy can easily be dissimulated and that in the absence of ascertainable propriety, what matters most is the specific name attached to a particular act. So when Cardinal Pandulph sternly tells Constance to desist from cursing the king of France when he wavers in his support of her cause, the papal legate asserts that her curses are illegitimate because (unlike his own) they have no 'law and warrant' behind them. Constance scornfully retorts that

> when law can do no right,
> Let it be lawful that law bar no wrong;
> Law cannot give my child his kingdom here,
> *For he that holds the kingdom holds the law*;
> Therefore since law itself is perfect wrong,
> How can the law forbid my tongue to curse?   (III.i.185–90, emphasis mine)

Constance does not clarify the law to which she refers, and her statement could easily be construed as a blasphemous defiance of the pope, much like the crime of which John stands accused. Her point, however, whether aimed at Innocent III or John, is clear enough. There is a tautological connection between legality and morality: what is legal automatically becomes moral and vice versa. Her argument does not elicit a response from the cardinal, who simply reiterates the consequences for Philip if he will not wage war against John. But the text compels us, through this and other speeches, to challenge the very cast of appearance, the cast that passes on the *basis* of its appearance, since appearance is the law, and the law is, not only a 'perfect wrong,' but also an ass, ensuring that 'history,' as my epigraph from *Pericles* tells us, can just as easily be dismissed as a disdainful lie as it can be embraced as the truth.

If Constance and Eleanor are unlikely bedfellows in their argument for rhetorical supremacy, their shared voice nonetheless continues to echo through the Shakespearean canon and is later picked up by Emilia who, in one of her many spirited conversations with a drooping Desdemona, states her argument *for* sexual infidelity in the face of Desdemona's repeated piety. Fidelity, Emilia argues, is a relative term, and must be put in perspective before being judged. If by losing one's fidelity one gains the world, then that is a bargain worth making, especially because one can then cancel the (im)morality of the earlier transaction in this brave new world: 'Why, the wrong is but a wrong i' th' world; and having the world for your labor, 'tis a wrong in your own world, and you might quickly make it right' (IV.iii.80–3). Emilia emphasizes the importance of first principles for any argument. After all, different starting points tend to different ends, and conclusions depend on the assumptions made from within a certain framework. If the framework is John's, then Arthur is the enemy and Constance a liar, but if the framework is Constance's, then John is illegitimate, and despite holding the crown of England, should be deposed.

In an essay on Nietzsche, Paul de Man points to just this awkwardness in determining 'reality.' De Man cites Nietzsche's questioning of that 'most fundamental 'value' of all, (Aristotle's) principle of noncontradiction, ground of the identity principle':

> In short, the question remains open: are the axioms of logic adequate to reality or are they a means and measure for us to *create* the real, the concept of 'reality,' for ourselves? ... To affirm the former one would, as already stated, have to have a previous knowledge of entities; which is certainly not the case. The proposition therefore contains no *criterion of truth*, but an imperative concerning that which *should* count as true.

And, de Man adds:

> We are dealing with the more elusive oppositions between possibility and necessity ... and especially between knowing and positing ... [T]he question [is] whether the identity-principle is an obligatory speech act or a fact merely susceptible of being spoken.[38]

Eleanor, Constance, Emilia, the Bastard, John, and even to a certain extent Iago, would agree with Nietzsche and de Man: the propriety of names depends on a framework within which they are deemed either right or wrong. In the absence of a point of origin or fount of legitimacy (in the Bastard's case, his father and his 'father' are both dead), all legitimacy becomes merely contingent and susceptible to replacement, with particularly devastating consequences for royalty. This devastation is the moving force behind much of history and certainly behind many of Shakespeare's history plays, but nowhere is it spelled out as clearly as it is in *King John*. The necessity of catachresis proves devastating to the certainty of language, and the most recognizable figure of that devastation in this play is the figure of illegitimate sexuality, the figure of the Bastard. *King John* uses the Bastard in order to present most fully the ineluctably catachrestic cast of all royal performance; this is a lesson the Nigerian princesses in *Blacknesse* would have done well to learn.

Bastardy thus threatens to blow up the play in our faces and repeatedly figures battles for legitimacy as battles of reading. With an irony worthy of catachresis, the papal legate himself recognizes this power of language to name as it pleases, without consideration of person or place. Almost incidentally, Cardinal Pandulph notes that if John murders his rival Arthur, then the people will rebel against their king and will legitimate their antipathy by a reading of the stars:

> No natural exhalation in the sky,
> No scope of nature, no distemper'd day,
> No common wind, no customed event,
> But they will pluck away his natural cause
> And call them meteors, prodigies, and signs,
> Abortives, presages, and tongues of heaven,
> Plainly denouncing vengeance upon John.   (III.v.153–9)

The people will read the stars in order to find a reflection, and thus, retrospectively, a vindication, of their anger. This, of course, is the very principle of catachrestic language: words always mean less than what they have the *ability* to mean. Language can be set in stone only if stoniness is itself shut down as a word to be interpreted. Cardinal Pandulph – almost as canny a theorist of language as the Bastard – insists that the catachrestic cast of language will enable people to interpret the 'natural exhalation[s] in the sky' as prodigies importing meaning. That meaning, however, will always be made to adapt to any given situation. In other words, the celestial signs will always mean what we want them to mean; in this case, the cardinal suggests, the stars will propagate vengeance against King John. 'Customed event[s]' will be counted uncustomary and the 'signs' of such a misreading will be indistinguishable from the map of reading. The *same* signs will be read as presages of good fortune in times of grace and as bad omens in times of ill.

This 'abortive' endeavour to make language mean what it says ensures an end to the play's narrative – King John dies and his son, Prince Henry, is poised to take over as king – but it also confirms the play's rhetorical infection by the '[a]bortives' of bastardy. Appropriately enough, despite never being or even wanting to be king, the Bastard has the last word in this play about a king. True to his own catachrestic nature, that word is itself 'true': 'Nought shall make us rue, / If England to itself do rest but true' (V.vii.117–18). This last desperate plea for the truth is bound up with an attempt to preserve English royalty from future sources of indeterminacy, but as the pleader of the plea has amply demonstrated, bastardy is an integral part of the English court and catachresis is the lasting trace of the violence that language performs in order to confer legitimacy. The legitimacy of names with which the play seeks to end is undermined by the Bastard himself: when questioned by Hubert about his identity – 'Who art thou' – the Bastard answers 'Who thou wilt' (V.vi.9). Since every act of naming is necessarily an act of misnaming (there being no factor by which its truth can be determined), every name is as equally valid and invalid as the other. The figure of illegitimate sexuality makes this argument for catachresis repeatedly and forcefully; indeed, in some ways, he is in the best position to do so.

Catachresis thus extends the allegedly individual realms of sexual and racial abuse to also include one another. *Othello* creates a discourse around race that points both to the substitutive nature of racial difference and to the catachrestic nature of that substitution. *King John*, meanwhile, personifies sexual illegitimacy in the Bastard, who is then used as a figure for racial and lineal illegitimacy. These two plays present us with a sustained meditation on the sex-race link. Iago attaches blackness to the sin of sexuality in order for the latter to signify through the former – sexuality becomes racialized – while for the Bastard, illegitimate sexuality marks the difficulty of arriving at lineal certainty – racial illegitimacy is sexualized. Iago and the Bastard, both central characters in plays not named for them, enact the catachrestic impulse of naming and misnaming, of naming *as* misnaming. The use of terms like 'race' and 'sexuality,' itself catachrestic in studies of

Renaissance literature that analyse texts in which these terms are not used, is nonetheless necessary since it enables us to study Renaissance literature in the first place. In conversation with one another, these two plays forge an epistemology of race and sexuality in Renaissance England in which desire and race are identified as sites of linguistic corruption that continually reflect and replace one another. This reflection and replacement are necessarily abusive moves, but without them, neither the plays' language nor our own would exist.

5

Encore! Allegory, *Volpone, The Tempest*

If [the readers] do not meddle with the allegory, the allegory will not meddle with them.

William Hazlitt, *Lectures on the English Poets*[1]

Truth and *Goodnesse* are plaine and open: but, *Imposture* is ever asham'd of the light. A Puppet-play must be shadow'd and seene in the darke; for draw the Curtaine, *Et sordet gesticulatio.*

Ben Jonson, *Timber, or Discoveries*[2]

During the first half of the fifteenth century the person now designated the Wakefield Master made masterly revisions to the Nativity story in the Towneley cycle of mystery plays. The most famous of these revisions took the form of the *First* and *Second Shepherds' Plays*, which presented the story of Christ's birth in two different, yet similar, settings: the shepherds are directed to Bethlehem to adore the Child, and once there, leave off their coarse ways to join together in singing harmonious hymns to the Lord. There are several remarkable features in these plays, not least of which is the fact that they present two versions of the same story in the same cycle of plays written by the same person; it is as though Christ were born twice. Interestingly, this possibility is not too far from the truth, and the *Second Shepherds' Play* sets up a pattern of doubleness that gets at the heart of the mystery lurking in the mystery plays.

Early in the *Second Shepherds' Play*, three weary shepherds lie down to rest along with a no-good lowlife called Mak, who decides to make off with one of their sheep. He takes it home to his wife, Uxor, who comes up with a plan to hide the sheep until the shepherds depart:

> UXOR: A good bowrde have I spied, syn tou can none.
>   Here shall we hym hyde to thay be gone;
>   In my credyll abyde. Lett me alone,
>   And I shall lyg besyde in chylbed, and grone.
> MAK: Thou red;
>   And I shall say thou was lyght
>   Of a knave childe this nyght.   (332–8)

The uxorious husband (a stock source of medieval humour) and his wife decide to wrap the sheep in swaddling cloths till the coast is clear, at which point they will slaughter the 'babe' for food. After thus disposing of the sheep and deferring gratification for its flesh, Mak steals back to the sleeping shepherds and insinuates himself once again into their somnolent brotherhood. Shortly thereafter, one of the shepherds wakes to a premonitory dream that he has been robbed, and suspicion immediately falls on Mak. The shepherds go to Mak's house to search for their sheep, and are greeted with the sight of a newly delivered 'child,' an indignant Uxor, and a paternal Mak singing a lullaby to the newest addition to his flock. The shepherds level their accusation at Mak and his wife, who deny it strenuously; in a moment of exquisite irony, Uxor tries to settle her innocence once and for all by claiming, in a tone that Lady Macbeth later echoes: 'If ever I you begyld, / That I ete this chylde / That lygys in this credyll' (535–8), which, of course, is exactly what she intends to do. Faced with a truth that hides a lie and which the shepherds do not know as yet to be a truth, the three would-be prosecutors are chastened into submission and leave Mak alone with his wife and newborn child.

Soon after leaving, however, they realize they have been indecorous in not giving the newborn baby a gift and return once more to pay him a token of their affection. When the shepherds re-enter the house – to Mak and Uxor's surprise – they lift the cloth from the baby's face, and the 'revelation' that follows is a source of both horror and humour:

> III PASTOR: Gyf me lefe hym to kys, and lyft up the clowtt.
>   What the dewill is this? He has a long snowte.
> I PASTOR: He is merkyd amys. We wate ill abowte.

II PASTOR: Ill-spon weft, iwys, ay commys foull owte.
Ay, so!
He is lyke to oure shepe! (584–9)

The shepherds finally realize that the baby is the sheep stolen from their flock: the long snout is a dead giveaway. Soon after making the double discovery of the sheep and their earlier naivety, and punishing Mak (they toss him in a blanket), the shepherds fall asleep once more, worn out by the day's excitement.

In this their second sleep, an angel appears to the shepherds, singing of a birth in Bethlehem and urging them to go and pay their respects to the child who will deliver them from the devil:

ANGELUS: Ryse, hyrd-men heynd! For now is he borne
That shall take fro the feynd that Adam had lorne;
That warloo to sheynd, this nyghte is he borne.
God is made youre freynd now at this morne.
He behestys
At Bedlem go se:
Ther lygys that fre
In a crib full poorely,
Btweyx two bestys. (638–46)

The new child – the Saviour – bears an uncanny resemblance to the sheep-child, if not on account of his own snout, then by the proximity of the two snouts between which his crib is said to lie; the scene also plays off the association of Christ with *agnus dei*, the lamb of God. The shepherds nonetheless proceed to adore this child, and the play ends with the Virgin Mary's gracious thanks to the shepherds, a promise of her intercession for their well-being, and a song in praise of the new Lord.

The mystery plays were meant to present the ineffable mysteries of life in vehicles (literally, since the plays were often mounted on moving platforms) that could be easily comprehended by actors and audiences alike. English was used, which added to the popularity of these plays that allegorized the story of Jesus and enacted the eternal verities of damnation and salvation. The *Second Shepherds' Play* plays its role in this cycle by allegorizing the birth of Jesus. In the process of presenting its allegory, however, the *Second Shepherds' Play* prefaces the birth of Christ with the story of a false birth in which a child turns out to be a stolen sheep. If the Wakefield Master's play is anything to go by, then allegory turns out to be a narrative structured around the tension between surface deceit and inner truth that works in the mode of repetition. The narrative exists on at least two levels, one dealing with an individual story and another pointing to the religious, social, and political implications of that story; the movement of allegory is thus the movement between two stories, one of which is more apparent than the other, but the other of which is the more important and towards which the allegorical movement tends.

Anticipating this need, Edmund Spenser's *Faerie Queene* – arguably the most famous instance of allegory in Renaissance England – defines this particular aspect of allegorical movement and formalizes the terms introduced in the *Second Shepherds' Play*. In his prefatory letter to Raleigh, Spenser expounds the 'intention' of his poem:

> Knowing how doubtfully all Allegories may be construed, and this book of mine ... being a continued Allegory, or darke conceit, I have thought good aswell for *avoyding of gealous opinions and misconstructions, as also for your better light in reading* thereof ... to discover unto you the general intention and meaning. (1, emphasis mine)

For Spenser, an allegory needs to be explained, and the metaphor for that explanation is repeatedly one of illumination. The 'darke conceit' of allegory needs light in order to be read correctly; without proper illumination, its meaning is too 'doubtfull' – etymologically linked to the notion of 'doubleness' (or *dubitare*) – to be construed. Spenser's letter provides that illumination to the reader of his text, but this illumination implies also the inevitable darkness of the allegorical condition, the fact that despite appearing as the vehicle of light, allegory operates in the shadows of darkness. In other words, Spenser glorifies allegorical light even as he glosses over the realm of darkness in which allegory exists. The letter to Raleigh serves as the remedy for a textual condition that is never defined as sick, but which is nonetheless recognized as being in need of amelioration.

The project of bringing to light an allegorical darkness is therefore a tautological one: allegory needs to be dark in order that it may be brought to light, and Spenser describes his letter as the illumination necessary to pierce the dark textual veil of allegory. This tautological formulation suggests that allegorical light needs allegorical darkness in order to succeed – and even exist – as allegory. The *Faerie Queene* therefore matches the *Second Shepherds' Play* double for double, offering its twinning of Duessa and Una to correspond to the doubling of Uxor and Mary, each set sexualizing allegory even as it allegorizes sexuality. Like all allegory, Spenser's version has a stake in its own darkness and needs to produce it so that it can all the more effectively provide us with the illuminating key. It is unable to exist in the light alone even as the myth of the enlightening and enlightened allegory continues to be the most durable myth surrounding the trope. Allegory, as we shall see, has a tendency to repeat its problematic terms in its explication. Even as it appears to move from the dark to the light, the dark is itself kept in the dark, creating a sense of claustrophobia at the same time as it plots a sense of narrative movement. This complicated allegorical cycle that Spenser sketches in his letter to the reader is reflected in the structure of the Shepherds' play, not only by the fact that there are two narratives, one of which is arguably more significant than the other, but also because the urge to repeat is everywhere embedded in the play. Both versions of the story use largely similar characters, the shepherds fall asleep at two crucial moments and their waking hours after each sleep are filled with chasing after lost sheep (or lambs). Twice the shepherds fall asleep, twice they have a dream, twice they make a journey, see two babies, and arrive twice at a revelation. The first revelation comes when the cloth covering the 'baby' is lifted by the shepherd and the child is revealed to be a sheep. This lifting of the veil is later paralleled by the revelation of Christ asleep in the manger in his swaddling clothes, when the shepherds lift his veil in order to ensure that he will, in turn, lift the veil of sin that shrouds humanity.

This veil is perhaps the most important component of allegory inasmuch as it marks the point at which the surface narrative slides into the trope's deeper implications. Both Spenser's letter to the reader and the *Second Shepherds' Play* point to the narrative importance of a veil that can and should be lifted to reveal the truth (or even the Truth). In both cases involving the shepherds, the veil is the crucial marker of division between a surface narrative (the baby is human) and a hidden truth (the baby is a sheep, or else, the Saviour). The truth is meant to lie behind the veil, both in Mak's house and in the manger, and the truth in both cases is that the *bairn* in the barn is not a child as we know it. The two unveilings are meant to parallel one another: the first veil reveals the real sheep while the second unveiling discovers the Lamb of God. But equally, if the first unveiling reveals the shepherds' foolishness, might not the second one do the same? Rather than giving us the truth, could the unveiling reveal merely that a veil can hide deceit (the child is a sheep) just as well as it can conceal the truth (the child is the Son of God)? In which case, might the truth itself be a case of foolish misreading? After all, there is no guarantee that the second child, though not a sheep, will not eventually get the shepherds' goat. By all accounts, the birth of Jesus signifies only a false moment of deliverance since only the *Second* Coming will ensure an end to the great cycle of sin and redemption. Lifting the veil does not therefore put an end to superficial or 'false' reading; instead, it plunges reader and shepherd alike into the abyss of an interpretation whose end is uncertain. Even as it marks the frontier between two worlds of meaning, the veil is unable to reveal which world is the more true. Instead of an end, therefore, perhaps Spenser's readers and the Wakefield Master's allegorical shepherds are condemned to a fate of endless repetition.

The endlessness of this repetition is made clear in the parallel between two worlds of allegorical meaning in the *Second Shepherds' Play*, each represented by a woman. While Uxor generates prodigiously Mary has only one prodigy. Uxor's body is both sexualized and ravaged as she is delivered of another 'knave.' Mary's body, on the other hand, is closed, intact, and virginal despite the great breach in nature signified by the birth of her child. The play moves from its image of uxorious gaping sexuality to pure virginity as part of a larger allegorical movement from surface to depth, and from deceit to truth. This movement is a reflection of the theological allegory of the word as it approaches the Word, but is made flesh in a play that insists on the circularity of the allegorical process, casting Mary in Uxor's role and vice versa. The cycle of repetition then guarantees, not an arrival at the Truth, but the inevitability of the journey and the unreliable coordinates of the destination. Both Uxor and Mary centre their li(v)es around the cradle and the baby in it, but the latter's tale is more successful *as a story* than the former's and has spawned millions of believers. Even as the *Second Shepherds' Play* valorizes the second birth as a singular, true, and unique event, it nonetheless presents it as the echo of a story that has already been told. The tale of the shepherds takes us to Jesus but does not guarantee that the virginal Mary is not merely Uxor with better make-up, one who has been able to disguise herself and her child more cunningly.

The ideas of veiling and circularity, I argue, are central to the trope of allegory in which the tropological impulse makes it impossible to arrive at a certainty that does not immediately question itself. More-over, this deconstruction of certainty is inevitably tied, as it is in this play, to the construction of sexuality. The crux on which the plot of the *Second Shepherds' Play* hinges is whether Mary's sexuality and its off-spring are more 'true' than Uxor's. By depending on the fact that Mary's sexuality is, in fact, the *lack* of sexuality, allegory validates it as the truth while condemning Uxor's much-opened body to the status of deceit. Uxor's splayed legs nonetheless act as the veil beneath which Mary's virginity is carefully preserved, but the purity of this virginity is irrevocably tainted by the droppings of rampant sexuality. Purity finds itself in the same bed as impurity, and allegory undermines the distinction between the two.

In such a schema, allegory is not so much sexual as sexuality is itself insistently allegorical; neither trope can arrive at a stable point of refer-ence that does not disguise its premise as its end. The sexuality that crucially supports the allegory of this play is structured as a textual narrative in which a proper reading reveals the kernel of truth within the portal of flesh. But this act of reading – of interpreting the two dreams, for instance – is always an act of *contingent* reading and the trope that is read as pointing the way toward interpretive certainty points out nothing more (or less) than the certainty of continual inter-pretation. This chapter will explore the problematic of readability and obscurity, sexuality and allegory, in two plays – Ben Jonson's *Volpone* and William Shakespeare's *Tempest* – both of which explicitly drama-tize the veil separating two realms of interpretation. In the process, each play makes clear the interface between the rhetorical structure of allegory and, to borrow Joel Fineman's formulation, the structure of allegorical desire.[3] Notably, this interface is foregrounded also in Quin-tilian's *Institutio Oratoria*, which allegorizes allegory in the workings of sexuality.

Lesbia or Lesbian?

Wheresoever manners and fashions are corrupted, Language is. It imitates the publicke riot. The excesse of Feasts, and apparell, are the notes of a sick State; and the wantonnesse of language, of a sick mind.

Ben Jonson, *Discoveries*[4]

The *Institutio Oratoria* begins by defining allegory (*inversio*) as that which 'either present[s] one thing in words and another in meaning, or else something absolutely opposed to the meaning of the words' (VIII.6.44). The split between word and meaning that this definition registers is central to the trope: allegory is that which *officially* exists on two different planes of meaning. It is in this sense akin to metaphor, which is why allegory is often referred to as 'a long and perpetuall Metaphore' (Puttenham, *Arte of English Poesie*, 187). The local division of meaning that metaphor enacts is stretched out across entire sentences and speeches by allegory so that what begins as a single deviation from sense and logic becomes nothing short of spatial, temporal, and causal inversion. Allegory destabilizes our notions of certainty by confronting them with 'something absolutely opposed' to it. *Inversio* represents less a chiastic inversion of ideas based on a reciprocity between two terms, and more an overthrow of sense that threatens the concept of order itself.

Allegory is thus not always about a movement toward lucidity. Quintilian criticizes this lack of clarity, especially while speaking of the allegorical 'riddle': 'When ... an allegory is too obscure, we call it a riddle: such riddles are, in my opinion, to be regarded as blemishes, in view of the fact that lucidity is a virtue; nevertheless they are used by poets' (VIII.6.52). The recalcitrance of poets who insist on using obscurity despite (and perhaps because of) its unclear nature, infuriates Quintilian, who tries to instill a modicum of order into an otherwise wild world of words. If poets can be dismissed for having stubbornly fertile imaginations, orators are less easy to ignore since their use of obscurity cuts closer to home. Hence Quintilian's most fascinating example of an allegorical riddle, and of the impropriety latent within the practice of allegory itself, and also of the potential blemish in allegory that most threatens to taint the trope, comes from the speech of an orator:

> Even orators sometimes use them [riddles], as when Caelius speaks of the 'Clytemnestra who sold her favours for a farthing, who was a Coan in the dining-room and a Nolan in her bedroom.' For although we know the answers, and although they were better known at the time when the words were uttered, they are riddles for all that; and other riddles are, after all, intelligible if you can get someone to explain them. (VIII.vi.53)

The example in this passage derives from a speech of the orator Caelius denouncing Clodia as a 'loose' (Clytemnestra-like) woman. The wife of Caecilius Metellus Celer, sometime consul of Cisalpine Gaul,

Clodia was sexually involved with, among others, Caelius and Catullus. She was a contemporary and enemy of Cicero, who bitterly denounced her while defending his friend and her former lover, Caelius Rufus, on a charge of attempted poisoning that she brought against him.[5] Before exploring the allegorical 'sense' of Caelius's accusation cited by Quintilian, it is worthwhile to explore Clodia's association with the poet Catullus.

It has long been acknowledged that Clodia was both the inspiration for and the recipient of Catullus's 'Lesbia' poems. Interestingly, Clodia is first addressed as Lesbia in Poem 51, which is a translation of one of Sappho's poems; 'Lesbia' is a metrically equivalent substitute for 'Clodia.'[6] However, Sappho's original poem has no vocative, and 'Lesbia' is Catullus's own substitution, his private perversion of the original, his catachrestic naming of the recipient of a certain brand of Sapphist poetry. This deviation at the textual level, I suggest, nudges us toward the trace of perversion at the sexual level as well. Even though the OED does not list 'Lesbia' as an etymological source for the modern term 'lesbian,' the connection between a bold, sexually unconventional protagonist of a Sapphist poem and a modern 'lesbian' does not demand too insurmountable a suspension of disbelief.

Clodia is accused, in Quintilian's disapproving citation of Caelius's riddlingly allegorical speech, of being 'a Coan in the dining-room and a Nolan in her bedroom.' According to the Oxford Latin Dictionary, a Coan signified an inhabitant of Cos, an island famous for its devotion to Venus and an investment in sensual delights like art. To be a Nolan, on the other hand, signified not only habitation in Nola, a rather strait-laced town in the interior of Campania, but also a specific psychological temperament: the term derives etymologically from the combination of ne and volo, to be unwilling. We can thus translate Caelius's statement as saying that Clodia was Venus-like in the dining-room but more prudish in the bedroom; that she was sexy and attractive on the outside (or while in company), but frigid and conservative on the inside (within the confines of her bedchamber). Even as this instance registers Clodia's lack of interest in Caelius (thus, perhaps, providing more fodder for her association with 'lesbianism'), the allegorical accusation levelled by Caelius also points to a fundamental aspect of allegory itself: like Caelius's Clodia, allegory is predicated on a division between interior and exterior, on a confusion of signals that makes its 'message' difficult to read. However, even as the riddle is condemned for confusing the reader (and the listener), Quintilian also suggests that this confusion is not insurmountable. As long as someone is willing to explicate the riddle, the message on the inside can always be attained; the truth of the bedchamber can always be penetrated if there is an explanatory torch to light the way.

Rather than existing as a factor external to the riddle, however, this light emerges from within the darkness of the trope precisely in order to drag it out of the dark. Far from being extrinsic to the allegory, the light at the end of the tunnel surfaces from within its depths. As such, its explanation is always rooted in the riddle itself and any light it might shed on that riddle is both implied and implicated by the dark problem. This implication, however, has to be forgotten in order to posit the light as the answer – the extratextual explanation – of any given riddle. As is the case with Spenser's letter to the reader, allegorical illumination has to repudiate its investment in allegorical darkness even as it can only emerge from it; once attained, the light has to seem absolute even as its very existence is differential. In Quintilian's example, this light is provided by a lesbian whose figure then retroactively explains (her) sexual deviance and unreadability. Caelius's speech is criticized for being too riddling even as its hidden meaning is deemed easy to read. In other words, the surface narrative positioning Lesbia between a Coan and a Nolan leads to the true signification of sexual inversion that then 'explains' the position of Lesbia in the riddle, providing illumination where there had once only been darkness. The veil that separates Lesbia's dining room from her bedroom has to be lifted in order for the allegorical riddle to be explained. Equally, this lifted veil has to definitively differentiate what lies before from what lies behind it, casting the former as the truth and the latter as the darkness to be shunned. The veil that protects Lesbia's bedroom is lifted in order to discredit her sexually and identify her as what we would now call a 'lesbian.' That identification is achieved primarily by producing the riddling figure of Clodia to figure the very process of allegory. Like allegory's movement from darkness to light, Caelius's riddle can also be read as moving from obscurity to knowledge as soon as we have access to the sexual connotations of what it might mean to be a Nolan in the bedroom while playing at being a Coan in the dining room. The specifically *allegorical* impulse of allegory is set in motion when the trope encounters its own inevitable investment in what Quintilian terms 'an element of obscurity' (VIII.vi.58). This element of obscurity resists the formation of allegorical light even as it is the thing that most encourages such a formulation. Obscurity must be made to mean, even and especially when it stubbornly holds out against the fixity of meaning.

In the case of Clodia, allegory's investment in obscurity highlights the tropological nature of the sexuality involved in making sense of its protagonist. Clodia's sexual identity is always a convention identifiable only by a convention of reading, even as her identity has to be fixed in order to translate the allegorical riddle into essential truth. Thus the contradiction of allegory remains that it posits a realm of stable meaning lying just beyond the realm of riddling instability, repudiating tropology even as the urge to mean is built into the trope of allegory. Quintilian is convinced that all riddles are 'intelligible if you can get someone to explain them,' but this intelligibility is nonetheless tainted by the obscurity of the message that it attempts to unravel. Allegory is thus neither the riddle nor its solution; rather, it figures the relationality between the two. An allegory has to involve a surface that both exists on its own *and* creates the illusion of something lying behind it. Reading allegory is always to read obscurity even as obscurity is apparently extinguished by the onset of 'clarity.'

This sense of allegorical obscurity is even more pointed in the *Ad Herennium* than it is in the *Institutio*. The pseudo-Ciceronian text ties its understanding of allegory to the larger concept of irony, and the distance between words and their meanings.[7] Like the *Institutio Oratoria*, the *Ad Herennium* points to a gap in signification that defines the differential relation constitutive of sexuality;[8] while the *Institutio* suggests that Clodia is both the reason for and consequence of being a Coan in the dining room and a Nolan in the bedroom, the *Ad Herennium* goes even further in positing the link between a riddling textuality and an obscure sexuality. It gives us an example of allegory drawn by contrast: 'If we should call ... an intemperate and adulterous man "Hippolytus"' (IV.xxxiv.46). The 'contrast' in this example derives from the ironic distance between a hypothetical man's alleged intemperance, and Hippolytus's 'real' chastity for which he was punished. Hippolytus is accused by his stepmother Phaedra of attempted rape after he rejects her sexual advances, and is put to death. This 'otherness' of meaning – the man called Hippolytus is other than Hippolytus was – is the very hallmark of irony and here, it is also the mark of an allegorical statement that derives its sense from the dishonesty inherent in (female) sexuality. Hippolytus becomes the type of man whose chastity can only be recovered by uncovering it; in the *Ad Herennium*, he becomes both an example of allegory and an instance of allegory gone awry.

Phaedra's sexual accusation veils Hippolytus's innocence even as Hippolytus's nominative innocence veils the unknown man's intemperance. Allegory veils even as it is itself veiled, and in both these texts, that veiling is the central tenet of the allegorical imperative. While the *Institutio Oratoria* suggests that Clodia's unnatural sexuality derives from the distance between her dining room and her bedroom, the *Ad Herennium* insists that Hippolytus is distanced from his true position of chastity by means of allegorical inversion. This otherness of meaning, of meaning hidden by a veil, is crucial to both allegory and sexuality. In fact, sexuality is produced by a riddling language precisely *as* that something hidden behind a veil; it both leads to allegorical revelation and is the revelation itself.

However, this revelation is presented in both classical texts as an undesirable, even traumatic event. Clodia is held up as a Clytemnestra figure who is not to be trusted while Hippolytus is engaged as the tragic victim of false sexual allegations. Even if the allegory in both these instances is meant to reveal enlightening ends, their means are obscene. This obscenity is defined precisely by the sense that both Jacques Lacan and Slavoj Žižek ascribe to the obscene: the ob-seen, the scene that is not seen, and in these texts, the scene that is covered over with a veil.[9] Allegory insists that the veil be lifted in order to reveal meaning, but the production of meaning – though intended to create stability – is itself a traumatic event that needs to forget its trauma in order to signify. This trauma of signification is evident in the *Second Shepherds' Play* where Mary has to be a virgin in order for Jesus not to be a sheep, and in the *Institutio Oratoria* where Clodia's metrical equivalence with Lesbia is only a measure of her tropological equivalence with a figure of inverted (or allegorical) sexuality.

Hazlitt's epigraph to this chapter – 'If [the readers] do not meddle with the allegory, the allegory will not meddle with them' – thus acquires urgency in light of this trauma of allegory. Is it ever possible to keep the veil in place rather than lift it? To stay near the surface of a narrative rather than straying near the allegorical depths? Is allegory meddlesome only if, as Hazlitt suggests, one meddles *with* it? Can one ever be free of allegory and its traumatic revelations? Can allegory ever reveal anything other than the trauma of revelation? Hazlitt's statement suggests that one can walk away from allegory, choosing not to engage it at all. In his formulation, there are two distinct realms that do not necessarily intersect with one another – the realm of the reader and the realm of the allegory – with a common area being provided by perverse readers of the trope; allegory is here posited as a menacing figure that warns the reader not to meddle (or 'mess') with it. But even as Hazlitt appears to be suggesting the separability of reader and allegory, he also invests allegory with a life of its own, ascribing to it an agency equal to human initiative. Not only do human beings have the option of ignoring allegory, but allegory too has the choice of ignoring human beings. This infusion of agency blurs the demarcating line between reader and trope, allowing us to hark back to Moth's suggestion in *Love's Labour's Lost* that a person is always a trope. We might then read 'meddl[ing]' to mean 'troping,' an activity that turns the meaning of a transparent surface, disturbing the original and presenting only its distortion; this distortion is itself a literal translation of 'trope.' As such, Hazlitt's original formulation, 'If [the readers] do not meddle with the allegory, the allegory will not meddle with them,' suggests also that 'If [the readers] do not trope the allegory, the allegory will not trope them.' Meddling is thus not something done *by* a reader *to* an allegory; rather, it is the allegorical condition that reveals itself also to be the human condition. In other words, allegory cannot exist outside the arena of meddling. Readers who meddle with allegory also create allegory and vice versa. This act of creation posits a necessary interaction between reader and allegory so that the one cannot exist without the other. Hazlitt's supposed dichotomy then is really an interpenetration of trope and person; perhaps typically, this tropological confabulation lies hidden behind a veil of apparent freedom from tropological interpellation. Like sexuality in both the *Ad Herennium* and *Institutio Oratoria*, Hazlitt produces subjectivity as at once hopelessly distant from and abjectly created by allegory.

Maureen Quilligan dwells on this sense of veiled allegorical alienation when she notes that 'the "other" named by the term *allos* in the word "allegory" is not some other hovering above the words of the text, but the possibility of an otherness, a polysemy, inherent in the very words on the page; allegory therefore names the fact that language can signify many things at once.'[10] Quilligan dismisses the possibility that the allegorical 'otherness' of language might refer to things 'hovering above the words of the text,' and situates otherness firmly within a language in which signifiers do not always make sense even as they crucially depend on the existence of knowable signification. The *Ad Herennium*'s definition of allegory as 'a manner of speech denoting one thing by the letter of the words, but another by their meaning' (iv.xxxiv.46) refers, in light of Quilligan's understanding, to an exercise that takes place wholly *within* the text. Unlike Hazlitt's epi-graph, which seems to set up a relationship between allegory and a reader *outside* the allegory, Quilligan locates allegory as a purely tex-tual phenomenon in which words interact with other words to pro-duce ambiguity. This open, or public, alienation, is almost an exact rendition of allegory's compound etymology. Derived from the Greek *alleon* (cf. the Latin *alienus*), allegory contains within itself an otherness from itself that is crucial to its functioning. The term allegory, however, also derives from the Greek *agora* (literally, the 'assembly'), which notes the *public* face of the trope. The publicness of the allegorical mode condemns it to being, among all others, the most political of tropes; its alienation also marks it as the most rhetorical of figures. Allegory involves an endless immersion in rhetoric while our under-standing of politics seeks an end to that immersion. Allegory's public face earns it a publicity that politics revels in, but its alien rhetoric undermines that publicity by refusing to provide univocal answers. Far from providing certain truths, allegory imparts only the limitless pleasure of a lack of limits.

This lack of limits is also a source of anxiety because of its potentially unending nature. While classical rhetoricians highlight this anxiogenic underbelly of allegory, English Renaissance rhetoricians seem to revel in allegory's investment in ambiguity. In fact, this revelry prompts George Puttenham to cite an *insufficiently* ambiguous poem as an instance of a 'mixt,' or undesirable, allegory:

> The cloudes of care haue couered all my coste,
> The stormes of strife, do threaten to appeare:
> The waues of woe, wherein my ship is toste.
> Haue broke the banks, where lay my life so deare.
> Chippes of ill chance, are fallen amidst my choise,
> To marre the mind that ment for to rejoyce.
> I call him not a full Allegorie, but mixt, bicause he discouers withall what
> the *cloud, storme, waue*, and the rest are, which in a full allegorie should not
> be discouered, but left at large to the readers iudgement and coniecture.

(*Arte of English Poesie*, 188)

For Puttenham, a full allegory is one in which the hidden terms are not identified explicitly but are left as a code for the discerning reader to decipher. In this reading, allegory is primarily concerned with address-ing a community of 'knowing' readers who take pleasure in their identification of the text as always coded; an easy explanation only 'marre[s] the mind that ment for to rejoyce.' And even though Puttenham indicates that this identification may be limited to a few people, he nonetheless identifies allegorical ambiguity as the most prevalent aspect of discourse, both formal and plebian. Nicknaming allegory the figure of 'false semblant or dissimulation' (the very definition of Duessa in the *Faerie Queene*), the *Arte* proceeds to state that the 'vse of this figure is so large, and his vertue of so great efficacie as it is supposed no man can pleasantly vtter and perswade without it'; so much so that 'not only euery common Courtier, but also the grauest Counsellour, yea and the most noble and wisest Prince of them all are many times enforced to vse it' (186). The cohabitation of the common courtier and the prince, drawing together as it does both Castiglione's notion of courtly *sprezzatura* and Machiavelli's belief in hidden council, builds a picture of allegory as a composite of theatrical masking and politic dissimulation (Dante's 'beautiful lie').[11] Unlike Quintilian, who believes that allegory can be rendered transparent given a right knowledge of the textual conventions, Puttenham prefers the hiddenness of meaning to transparency since it is the more challenging textual condition.

Allegories are thus, above all, tropes invested in creating the illusion of referential transparency even as they insistently come up against the opaque textuality of that referent. The two plays that this chapter looks at are allegories that confront and enact the vicissitudes of the allegorical process. Both plays involve circular narratives pivoting crucially on an unveiling scene that promises to reveal its truth through the very act of unveiling. In the process, however, they reveal how the referent allegedly unveiled by allegory remains unavailable despite the promise of its accessibility. The tropological cast of both plays echoes the understanding of allegory derived from the handbooks of rhetoric. Like Quintilian, Cicero, and Puttenham, Jonson and Shakespeare also understand allegory as possessing certain key features:

1. Allegories are extended tropes that physically enact the imperative to veil and unveil.
2. Allegorical narratives divide themselves into two realms, one occupied by the text's worst fears, and the other hosting eternal truths toward which the text gestures; the former has to be shunned as soon as the true allegorical meaning has been unveiled. As the rhetorical handbooks suggest, these worst fears are usually figured by and as the realm of sexuality.

3. Allegories enact circles of repetition in which it is difficult to distinguish ends from means even as that distinction is crucial to allegory's sense of itself.

Content with Style?

'Ah, I see your confusion,' Ghani said, his poisonous smile broadening, 'You European-returned chappies forget certain things. Doctor Sahib, my daughter is a decent girl, it goes without saying. She does not flaunt her body under the noses of strange men. You will understand that you cannot be permitted to see her, no, not in any circumstances; accordingly I have required her to be positioned behind that sheet ...
  A frantic note had crept into Doctor Aziz's voice. 'Ghani Sahib, tell me how I am to examine her without looking at her?' Ghani smiled on.
  'You will kindly specify which portion of my daughter it is necessary to inspect. I will then issue her with my instructions to place the required segment against that hole which you see there. And so, in this fashion the thing may be achieved.'

Salman Rushdie, Midnight's Children[12]

As Dr Aziz soon discovers to his horror and delight, there is a certain erotic pleasure to be gained from veiled holes: the taboo enjoined by the veil heightens the anticipated pleasure of the hole. Allegory performs a similar function of heightening the rhetorical stakes by promising that meaning exists in a veiled space just beyond the realm of the fully visible text. The hole that promises plenitude bases its promise on a visible lack that nonetheless sharpens the desire for gaining access to the full picture. Aziz is shown successively a toe, an ankle, a forehead, a belly, a breast, and a behind. The canny Ghani (soon to be Aziz's father-in-law) knows that the promise of tangible physicality on the other side of the veil will keep the good doctor probing (and, by extension, the good reader reading). In order to achieve the 'thing' itself, there is no more certain ploy than first to produce an object of desire as desirable precisely because it is not fully visible; limited visibility ensures unlimited desirability.
  The realm of the invisible is thus necessary to ensure visibility itself – indeed, to create visibility as desirable even as it is the invisible that kindles desire. Allegorical veiling performs the miraculous feat of being legal about its illegality; in Rushdie's text, the daughter's bodily 'exposure' is achieved at the express command of the father even as it

is framed as a defence against illegality: 'You European-returned chappies forget certain things ... [M]y daughter ... does not flaunt her body under the noses of strange men.' What should have been a routine medical examination is here turned into an erotic spectacle in which the body is not seen even as it is created as the thing one most desires to see. The power of the veil is the power of partial vision that allegory exploits to keep its newness in mint condition.

This minting is related to a treasure that acquires value only if it is not seen or rather, if it is seen to be in short supply. Ben Jonson's Volpone adopts this ploy and creates a fortune by allegedly already having a fortune. The Fox keeps his treasure veiled and several wealthy people contribute to it in the hope of inheriting the entire amount. Volpone's concealment of his treasure is designed to increase speculation about its magnitude, but he also has to keep himself veiled in order to convince hopeful heirs of his desperate illness. His cloaked 'disease' is thus both the gold that he hides and his health which, if revealed, would put an end to the accumulation of gold. The play hovers over Volpone's gold and his obsession with it, both of which are enshrined behind a veil.[13] In fact, in an interesting parallel with Quintilian's Clodia, Volpone too is closely observed in his bed(room) where, with the exception of the Mountebank episode and the final trial, he remains throughout the play.

More than the gold itself, it is the *means* employed to keep the hole hidden – indeed, to ever increase its depth – that delights Volpone. The seemingly endless pleasure to be derived from hinting at treasure lying beyond a curtain makes Volpone disagree with Mosca's advice that the fraud should stop. In response to Mosca's statement that 'We must here be fixed; / Here we must rest. This is our masterpiece; / We cannot think to go beyond this' (V.i.12–14), Volpone (who, according to one critic, is 'unnerved by endings, [and so] dwells in perpetual teasing of desire')[14] suggests yet another plan, a coup d'état that he thinks will top all his past successes: he will feign his own death and have Mosca parade as his successor in order to rub the salt of loss into his victims' wounds. After instructing Mosca on how to carry out the plan, Volpone places himself 'behind the curtain, on a stool, [to] hearken' (V.ii.84) to his latest drama and to drink the draught of delight to the lees. After Mosca has done his bidding and baited Corvino and Corbaccio sorely, Volpone leaps out, enthralled by his parasite's performance and embraces Mosca: 'My witty mischief, [*Coming from behind curtain*] / Let me embrace thee. O that I could now / Transform thee to a Venus' (V.iii.102–4).

When he emerges from behind his curtain, Volpone displays not just a fascination with schemes, but also an attraction for the vehicle of his scheming, Mosca. Wishing he could transform his parasite into a 'Venus,' Volpone hints that this attraction might be passionate enough to be sexual, and indeed, many critics have used this sentence as a base from which to explore the homoerotic overtones of the Volpone-Mosca relationship.[15] What I want to explore here is not only how these overtones might specifically be set up in the context of allegory, but also the way in which allegory is itself structured by the veil and its contents.

Almost the entire play takes place on or around Volpone's veiled bed. His would-be inheritors come to his bedchamber to woo him, and Mosca, adding inimitable flourishes to the plan as he goes along, beckons them closer to the bed the more he wants to convince them of Volpone's fatal 'disease.' The bed is the place of Volpone's illness and becomes the physical space most closely identified with the play's protagonist, a fact Mosca frequently reinforces by returning him there: 'To your couch, sir; you / Make that place good' (III.viii.19–20). The bed is, literally, Volpone's veil, and it hides the fact that its inhabitant is well by pretending that he is an invalid; it creates the glow of gold by setting it in a pall of death. When Volpone attempts to *escape* his veil – when he emerges into the clear light of day as a mountebank – his 'escape' continues to be cast in the rhetorical mode of disguise, and the text implacably returns him to his place behind a curtain by emphasizing that allegory cannot shed its own veil quite so easily.

Volpone stirs abroad in the guise of a mountebank named Scoto of Mantua in order to woo the nonpareil beauty, Celia. During his superb performance as the mountebank perched just beneath Celia's window, Volpone holds forth on the advantages of his wares:

To fortify the most indigest and crude stomach, ay, were it of one that through extreme weakness vomited blood ... for the vertigine in the head ... the *mal caduco*, cramps, convulsions, paralyses, epilepsies, *tremor cordia*, retired nerves, ill vapours of the spleen, stoppings of the liver, the stone, the strangury, *hernia ventosa, iliaca passio*; stops a *dysentria* immediately; easeth the torsion of the small guts; and cures *melancholia hypocondriaca*, being taken and applied according to my printed receipt. For, this is the physician, this the medicine; this counsels, this cures; this gives the direction, this works the effect; and, in sum, both together may be termed an abstract of the theoric and practic in the Aesculapian art. 'Twill cost you eight crowns. (II.ii.98–114)

Not only is this an astonishing medical catalogue, but it is also an astonishing *rhetorical* catalogue, combining 'theoric' and 'practic' nicely to maximum effect. Just as the rhetorical handbooks detail appropriate tropes to produce particular effects, so too does 'Scoto' list the salutary effects of his oil. Like Hermes, who straddles both the worlds of persuasion (amply chronicled in the *Odyssey*) and medicine (his symbol is the caduceus), Scoto uses his bag of rhetorical tricks to persuade the audience of his medical prowess, offering to effect a physiological change paralleling the psychological change that rhetoric is supposed to induce.[16] However, both claims are doomed to failure in this play. Volpone's rhetoric fails to get Celia just as surely as Scoto's unguent fails to cure the hernia. The attempt to create a gold-filled hole is here revealed as nothing more than the failure of disease to gild itself sufficiently; once Volpone sets up a world that derives its health from a *lack* of health, *Volpone* is only able to fill that lack with disease and failure. Just as the handbooks of rhetoric create sexuality as the figure for an impossible rhetoric, so too does the text of this allegory create disease as the inevitable outcome of the veil of signification; rather than creating a desirable void, Volpone's world becomes associated with an image of disease that is produced as a result of its being veiled. When Volpone asks, early on: 'What should I do / But cocker up my genius and live free / To all delights my fortune calls me to?' (I.i.70–2), he determines to amass a fortune by pretending there already is one, and this is the circularity within which the plot and its disease operate. Volpone paradoxically seeks to 'cocker up' his genius in order to live free, but true to its allegorical bent, the play suggests that this opposition is really only a repetition.

Volpone thus contributes to a study of allegory in three ways: it emphasizes the importance of a veil, it suggests the relationship between disease and the condition of being veiled, and it points to the inevitable fact that this disease, far from being contained, will erupt at several moments and in different registers throughout the play. Thus it is that Corvino, intensely jealous of his wife's chastity, nonetheless himself leads her to an ailing Volpone's bed, convinced of the old man's impotence.[17] The self-cuckolded husband leads his wife to the symbol of alleged impotence lying at death's door in a veiled bed.

Volpone's impotence is itself a veil that attracts the gold of Celia even as it is the veil that needs to be shed in order to enjoy Celia's gold. And so Volpone, in the grip of sensual craving, leaps from his sick-bed in order to demonstrate his potency to the horrified Celia. As soon as Volpone sheds his veil, though, the allegory that he has hitherto inhabited comes crashing to a close. Volpone's tearing of his physical veil ensures also the tearing of his rhetorical veil and the play leaps toward its inevitable end as the fizz of allegory evaporates into the ether of plain sight. Immediately after Volpone leaps from his bed, the good and aptly named Bonario, witnessing this dastardly behaviour, leaps into the room from behind another curtain and the play, along with its protagonist, fears it has been 'unmasked, unspirited, [and] undone' (III.vii.278).

This image of being 'undone' comes as soon as Volpone succumbs to the temptation of revealing himself and his formidable potency, determining to rape Celia rather than be thought impotent. However, this emergence from darkness only forces him into even greater seclusion. Volpone now not only has to insist that he is too ill to move, but specifically, that he is too impotent to ever assay against anyone's chastity; his burst of virility ensures his embrace of impotence. In fact, the only other time Volpone leaves his bed is to be presented *as* impotent in a court of law and so convince the judges of his physical inability to stage a rape. Volpone's worst nightmare of impotence is presented as visually 'true' to the *Scrutineo*, and as rhetorically true in the rest of the play. Trying to lead a sexually active life only ensures the passivity of lying behind a veil; as the incident of the mountebank makes clear, there is an inverse link between active rhetoric and passive sexuality. Rhetoric is seen to be by its very nature effeminate and effeminizing,[18] and when the rhetorical mode is allegorical – when the text is split into layers of reality separated by a curtain and deemed *inversio* – then what lies behind the veil is a 'disease' for which even Scoto's oil does not possess the cure. Every attempt at lifting the veil only reinforces the *effect* of greater concealment; it is as though allegory is incapable of allowing its veil to be lifted, either because that would spell its end, or because what it has consigned to lie behind the veil is too horrific to be displayed in the harsh light of day.

And so Volpone and Mosca frenziedly rewrite the allegorical cast of their play in order to ensure both their own survival and the durability of the veil. Despite their best attempts, however, master and servant are exposed to the scrutiny of the *Scrutineo*, the veil of their disguise is rent, and by punishing them, disease is finally purged from Venetian society. Under normal circumstances, this narrative end would also spell the end (or goal) of allegory: Mosca and Volpone are revealed to be ethically depraved rather than physically diseased and the reader (or playgoer) is given a moral by which to lead his or her life. Rather than spelling the end of allegory, however, the narrative end of the play is a superb instantiation of allegory's inability to exist in an unveiled condition. Much like Volpone, allegory too does everything in its power to stay veiled, or at least to keep its veil in place (which is not the same thing); even as it is poised to lift the final curtain and render the truth of a text in which the main characters are named for animals and birds, the play slips back once again into an allegorical mode. Mosca is sentenced to whipping and perpetual imprisonment in Venetian galleys, while Volpone is sent off to join a hospital of 'incurables' since, the judges argue, 'the most was gotten by imposture, / By feigning lame, gout, palsy, and such diseases, / Thou art to lie in prison, cramped with irons, / Till thou be'st sick and lame indeed' (V.xii.121–4). The law tries to enforce a metaphoric correspondence between Volpone's fiction and his reality, sentencing the fox to a mortification that, quite literally, equals his crime. The metaphorical cast of Volpone's and Mosca's punishment tries to make what lies behind the veil correspond to what lies in front, but this attempted correspondence only ensures a two-way traffic between disease and medicine, between what lies behind the veil and what emerges from it. The 'perpetuall metaphore' of allegory ensures that any alignment between fiction and fact results in both the fictionality of fact and the facticity of fiction.

If one of the highlights of allegory, therefore, is an inevitable insistence on its own reinscription, then *Volpone* thematizes that tendency by showing that allegory can never have a referent external to itself even as the referent is allegorically instituted as the end of allegory. What lies behind the veil is both constituted by, and is constitutive of, what lies in front, and if what lies behind the veil is consistently coded as diseased in this play, then that has an impact on the entire play – from the travelling Peregrine who is mistaken for a 'wench' in man's apparel, to Sir Politic Would-Be who continuously devises plans to sell 'red-herrings' to the state, to Lady Politic who reads the pornographic Aretino, to the *Avocatori* who are willing to sell their daughters to the highest bidder – in which there is no remission from disease. That this 'disease' is too dreadful to be seen is indicated by the vital importance of veils in this play and by the sexual impotence of what is located 'behind' the veil. Even when he 'unveils' himself for Celia, Volpone can only offer her more veils – theatrical ones, in which they will role-play as gods and people from exotic lands.

This inability to ever escape the veil ensures that even as allegories tend toward a centre of truth and beauty, their rhetoric continually moves away from it. It is ultimately this 'split,' characteristic of allegory, that makes any final teleological meaning impossible.[19] Medieval understandings of allegory pivot on the fact that as soon as one is able to pick the 'true' narrative thread apart from the 'fictional,' one sheds the fiction altogether and immerses oneself in the truth.[20] The *aim* of allegory, in this understanding of the term, is its own destruction; it is to demonstrate that in itself, it is nothing. Unlike metalepsis, where failure is the mark of tropological success, allegory calls into question the very notion of success and failure, insisting always that the thing for which allegory is celebrated is really the mark of nothing. Allegory promises a truth that it can deliver only in the form of the lack of a final truth. As such, allegorical nothingness is also obsessively a sexual 'nothingness' (the no-thing-ness of sexuality) coded as diseased impotence in *Volpone* and as Clodia's lesbianism in the *Institutio Oratoria*. In both texts, this no-thing provides the allegorical 'truth' even as it is the thing the texts attempt most to repress. In the grip of the allegorical injunction to repeat, Jonson returns to this idea of sexual nothingness in *Bartholomew Fair* where the allegorical Zeal-of-the-Land Busy unveils the puppet's genitals in order to reveal the truth of its sex, and comes up with nothing.[21]

Dark or Light?

...
Ban
Ban
Cal-
iban
like to play
pan
at the Car-
nival;
...

Edward Kamau Braithwaite, *The Arrivants: A New World Trilogy*[22]

If one of allegory's prime markers is the need to unveil itself, then *The Winter's Tale* stages just such an unveiling when it reveals Hermione's statue at its conclusion.[23] This unveiling – coterminous with the production of allegorical meaning – also aligns itself with a de Manian understanding of allegory, in which the trope's 'emphatic clarity of representation does not stand in the service of something that can be represented.'[24] Allegory is a trope gone to waste since all its conjurations are in the service of a truth that continually eludes representation: Hermione's statue turns out to be a live queen whom everyone had presumed dead, and whose life can now only be presented *as* death. This sense of rhetorical waste is also tied to a sense of sexual waste: Hermione is 'killed' because Leontes suspects she has been wanton with her chastity. In *De Garrulitate*, Plutarch echoes this wasteful sentiment: 'Just as ... the seed of persons too prone to lusts of the flesh is barren, so is the speech of babblers ineffectual and fruitless.'[25] Echoing the sentiment of *Volpone*'s mountebank scene, Plutarch suggests that an investment in 'too much' language results in fruitless seed.

In *The Winter's Tale*, this fruitless seed is amply in evidence as Hermione is 'killed' by news of her son's death and her daughter's exile. Hermione's vacillation between life and death is also a vacillation between what Leontes sets up as fallen and redeemed sexuality. Allegory posits the idea of difference along the lines of a divided realm in which one part – if we are to follow the *Second Shepherds' Play* – represents rampant sexuality while the other promises purity. This idea of division can be mapped onto a variety of configurations – narrative, moral, and sexual. For Ben Jonson, as the second epigraph to this chapter makes clear, the crucial distinction is between truth and imposture: while the one happily exists in the light, the other cravenly shrinks from it. Art in general (represented by the puppet-play) seems to fall under the category that mistrusts the light; by extension, rhetoric is seen as the realm of sordid shadows. For Ben Jonson, then, darkness is the realm opposed to the light. Such an understanding seems in direct contrast to allegory's (disavowed) investment in its shadows as productive of a utopian illumination. In allegory, dark and hidden terms are the truly enlightening ones; the rhetoric that opposes darkness and light is thus complicated by an allegorical mode that switches around the connotations of those words. In Ben Jonson's *Volpone*, this confusion is reflected in the imbrication of crime and punishment: Mosca and Volpone continue to live on in allegory even as the play pretends to have stripped away their allegorical cover. *Volpone*'s investment in allegorical bestiality (most of the characters are named after animals and birds) is coupled with an investment in a beastly sexuality marked as impotent. *The Tempest* deals with similar problems of tropological import: even as the play lifts its allegorical veil in order to make meaning clear, it only succeeds in further obfuscating its own thing of darkness which begins to look startlingly like the inhabitant of Volpone's bed and Clodia's bedroom.

At the centre of both the obfuscation and the attempt at clarity is Prospero. For twelve years, he and his daughter Miranda have been living bereft of all 'human' company on a remote island; their interaction with the native inhabitants – Caliban and Ariel – has prompted several commentators to recuperate *The Tempest* under the rubric of 'post-colonial' studies.[26] In this view, Prospero becomes the representative of a burgeoning English imperialism and Caliban (even more than Ariel) the dispossessed 'native' whose land and language have been taken away by brute force and cultural imperialism. *The Tempest* thus becomes an allegory that is itself read allegorically: the play consists of two tales about two intersecting worlds, the one now commonly understood as the tale of colonialism and the other as the tale of resistance to colonialism. Critics read this latter tale of postcolonialism in an attempt to uncover, or bring to light, the play's 'true' narrative of colonial oppression, thereby enacting the allegorical movement away from deception and towards the 'truth.'

But rather than putting pressure on the allegorical commonplaces of light and dark, deceptive and true, such a reading merely recreates long-standing allegorical coordinates. The postcolonial attempt to rewrite colonial writing falls into the same trap as that of the colonial enterprise, creating a discourse imprisoned within a paradigm of inversion.[27] While embodying and enacting the allegorical impulse, the postcolonial unveiling of the colonial project does nothing to resist the distinctions between black and white and does not complicate a situation that has been constituted by an elaborate set of discursive formations; in fact, it creates a discourse of resistance that reifies adherence. In an influential article that has often been read as providing support for the postcolonial reading of the play, Paul Brown in fact cautions us against any simple-minded unveiling by noting that 'colonialist discourse does not simply announce a triumph for civility, it must continually *produce* it.'[28] Imperialism, like most other textual strategies, does not operate at a simple level and this is evidenced astoundingly by the fact that Caliban was read, in the late nineteenth and early twentieth centuries, as the symbol of an imperialist *domina-tor*, and only in recent decades has he been recovered as an oppressed native.[29] The emphasis on rewriting, as we have already seen, is constitutive of allegory and essential to its production, but the allegory I want to look at is not (just) the colonial one; rather, it is an allegory that functions around the coordinates of language, sexuality, and colonialism, all of which are crucially linked by a veil and none of which can be understood simply by reversing its earlier effects. *The Tempest* enacts its allegory by profoundly unsettling the 'thing of darkness' that postcolonial criticism has routinely understood as denoting Caliban in particular and the colonial endeavour in general.[30]

Quite apart from representing the 'oppressed native,' Caliban figures the allegorical imperative to repeatedly reconfigure texts. Revelling in the dross of his master's lessons – 'You taught me language, and my profit on't / Is, I know how to curse' – Caliban recognizes and fully articulates for us the extent to which his life is a linguistic phenomenon. Caliban's delighted song: ' 'Ban, 'Ban, Ca-Caliban / Has a new master, get a new man' (II.ii.184–5), of which the epigraph to this section is an adaptation, anticipates a brave new world in which Caliban will speak his own version of Prospero's language. But crucially, Caliban's language also slots itself into the allegorical mode, which somewhat undermines Prospero's mastery of both the island and of rhetoric. Unlike Miranda, and certainly unlike Ariel, Caliban speaks the master's language, but Prospero's 'success' also potentially undermines him as Caliban sets off to rewrite his allegory and makes Stephano a new 'god' presiding over a new religion in which the bottle will equal 'the book.' This acquisition of language by Caliban really marks the failure of Prospero's project since Caliban's skills far exceed the parameters entailed by that project. As a result, the language of the master and the slave continue to rewrite each other in the play with uncertain results. But uncertain results are anathema to Prospero who writes (or at least directs) his own play within this play in order to make a very specific and unequivocal point about playing; this play defines for us more clearly the frustration that Prospero feels with his slave and the 'thing of darkness' over which he seeks control.

The masque of Prospero serves as Prospero's mask at the betrothal of his daughter Miranda to Ferdinand, the son of his enemy. Despite having arranged for them to meet and fall in love – an early instance of an 'arranged marriage' – Prospero nonetheless continues to play his cards close to his chest, revealing nothing of his future plans. Prospero tests Ferdinand's mettle and intention, and only after he is satisfied with both does he allow his daughter to mingle freely with the prince of Naples. But not too freely. Prospero's one condition to their betrothal and his approval is that they will not have sex before the appropriate time: 'If thou dost break her virgin-knot before / All sanctimonious ceremonies may / With full and holy rite be minist'red, / No sweet aspersion shall the heavens let fall / To make this contract grow' (IV.i.14–19). Like Aziz, Ferdinand too is quite enamoured of his future father-in-law and promises not to 'violate' Miranda, but Prospero emphasizes his condition again: 'Look thou be true; do not give dalliance / Too much the reign. The strongest oaths are straw / To th' fire i' th' blood. Be more abstemious, / Or else good night your vow' (IV.i.51–4). After this final warning, Prospero mounts the masque to provide a salutary example to the young couple, and summons only the most chaste and natural gods to perform it.

Consisting of set-pieces of poetry and magnificent costumes, the masque is performed by three of the most 'natural' goddesses – Iris, goddess of the rainbow, Ceres, goddess of agriculture, and Juno, 'the Queen o' th' sky.' The goddesses gather to heap blessings of fecundity on the newly betrothed couple but this fecundity pointedly excludes an active sexuality. In fact, Ceres's 'condition' for being part of the masque (which is itself part of the masque) is that Venus and Cupid should not be present, a point about which Iris assures her:

Be not afraid. I met her Deity
Cutting the clouds towards Paphos; and her son
Dove-drawn with her. Here thought they to have done
Some wanton charm upon this man and maid,
Whose vows are, that no bed-right shall be paid
Till Hymen's torch be lighted; but in vain,
Mars's hot minion is return'd again;
Her waspish-headed son has broke his arrows,
Swears he will shoot no more, but play with sparrows,
And be a boy right out.   (IV.i.92–101)

According to this narrative, Venus and Cupid have already tried to

corrupt the young couple and have now retired in disgust at their failure, swearing never to play at the arts of seduction again (even though
it is endlessly ironic that Cupid should have given up archery to play
with lecherous birds instead, reinserting the taint of sexual excess just
as the masque thinks it might have purged it). The goddesses therefore
gather not only to enjoin the vow of abstinence on Miranda and Ferdinand, but also to celebrate the couple's first victory over the malignant
force of Venus and Cupid.

However, even as Prospero tries to keep sexual desire at the furthest
remove from Miranda and Ferdinand, the masque is nonetheless structured around sexuality in the mode of abstention; as though to mark
the lurking danger of untamed desire, the masque is rudely interrupted by the memory of the danger posed to the civility of the island's
inhabitants (as remarked in the masque) by Caliban's uncontrolled
desires. The masque comes to an abrupt end as Prospero remembers
Caliban's plot against his life and this ugly remembrance takes over
from the virginal spectacle. For Francis Barker and Peter Hulme, the
play's 'dramatic' climax comes at this point of the masque's disruption
when Prospero's play has to wrench itself away from the realm of an
idealized representation.[31] But the play's *rhetorical* climax, I suggest,
comes at the moment of its unveiling scene. Shortly after the visual
demonstration of chaste love has come to its sudden end, Prospero
meets a group of the travellers he has caused to be shipwrecked and
proceeds to reveal a carefully engineered 'miraculous' sight to Alonso
and his motley crew; drawing aside a curtain, Prospero *'discovers*
Ferdinand *and* Miranda *playing at chess.'* This 'discovery scene,' so different in tone from the one in *The Winter's Tale*, is met with the same
wonderment; a 'most high miracle,' Sebastian calls it.

Miranda and Ferdinand are 'discovered' playing chess, and they are
playing chess, one presumes, because they have been forbidden from
indulging in more pleasurable sport. What allegory 'unveils' here is a
sight that symbolizes the repression and substitution of desire: the lovers play a game of chess instead of playing at the games of sex. Like
Volpone, who is confined to the couch of impotence and damned the
minute he leaves it in his own person, Miranda and Ferdinand detail a
relation to allegory that insists on the necessity of the veil in order to
isolate sexuality. Desire in both plays becomes that which the realm of
representation has to banish from itself precisely because it is created
as the figure that insistently threatens to defile the representational
matrix. Sexuality is both activated and suppressed by a language that

cannot deal with its excess, and the figurehead of that mechanism of activation and repression in this play is Prospero.

The way in which this control is most explicitly (and therefore least allegorically) presented in the play is in the narrative of colonial domination. Prospero as the wielder of imperial might is read as exerting control over the native population, terrorizing them into doing his bidding. This imperial power is exerted most forcibly, it is argued, over Caliban, the darkest of the natives inasmuch as he is presented as being the least developed and the most dangerous. But Prospero's 'thing of darkness' that he later claims as his own does not, I suggest, refer to the skin colour of Caliban – or at least not to the skin colour of Caliban alone – but rather to a larger 'darkness' that terrifies the master of the island. This 'thing of darkness' covers at least the realms of linguistic and sexual activity over which Prospero is repeatedly exercised. While acknowledging his 'thing of darkness,' Prospero holds forth:

> This misshapen knave –
> His mother was a witch, and one so strong
> That could control the moon, make flows and ebbs,
> And deal in her command without her power.
> These three have robb'd me, and this demi-devil
> (For he's a bastard one) had plotted with them
> To take my life. Two of these fellows you
> Must know and own, this thing of darkness I
> Acknowledge mine.
>
> (V.i.268–76)

The designation of Caliban's 'darkness' is crucially tied to his designation as a 'bastard' and the offspring of a witchlike mother; like *Othello*, this designation serves to racialize sex and sexualize race – Sycorax's Algerian provenance makes her Othello's kissing cousin. For Prospero, Caliban's crime seems to be as much his descent from Sycorax as it is the plot to kill his master; Caliban's ontology seems as, if not more, frightening than his current anarchy.

In this 'acceptance' speech, Prospero spends what seems like an inordinate amount of time detailing the character of Caliban's mother even as his ostensible object of discussion is Caliban himself. Far from being irrelevant, however, Prospero's investment in these details reveals a textual tic that eventually leads to what we may call Prospero's investment in allegorical chastity; these details about Sycorax, then, are crucial to approaching Prospero's thing of darkness. Sycorax's 'crime' also figures prominently in Prospero's obsessive narratives about his arrival on the island and his rescue of Ariel from the witch's clutches. Every time Prospero tells this tale – mostly while bullying Ariel into performing his will – he begins with an account of Sycorax's monstrosity, a monstrosity that seems to have a direct relationship to his own potency:

> I must
> Once in a month recount what thou hast been,
> Which thou forget'st. This damn'd witch Sycorax,
> For mischiefs manifold, and sorceries terrible
> To enter human hearing, from Argier
> Thou know'st was banish'd; for one thing she did
> They would not take her life.   (I.ii.263–9)

An air of mystery envelops Sycorax as Prospero accuses her of having performed crimes too terrible to be named, crimes too terrible to be entered into the register of language. These crimes include giving birth to Caliban and doubling the population of monsters on the island, a feat that Caliban has tried to repeat in the past through his alleged attempt to rape Miranda and produce ever more Calibans.[32] Both in this speech to Ariel and in his earlier attempt to 'acknowledge' Caliban, Prospero registers a horror of Sycorax's sexuality. Not only has she produced a 'bastard' child, but the very fact of her pregnancy fills Prospero with unspeakable dread. Editors routinely gloss the 'one thing' Sycorax did as the pregnancy that earns her immunity from hanging, but clearly this 'one thing' also refers back in time to the very act of sex of which Caliban is an offshoot. Sycorax has not only had illegitimate sex, but she has also spawned an image of illegitimacy in Caliban. Prospero's 'fear' of Caliban's plot against his life – the very fear that rudely disrupts the masque of chastity – might thus easily be read as a fear of what Caliban *represents*, both genealogically, and in himself.

Sycorax's 'one thing' is also itself another thing, a textual echo of the moment in Prospero's interrogation of Miranda when he tests her memory: 'What seest thou else / In the dark backward and abysm of time?' (I.ii.49–50). Prospero describes Miranda's father as the 'Duke of Milan,' and when Miranda comments on this third-person nomination of her father, asking if the duke of Milan is indeed Prospero and her father, Prospero's response rehearses a stock source of Renaissance humour: 'Thy mother was a piece of virtue, and / She said thou wast my daughter' (I.ii.55–6). The darkness of Miranda's memory is allegorically illuminated by Prospero, but only by calling into question the virtue of Miranda's mother, the other person in this play who is described as having had sex, at least once. The 'one thing' of sex has to be repudiated – or at least called into question by Prospero – since it threatens to ruin his carefully constructed allegory for Miranda in which a game of chess is revealed to be allegory's illuminated (but textually opaque) referent. Sycorax and Miranda's mother have had to die for their 'one thing,' but the image of their crimes lives on – or so he fears – in their children. Prospero attempts to purify both Caliban and Miranda of their sexual mark but the play narrates his explicit failure with the one, and his impending failure with the other: while Caliban starts writing his own allegory, Miranda is barely able to conceal the rippling underbelly of desire in her game of chess.

In his essay on 'The Print of Goodness,' Jonathan Goldberg points to the wide-ranging implications in this play of the 'one thing' that is sexuality:

> While that 'one thing' [that Sycorax did] would appear commonsensically to be Prospero's way of not quite naming the sexual act that resulted in her pregnancy, his very prolixity and evasiveness also constitutes that sex act as an unspeakable one. Sex with the devil is perhaps also to euphemize and name what is unnameable in these moments that hover around 'things' and 'its.' It is also to glimpse sexual possibilities that are far from the norm.[33]

Prospero is unable to name sexuality because the very name, he fears, will taint him. This is the fear that prompts the staging of the masque, and the same fear suggests the designation of Caliban as bestial. Prospero has already lost control of Caliban's tongue, and here, that loss is figured as a rampant sexuality that Caliban has inherited from his other parent, Prospero's mirror double, Sycorax. Finding himself trapped in an allegory in which the twin narratives are inhabited by himself and Sycorax, Prospero attempts to seal off his world from the contaminating influence of hers, but Caliban's physical presence in the play asserts the intrusion of sexuality even and especially during a masque of chastity.

Mark Thornton Burnett suggests that 'judging from *The Tempest* as a whole, it would appear that the overriding imperative is less a representation of monstrosity than the terror of reproduction itself.'[34] The witch is Prospero's mirror image – a magical being banished to an island with a single offspring. Sycorax's sexual reproduction has produced Caliban while Prospero's attempt at linguistic reproduction has turned Caliban against him. The 'thing of darkness' thus brings together ideas of sexual and linguistic potency in which the one is figured as the other. Sycorax's language lives on in Caliban only to the extent that Prospero's does not. Caliban speaks a language that fills the current master of the island with horror because it uses allegory against itself. Like Clodia and Volpone, Caliban too embodies the conjunction of diseased language and sexuality, of diseased language because of diseased sexuality. Prospero's repeated response to this double threat is to explicitly forbid his daughter from engaging in sex, and by characterizing Caliban's interaction with Miranda as a threatened 'rape.' Prospero figures sexuality as monstrous, displacing it first onto the body of Miranda's mother, then Sycorax, and then onto her son Caliban. The magician unspeaks sexuality by rhetorically vilifying Sycorax while Caliban unspeaks civility by rhetorically repudiating Prospero.

Ultimately, both Prospero and Caliban use allegory against each other. While the 'slave' tries to explore the possibilities afforded by linguistic troping, the 'master' tries to shut down on the possibilities that threaten his mask of chastity and civility. In response to Caliban's allegorical speech, Prospero writes a play in which the very idea of illegitimate sexuality is banished from the scene; the purified space is then preserved behind a curtain where a young couple chastely plays chess instead of embarking on the begetting of bastard offspring. Prospero enacts the allegorical imperative of creating an 'other side' of the veil that is inhabited by his worst fears. These fears account both for the masque in which Ferdinand and Miranda are enjoined to sexual abstinence, and for the creation of Caliban as an 'overly' sexualized monster; these two scenes are then cast on either side of the allegorical veil. The 'damn'd witch' provides Prospero with an alternative paradigm of power in which sexuality is rampant: the offspring of that bestial sexuality cannot speak a clean language, and the coupling of an unclean body with an unclean tongue provides Prospero with his terrifyingly vast and seemingly insurmountable area of darkness.

The Tempest may thus be described as a text 'about' imperialism because Prospero tries to control what he finds wild and savage, but what he finds wild and savage is not Caliban alone. Rather, Prospero's

fear exceeds the objective correlative of Caliban's alleged physical difference; there is a residue of horror which, 'however much it may take
its origins in the colonial situation, also exceeds it.'[35] Prospero's fear of
darkness is crucially figured in this text as a fear of procreation beyond
the master's control; this procreation occupies the registers of both language and sexuality and Caliban is made to bear this double burden.
The fear of darkness is repeatedly the fear of uncontrollable linguistic
and sexual reproduction, and Prospero tries to banish the cause of his
fear to a realm from which it cannot touch him any longer. Prospero's
curtain veils the sight of Ferdinand and Miranda's chastity but it is also
meant, crucially, to block out the sight of Caliban's 'monstrosity'; the
unceremonious intrusion of Caliban's realm into the space of chastity
triggers a panic attack that Prospero finds difficult to control.

The attempt proves so difficult that Prospero finally gives up on his
civilizing mission and acknowledges Caliban's 'darkness' as his own.
Despite coinciding conveniently with his impending departure from
the island, Prospero's acknowledgment points to an area of darkness
that is not wholly external. Rather, the 'thing of darkness' that was the
thing called Caliban is now also a thing called Prospero. While at one
level, Prospero's statement might imply complete ownership of Caliban, warts and all, at another level, his acknowledgment also impli-
cates him in that realm of uncontrolled and uncontrollable darkness.
'Owning' Caliban thus also entails owning up to Caliban and destroying the 'truth' of chastity that his allegory had initially set out to create.
Prospero's final acknowledgment of darkness also acknowledges his
failure to control allegory, or rather, Prospero's final acknowledgment
shows the triumph of rhetoric over the colonial attempt to create order;
this limitless rhetoric signals also a regime change in which Caliban
has the upper hand because he is never invested in either the fixity or
chastity of language. The sun has, in fact, set on Prospero's empire, not
in the sense of heralding an end to his colonial narrative, but rather by
heralding the end of the colonizing attempt to control the *production* of
narrative. Allegory is unable to destroy the bridge connecting the
fallen world of boorish Calibans to the civilized world of chess; the
darkness of the one insists on shedding light on the other. Unable to
either dispel or control this darkness, then, Prospero eventually has to
acknowledge its structuring presence. The chaste sexuality that Prospero's curtain casts as the truth of his allegory is both created and rent
by the allegorical figure of Caliban.

In both *The Tempest* and *Volpone*, then, uncontrolled sexual desire is conceived of as the 'thing of darkness' that fuels and finally under-mines the allegorical thrust of its narratives. Prospero attempts to freeze sexuality within his cave while Volpone hides it beneath mounds of gold. Neither ploy is successful in keeping darkness at bay, however. Instead, darkness becomes the shaping presence of what alle-gory desperately hopes to believe is the light. Allegory thus sets up the promise of an answer but remains always at the level of the question; this is what makes it a 'perpetuall metaphore.'[36] Even as an ontological understanding of allegory centres on the notion of twin strands that can be separated to show the plain truth of the one and the pure fic-tionality of the other, a rhetorical understanding of allegory compli-cates its own explication. Allegory leads not to a higher purpose, but rather to the end of purposefulness. The allegorical process, as this chapter, and indeed all reading and writing attest to, is an inevitable and unending one, and no one allegory can claim to be the whole truth. At most, allegory can undermine the value of allegorical 'truth' so that the process of reading might continue unabated.[37]

After Words: *Henry VIII* and the Ends of History

> It is not easie to write that Princes History, of whom no one thing may constantly be affirmed ... It is impossible to draw his Picture well who hath several countenances.
>
> Lord Herbert of Cherbury, *Life and Raign of King Henry the Eighth*[1]

The end of this book goes back to its beginning in metaphor, both completing and complicating a circle of desire that rhetoric insists on drawing around itself and drawing itself into. This circle is also the knot that Lord Herbert, in the epigraph taken from his *Life and Raign of King Henry the Eighth*, has to untie in order to convert a convoluted circle into a straight chronological line. Lord Herbert blames his trouble on the need for reconciling contradiction and singularity, veracity and variety. The king's many faces are a challenge to the historian since they defy the project of drawing a single face. But this lament about Henry's 'several countenances' is being made after the king's portrait has already been drawn: the difficulty of writing history is being noted after the history has already been written. 'It is not easie to write that Princes History,' Lord Herbert complains, and yet he is able to do just that. How is this feat accomplished and what are the conditions under which a knotted history may be made *historical*?

The conceptual parameters of Lord Herbert's project are explored in Shakespeare's treatment of the Henry VIII tale, at once identified as Shakespeare's last play and as one of his many collaborative endeavours.[2] Like Lord Herbert's *Life*, Shakespeare's *Famous History of the Life of Henry VIII* deals with the 'ends of history,' by which I mean both the ends *to* which history is deployed, and the markers *by* which history is made conclusively recognizable. This history, like Lord Herbert's, needs to keep at bay an infection that nonetheless provides the text with its material foundation. The 'several countenances' that both animate and dismay Lord Herbert make an appearance in Shakespeare's text, where the alternative title, *All is True*,[3] could either gesture toward a fixed history – 'All is *True*' – or toward an unfixable history – '*All* is True.' For Shakespeare, this double bind takes on the specific form of Henry's marital troubles: Katherine of Aragon, once Henry's sister-in-law and now his wife, is facing divorce proceedings, while Anne Boleyn, sister and daughter of Henry's former mistresses, is the new object of the king's affections. If for Lord Herbert the history of Henry VIII cannot be told with any singularity, then in Shakespeare that lack of singularity takes on the specific taint of incest and becomes Henry's primary reason for divorcing Katherine.

In the play, Henry seeks the opinion of scholars all over Europe; this debate would presumably have hinged on two seemingly antithetical biblical texts. Leviticus 18.16 states: 'You must not uncover the nakedness of your brother's wife; for it is your brother's nakedness,' and Deuteronomy 25.5–6 asserts: 'If brothers live together and one of them dies childless, the dead man's wife must not marry a stranger outside the family. Her husband's brother must come to her and, exercising his levirate, make her his wife, and the first son she bears shall assume the dead brother's name; and so his name will not be blotted out in Israel.'[4] The endless incompatibility between these two texts, the endless 'variety' these two readings gives rise to, informs the dilemma marking Lord Herbert's writing of history, as indeed it did the historical reign of Henry Tudor. Finding himself blocked by a potentially unending religious debate, the king of England finally turned to his trusted aide Cranmer, who hit upon an ingenious way of solving the problem for his king. As Richard McCabe describes it, 'By the clever expedient of declaring the Levitical prohibitions indispensable and affinity contractible solely through wedlock, Cranmer invalidated Henry's marriage to Catherine while simultaneously empowering his marriage to Anne.'[5] The path out of this marital mess, however, was a tenuous one, and did nothing to staunch the long-term legal implications of the matter: Henry's Succession Act of 1534, for instance, 'declared "the marriage heretofore solemnised between [Henry] and the Lady Katherine" to be "against the laws of Almighty God" and therefore null,'[6] and removed Mary from the line of royal succession; the Succession Act of 1536 'annulled Henry's marriage to Anne on grounds that included incestuous adultery ... it declared Anne's daughter, Elizabeth, a bastard ...' Henry's 1540 statute legitimized his union with Catherine Howard; and the Succession Act of 1543 formally reinstated both Elizabeth and Mary, although it placed them both behind Edward. None of these acts was formally repealed during Henry's lifetime, which means they all stood as 'true' historical documents even though logically they could not all be true; 'the original of [Henry's] will unaccountably disappeared by the time of his death.'[7]

Even after Mary's death and her own accession to the throne, Elizabeth continued to be plagued by the spectre of illegitimacy. As Bruce Boehrer notes, 'Elizabeth replaced her father's bewildering logorrhea with a profound and ill-tempered silence ... When the English commissioners at Cateau-Cambrésis reported that their French counterparts had questioned the use of negotiating a treaty with representatives of a monarch whose claim to her throne was so shaky, Elizabeth waxed furious ... "We may nor ever will permit any over whom we have rule or may have to make doubt, question, or treaty of this matter," she concluded ... Elizabeth clearly regarded her control over genealogical matters, both past and future, as crucial to her tenure on the throne.'[8] No matter how removed the debate might have been – an argument between her ambassadors and the representatives of the French monarch implies at least three degrees of separation – Elizabeth was well aware of its importance; she refused to entertain any inquiry about her legitimacy and sought to police strictly both the biological and geographical boundaries of her realm. However, the spectre of illegitimacy continued to loom large over England despite Elizabeth's refusal to entertain the question and despite parliament's attempts to repeatedly declare the queen 'rightfully, lineally, and lawfully descended from the blood-royal.'[9]

In what follows, I argue that these two problems – on the one hand, Lord Herbert's with the writing of history, and on the other, Henry's with the institution of legitimate marriage – might not be so different after all. Both deal with trouble emanating from 'several countenances.' Both seek to impose unity on diversity, if only fleetingly. And both attempt to negotiate a path between excess and its containment. In *The End of Kinship*, Marc Shell addresses just such a binary and locates it as the specific problematic of incest: 'On the one hand ... the urge to reproduce our own kind, no matter how; [and] on the other ... the urge to set limits on how we reproduce or to arrest reproduction altogether.'[10] 'Arrest[ing] reproduction altogether' – not writing (a) history – would be one way out of Lord Herbert's dilemma with variety, but the 'urge to reproduce' marks the proliferation of a historical text that has somehow overcome the lack of constancy by imposing and asserting its own constants. Such paradoxical desire results in what I will term, out of deference to Henry, an incestuous dilemma. And this incestuous dilemma – both a dilemma *about* incest and a dilemma that is *structurally* incestuous – receives interesting treatment in Shakespeare's late history of *Henry VIII*.

There are two questions to be asked of this latter text: first, how does one write a history of incest, and second, what is the relation, if any, between the text's production of history and the history of the text's own production and reception? How, in other words, does Henry's inability to manage his sex life within the 'acceptable' levels of kinship act as a paradigmatic metaphor for the history associated with Shakespeare's *Henry VIII*?

Inside Incest

The aim of Shakespeare's play seems to be to eulogize Elizabeth, who appears as a babe in swaddling clothes at the end of the text; the last scene takes place on the day of her baptism and Henry christens it a 'Holy-day.' But the play is also much more than that: after all, as the title indicates, it deals not just with a 'history,' but with a 'famous history,' a history made famous because it is the story of Henry VIII. In addition to eulogizing Queen Elizabeth, the play is also an attempt to write down the history of England under Henry VIII and, as the text makes clear repeatedly, to at once impart and eliminate the taint of gossip from that history. In the play, Henry decides to divorce Katherine of Aragon because he fears he has committed incest with her (she was his sister-in-law before becoming his wife). While their marriage had always been controversial – she was labelled a virgin and thus 'allowed' to marry her brother-in-law, the future Henry VIII, after her husband died – the controversy acquired an urgent sinfulness when Henry decided to marry Anne Boleyn.[11] At this juncture, Katherine's having been his sister-in-law and the 'consummated' wife of his brother Arthur is one of the primary reasons Henry cites to justify his divorce. This reason is explicitly (and officially) presented as a selfless one – Henry worries about the legitimacy of his marriage only when he discovers that the world considers his children bastards:

My conscience first receiv'd a tenderness,
Scruple, and prick, on certain speeches utter'd

By th' Bishop of Bayonee, then French embassador,
Who had been hither sent on the debating
[A] marriage 'twixt the Duke of Orleance and
Our daughter Mary. I' th' progress of this business,
Ere a determinate resolution, he
(I mean the Bishop) did require a respite,
Wherein he might the King his lord advertise
Whether our daughter were legitimate,
Respecting this our marriage with the dowager,
Sometimes our brother's wife. This respite shook
The bosom of my conscience ...   (II.iv.171–83)

Henry cites the doubts expressed by an external source as the cause of
his internal turmoil. The French bishop's scruple about Mary's lineage
affects the English king's conscience, and so Henry decides to enter
into divorce proceedings against Katherine. Such external citation and
the apparent interest in the well-being of a future generation is an
argument rehearsed repeatedly during the course of the play; in this
instance, it is interesting to note that Henry's 'conscience' follows a
rather remarkable trajectory.[12] It dates its official birth from the occa-
sion of Mary's marriage negotiations and becomes the primary reason
for divorcing Katherine, but not everyone in the play believes this
chronology since it leaves out the crucial appearance of Anne Boleyn.
Henry's courtiers, for instance, are suspicious of both the king and his
conscience and correctly make the link between Henry's conscience
and his concupiscence:

SUFFOLK: How is the king employ'd?
CHAMBERLAIN: I left him private,
   Full of sad thoughts and troubles.
NORFOLK: What's the cause?
CHAM.: It seems the marriage with his brother's wife
   Has crept too near his conscience.
SUFF.:   Aside.] No, his conscience
   Has crept too near another lady.   (II.ii.14–18)

In Suffolk's reading, Henry's conscience is pricked by the prospect of
English pleasure rather than the threat of French pressure. The slipping
conscience enacts a process of displacement that Henry frames initially
in terms of a geopolitical imperative: the suspicion of illegitimacy has
lost him an alliance with the French. But by this point in the play

Henry has already met and wooed Anne, and marries her after a sham trial in which Katherine refuses to participate.[13] The king's 'conscience' thus tries to salvage an affair of some dubiousness, seeking to camouflage carnal desire with the veil of moral and political necessity. The insistence on dispensing with Katherine is represented as a desire to produce a generation of legitimate heirs to carry on the rule of the kingdom. It is in this sense that Henry's 'scruple' is awakened when the duke of Orleans questions Mary's legitimacy, even though Mary – despite being the alleged cause of all this concern – is initially cut off from the line of succession after the divorce.[14]

Against this background of masked illegality, Shakespeare's play attempts to pronounce a benediction over the baby Elizabeth, born of the scandalous union between Henry and Anne. Aware of the burden of sexual scandal borne by the baby, Archbishop Cranmer uses the christening ceremony to try and convert that scandal into chastity by prophesying that the future queen will be:

> A pattern to all princes living with her,
> And all that shall succeed.
> ... In her days every man shall eat in safety
> Under his own vine what he plants, and sing
> The merry songs of peace to his neighbors.
> God shall be truly known, and those about her
> From her shall read the perfect [ways] of honor,
> And by those claim their greatness, not by blood.
> Nor shall this peace sleep with her; but as when
> The bird of wonder dies, the maiden phoenix,
> Her ashes new create another heir
> As great in admiration as herself,
> So shall she leave her blessedness to one
> ... Who from the sacred ashes of her honor
> Shall star-like rise as great in fame as she was,
> And so stand fix'd.   (V.iv.22–3, 33–43, 45–7)

Cranmer's paean outlines the circumstances under which one is finally able to 'stand fix'd,' the condition that one may deem 'historically verifiable' (the *OED* defines 'history' as a 'written narrative constituting a continuous methodical record'). This ability to be fixed, of course, is remarkable precisely because it is so glaringly *absent* from Henry VIII's reign, when both wives and religion changed as quickly as did the wind. As Gordon McMullan puts it: 'The restless displacement of queens, each change both conclusive and inconclusive, embodies the long-term process of Reformation: England moves from reign to reign in the hope of a religious resolution just as Henry moves from queen to queen in the hope of a son and heir.'[15] The lack of stability in Henrician England makes the attempt to locate calm an increasingly urgent endeavour, and Cranmer's prophecy partakes of that enterprise. Elizabeth plays a vital role in effecting the conversion from variety to stability, and in providing the illusion, as Frank Kermode notes, of 'the happy dynastic progress of English history ... a progress which might have been very different if Henry had not put away Katherine.'[16] In his essay, 'Aspects of the Incest Problem in *Hamlet*,' Jason Rosenblatt provides even more evidence of the historical imperatives riding on Elizabeth's birth:

> That the birth of Elizabeth transforms an otherwise sinful union into a virtuous one is confirmed by Andrew Willet in his commentary on Leviticus xviii. Willet repeats the most vicious slanders against Henry, including his purported involvement with Anne Boleyn's mother. He relished the ribald counsel of Francis Bacon, Henry's Vicar of Hell, and rehearses the accusation that Henry 'had first carnall knowledge of the mother and then of the daughter; and that he made his owne bastard daughter his wife.' Then, abruptly, he rejects all these scandals: 'The renowned fame, and prosperous raygne of the issue of this Marriage, our late most noble Soveraigne, Queen *Elizabeth*, doth cleare this suspition, and stop Papists slaunderous mouthes.'[17]

Elizabeth thus straddles the cusp between illegitimacy and legitimacy; indeed, she is bestowed with the power of retrospectively *converting* illegitimacy to legitimacy and of putting to rest any 'scruples' of conscience arising from biblical injunctions. In a play dealing with the tangled webs of incest and history, Elizabeth's presence becomes crucial as the one island of peace in an otherwise tumultuous ocean, the last frontier against 'Papists slaunderous mouthes.' However, her antiseptic power has perforce to take note of the wound itself: it is only after libel has been uttered that her name can be invoked to restore the peace. Perhaps aware of the great rhetorical burden placed on the baby's shoulders, Archbishop Cranmer (elevated to this position of spiritual authority because of his powers of close reading) assumes it will take a while for England to achieve stability after the incestuous ravages of Henry's reign. Thus, he locates calm several decades ahead in Jacobean England, when James I – Henry's great grand-nephew and son of the dreaded Mary Queen of Scots – will reign and proudly 'stand fix'd.'

The *lack* of fixity in Henry's England invests Cranmer's speech with the importance of reinstating a legitimate and constant history. This reinstatement is enacted by means of an elaborate metaphor that aligns Elizabeth with a 'maiden phoenix' consumed only by herself. Elizabeth's self-consumption is meant to be in stark contrast to Henry's active sex life in which he has not only consumed maidenheads but also lopped off the heads of maidens. The future queen's virginity is meant to signal the absence of the specific blemish that has so plagued her father's reign – Anne Boleyn was executed for allegedly having an incestuous affair with her brother even as Henry allegedly had an affair with Anne's mother and certainly with her sister before getting involved with Anne herself – and to indicate a containment of sexual desire as opposed to a desire continually overstepping its bounds. This containment is signalled in the passage by the image of a blissful, if slightly stupefied, England, in which every 'man' will be sufficient unto him or herself. But this end point, where Elizabeth is meant to achieve the purity that proved so elusive to her father and restore order in England, where she is meant to escape the cycle of incest that rotated ceaselessly in Henry's reign, is also the point where, perhaps unsurprisingly, Cranmer's rhetoric begins to slip. His prophecy tries to locate an end to sexual turbulence and the menace of incest by enthroning a monarch who will not live a life of the body. However, if Elizabeth is a 'maiden phoenix,' a one-of-a-kind bird that rises from its own ashes, youthful and renewed, then surely, designating *James* as the newly risen phoenix somewhat muddles the metaphor of purity. After all, the 'bird of wonder' that creates its own heir importantly creates *itself* as its own heir rather than giving birth to a different entity who might be thought of as a progeny separate from itself.

Cranmer's narrative tries to align itself with the purity of the phoenix, but the sexual closure that this myth seeks to evoke gets threateningly blurred with a closure from which no escape is possible.[18] If virginity – or nonbiological/nonsexual reproduction – is held up as the desirable antidote to incest, then figuring that purity with a bird that defines endogamous mating poisons the antidote irrevocably. Elizabeth's non-sexual life might be in stark contrast to Henry's sexual one, but they are positioned in rhetorically identical ways. The phoenix mating with itself is not incestuous so much as it is endogamous in a way that diverts it from an exogamous end; it figures the 'thing' of incest that runs through *Henry VIII* because it gives rise to sameness in the mode of difference. If getting rid of incest and *fixing* history, both in the sense of remedying and stilling it, is the aim of Cranmer's chronology, then signalling that end with the image of the phoenix perpetrates an endless cycle in which the 'effects' (or 'ends') are indistinguishable from the causes (or beginnings). The cloud of incest hangs over a history play in which the 'history' that relies on a continual projection outward in order to chart its chronology is undone by a phoenix that threatens to collapse an open circuit into the circularity of rhetoric.

In other words, what John Donne called the 'phoenix riddle' in his poem 'The Canonization' is *inherent* to the project of writing history, especially royal history, and especially during the Renaissance. Even as history might claim to engage models of multiplicity – the official adage of 'The king is dead. Long live the king,' for instance, points to what has often been termed 'the king's *two* bodies' in which the dead king refers to the individual while the live king represents the enduring institution of kingship – I would suggest that these 'two' bodies point to a rhetorical inflection of history that seriously compromises the *ends* to which history is deployed and which indeed have to be forgotten, like Lord Herbert's excitement, if history is to be written. The phoenix riddle confounds deciphering and what should be opposed concepts – virginity and incest – end up playing the same rhetorical game as each other. In this game, closeness attempts to counteract the threat of openness, but is unable to yield a different result. Establishing a rightful and lawful descent is the end of Cranmer's history, but far from being the marker of stability, James, figured relationally to Elizabeth by means of the phoenix, continues to instantiate the persistence of a closed metaphor.[19] Even as Cranmer arrives at a point of historical fixity, the text resorts again to metaphor: the play's understanding of history seems linked to the pervasiveness of metaphor and the epistemological impossibility of a fact divorced from its concomitant fiction.

The problem of rising from one's ashes is not the same as sleeping with near kin, but each gives rise to an endogamous endgame. Both situations collapse openness into extreme closeness, or rather, seek openness in a relationship that is in fact close. Such is the incestuous strategy of the phoenix and it ensures that Elizabeth's virginity, despite its purity, is nonetheless an illegitimate figure. This illegitimacy lies not only in the fact that she gives metaphorical birth to a king not directly descended from Henry, but also because James rises as what should have been, rhetorically speaking, Elizabeth. Even if Cranmer's history 'means' to suggest that James rises in Elizabeth's image rather than as herself, the phoenix cannot keep at bay the possibility that James might perpetrate yet another scandalously incestuous episode in the Tudor Family Drama. The spectre of Henry mating with sister and wife, mother and daughter, or of Anne coupling with husband and brother, continues to haunt England's future under James. The taint of incest is woven into the very figure that seeks to distance history from variety. If Elizabeth's 'safety' lies in her lack of sexual activity, then this lack is figured in the same terms as its excess: the phoenix bespeaks the dangers of both incest – endogamous coupling – *and* nonbiological reproduction. The narrative of *Henry VIII* insistently bears the mark of the phoenix, which is at once the mark that tries to write a pure history but whose re-markable presence always prevents that purity from being achieved.

The Lesson Unlearned

Even as the text grapples endlessly with the refusal of the phoenix to signify in a singular manner, the history of the play appears to have settled comfortably into a line of questioning that seems curiously to ignore the conflict altogether. From the time of James Spedding's first article in 1850 titled 'Who Wrote Shakespeare's *Henry VIII*?' critics have been exercised by the question of 'identifying' the author of the play, and most critics worth their salt have come down on one side or other of the question. Scholars like G. Wilson Knight root for sole Shakespearean authorship, while A.C. Partridge and J. Dover Wilson 'concede' Fletcher's hand; a few like H.D. Sykes rope in Massinger as well. In this game of pinning the tail, the donkey turns out to embody a certain investment in authorial veracity that seems completely disconnected from the play. I am not interested in adjudicating the matter and deciding who 'really' wrote *Henry VIII*,[20] but I find it ironic that this particular question should be the one to most exercise critics of the play since the text itself eschews an investment in certainty. Interestingly, such authorial speculation seems insistently to be linked to the aesthetic value, or lack thereof, of the play. Frank Kermode points to this tendency by stating that the assumption of dual authorship 'underlies the dearth of critical comment on the play itself; it is assumed to be of interest only in that it was a collaboration of such a kind that no unity of conception and design ought to be expected of it.'[21] And as the Arden editor, R.A. Foakes, adds, 'It is significant that support for Fletcher has nearly always been associated with condemnation of *Henry VIII* as bad or lacking unity, and belief in Shakespeare's authorship with approval of the play.'[22]

This aestheticization of the question of authorship both ignores the collaborative nature of early modern writing for the theatre, and invests authorial identity with the power of textual certainty.[23] The question of authorship – for long the primary question asked of *Henry VIII* – devalues the lesson about author-ity that the text itself dwells on. Peter L. Rudnytsky notes that 'the controversy [surrounding the play's] authorship strikingly mirrors the crisis of authority thematized within the play itself.'[24] The difference is that while the crisis in the play is unable to deny the rapacious sexuality that incestuously eats into its text, the authorship controversy seeks to rid itself of incest by clearly drawing the lines of demarcation between authors.[25] The way out of the play's insistence on incest is by transplanting the concerns of similitude and difference onto a different matter altogether.

In other words, while the 'authorship' of Elizabeth is itself an issue of some uncertainty in the play, the 'author' of *Henry VIII* needs, in most critical quarters, to be a matter beyond doubt. Even though, as Richard McCabe notes, 'what the play affords is a series of "choices" between apparently conflicting "truths" with no clear indication of how such a decision might be made,'[26] the critical tradition engaging *Henry VIII* deems it necessary to make that choice, and pass it off as truth. This tradition tries to explain what are seen as stylistic inconsistencies in the text,[27] but it does so at the expense of the rhetorical thrust of the play. The assumptions underpinning the search for authorial identity stem from a discomfort with the incestuous multiplicity of the play; the question of authorship, I suggest, becomes the most convenient method of focusing attention away from the idea of incest and achieving the fixity that eluded Archbishop Cranmer. The play is so steeped in incest that the singular question of settling authorship ends up repeating what it would repudiate. Just as the phoenix insisted on Elizabeth *and* James, the authorship question suggests Shakespeare *and* Fletcher: at least two authors in response to the demand for one. That the demand for singularity will yield multiplicity is a lesson that the play teaches us. Despite arriving at the same 'conclusion,' however, scholars refuse to acknowledge this as a lesson learned *from* the play.

Even as the 'answer' to the question of authorship is supported by the play's views on incest, these views do not themselves play a role in scholarly essays on the subject. Because *Henry VIII* does not support historical certainty, history has chosen not to support the play's uncertainties.

This lack of support for history is overwhelming in the play. As Howard Felperin points out, *Henry VIII* 'departs from history, that is from Holinshed, more radically than any of the earlier dramas – so much so, that the subtitle of the play, "All is True," makes one wonder whether Shakespeare is not ironically hinting that we revise our conventional notions of historical truth, even of mimetic truth itself.'[28] By telescoping, omitting, and creating its own historical 'order,' *Henry VIII* seems invested in a mode of historical *dis*order. The text alternatively titled 'All is True' gives us an historical understanding that radically questions the existence, value, and knowability of historical truth. It presents us with a text in which the 'fry of fornication' (V.iii.36) always threatens to disrupt the linear procession of history (James is not Elizabeth's son, even as Elizabeth might not have been Henry's daughter), and in which the entire question of historical legitimacy is thrown into rhetorical doubt. In *Henry VIII*, history is never innocent of rhetoric and the project of writing a 'fix'd' narrative is bedeviled by the slipperiness of sexual metaphor.

Equally, history has ignored these claims to historical uncertainty and has settled instead into finding a face and trajectory for 'Shakespeare' himself.[29] In such endeavours, 'Shakespeare' is most often identified with Prospero, the magician from his previous play, whose broken staff at the end of *The Tempest* is read as symbolizing the playwright's own farewell to the stage. As Jeffrey Masten notes, 'it is customary to end with *The Tempest*. That is, it has been customary to end discussions of the authorship of one particular Renaissance writer with *The Tempest*, because the play has been taken to encode an autobiographical commentary on authorship at the close of an authorial career: Shakespeare's farewell to his theatre, his art ... This interpretation has often made for an orderly autobiographical trajectory.'[30] Mark Taylor states that the notion of *The Tempest* being the 'final chapter in Shakespeare's autobiography, the most lucid and the most poignant, is harmless enough,' and cites Edward Dowden providing an early visualization of this authorship fantasy by asking: 'And who is Ferdinand? Is he not, with his gallantry and his beauty, the young Fletcher with whom Shakespeare worked upon *The Two Noble Kinsmen* and *Henry*

VIII?'[31] According to R.A. Foakes, 'it is partly because of this estimate that *Henry VIII* is still ignored in nearly all criticism of the last plays.'[32] Foakes then elaborates in a footnote that the play:

> [R]eceives noble tribute in G. Wilson Knight's *The Crown of Life* (1947). But it is not mentioned in E.M.W. Tillyard's *Shakespeare's Last Plays* (1938) or in Derek Traversi's *Shakespeare: The Last Phase* (1954), and is virtually ignored in much general criticism of Shakespeare's plays. It is worth noting that it cannot be fitted into the scheme of the earlier histories, and is not discussed in Tillyard's *Shakespeare's History Plays* (1944), or in Lily B. Campbell's *Shakespeare's 'Histories'* ...[33]

It is interesting that G. Wilson Knight discusses the play because he approves of it, and approves of it as *Shakespeare's* creation. All the other critics have reservations about both the play's quality and authorship, and neither Tillyard nor Campbell can fit it into the pattern of Shakespeare's histories.

Henry VIII thus remains as the surplus of the Shakespearean canon that comes after the 'real' artistic ending of *The Tempest*, and provides an unnecessary supplement to what is already a healthy banquet.[34] Such a reading of the play stems from the frustration of attempts to 'explain' or 'fit' it into an understandable scheme of things. The failure to read Henry Tudor as a metaphor for William Shakespeare, or *Henry VIII* as a 'fully' Shakespearean play, is premised on an unwillingness to read the rhetorical basis of history; this unwillingness ignores the play's insistence on the impossibility of writing an untainted history.[35] What Gordon McMullan has called 'the radical textuality of historical representation' is noted and then rejected as the critical reception of the play continues to base itself on a history that has itself forgotten the lessons of (the play's) history. Rather than being read as a sustained evocation of a fixity always haunted by its own undoing, therefore, *Henry VIII* is read instead as a play whose weak structural development needs to be explained by recourse to the question of authorship.

In the scene just preceding the description of Elizabeth as a phoenix, the play's lack of authority is linked explicitly to sexual corruption as the Porter (making an uncanny appearance after his *Macbeth* days) describes the crowds thronging the streets of London to watch Elizabeth being christened. When his men admit they are not equal to the task of controlling the crowd, the Porter roars at them:

What should you do, but knock 'em down by th' dozens? Is this Moor-
fields to muster in? Or have we some strange Indian with the great tool
come to court, the women so besiege us? Bless me, what a fry of fornication is at door! On my Christian conscience, this one christening
will beget a thousand, here will be father, godfather, and all together.
(V.iii.32–8)

The Porter's indignation is expressed in terms of sexual incredulity,
and he witheringly wonders if the women are being so forward in their
eagerness because there is a great sexual organ on display.[36] Both Elizabeth and Henry play their roles, as Cranmer makes clear, in a sexual
drama that poses and passes as the search for historical fixity. Elizabeth
is the offspring of one of Henry's many sexual escapades and her virginity is the subject of Cranmer's prophecy. The Indian's 'great tool'
draws together different kinds of corruption and mingles them till it is
impossible to tell one's father from one's godfather. This, of course, is a
very real dilemma in both Henry and Elizabeth's lives. The 'fry of fornication' outlined by the Porter, which seems to be definitive of rather
than unusual in Henrician England, has to be translated by Cranmer
from an expression of rampant sweat and sensuality into a beatific
morning after. The play needs to simultaneously capture and disavow
the spirit of England under Henry and point to a healthy England
under James even though that latter England continues to bear the
mark of the Henrician 'fry.' Even as it seeks to inject a note of purity
and untainted chastity, the phoenix produces almost exactly the opposite effect by throwing the issue of incest open to ever further rhetorical
debate. The ends of history are severely compromised by a rhetoric
that depends, even and especially when its stated intention is otherwise, on the unfixability of history. The trajectory away from uncertain
origins toward fixed conclusions is the trajectory of history in *Henry
VIII*. That this trajectory is also bound to veer from its chosen path is
the lesson that the play imparts.

This chosen path of historical certainty is repeatedly presented as an
unlocatable phenomenon refracted by rhetorical effects (like the exten-
sive third-person narrative), and producing a subjectivity continually
alienated from subjects.[37] Even names of places, which one might
expect to be recognizable and fixed within the historical context of the
play, are thrown into disarray. While describing the wedding procession of Henry and Anne, for instance, the Third Gentleman states that

the king and queen are attending a celebratory banquet at 'York-place.'
The First Gentleman responds:

```
1 GENT.:                              Sir,
     You must no more call it York-place, that's past;
     For since the Cardinal fell that title's lost.
     'Tis now the King's, and call'd Whitehall.
3 GENT.:                      I know it;
     But 'tis so lately alter'd that the old name
     Is fresh about me.                           (IV.i.94–9)
```

The freshness of names and the staleness of change are both captured
in this debate about the name of the palace, a debate that showcases
history as a continual rewriting haunted by its own shifting signification and incestuous affiliation. This affiliation produces a sense of ver-
tiginous unreality that is at the farthest remove from a fixable identity;
it partakes instead in the incestuous fabric that so annoys people in the
play, and when he is having difficulty obtaining a divorce from
Katherine, none more than King Henry himself.

It is endlessly ironic, then, that the play embodying the vicissitudes
of both history and historical narrative can itself be dated with such
'precision,' since its staging burnt the Globe down in 1613. It is 'rare,'
the *Riverside* assures us, 'to find so much converging testimony for any
event in Elizabethan or Jacobean drama.'[38] The final irony in this play
about irony is that the position of the text can be 'realized' with such
damning accuracy. It is this irony of ironies, however, that most closely
approximates the action of metaphor itself, since the date does not tell
us anything about authorship, and authorship does not reveal anything about the author. The phoenix rises from the ashes of the Globe
to disprove that its death is consequential,[39] and *Henry VIII* continues
to talk about history as a textual phenomenon that is historical despite
a flagrant disregard for chronology and an utter disrespect for historical presence. Such a rhetorical reading of history will make historians
of us all. Until that day, however, the end of *Henry VIII* should be read
as the end of history as we know it, which is of course never finally,
The End.

Notes

Foreplay

1 All quotations from Shakespeare's plays and poems are from the second edition of the *Riverside Shakespeare*, and will henceforth be referenced by act, scene, and line numbers.

2 This is the understanding that William Carroll, in *The Great Feast of Language in* Love's Labour's Lost, brings to his analysis of the play.

3 Goldberg, *Sodometries*, 18.

4 I owe enormous intellectual debts to texts that have shaped my understanding of both sexuality and rhetoric in the early modern era. Patricia Parker's work on rhetoric, especially in *Literary Fat Ladies*, has been groundbreaking in its emphasis on the sheer textuality of the text, even as she focuses more on the link between rhetoric and gender, rather than sexuality. Jonathan Goldberg's hugely influential *Sodometries* is a fine example of how not to give up on theory even in this age of the nonbeliever. Among the brilliant and influential books that deal, interestingly enough, with medieval sexuality, Carolyn Dinshaw's *Getting Medieval* tackles many of the same questions that interest this work, and actively questions the divide between sexual 'acts' and 'identities' so notoriously attributed to Foucault. Short of going into an extended analysis of the *History of Sexuality*, vol. 1, I will only state that the 'sexuality' I am exploring retains (even initiates) the 'discursive' production that Foucault was to attribute to post-Enlightenment sexuality. Louise Fradenburg and Carla Freccero's edition on *Premodern Sexualities* is also an important contribution to ways of thinking of sexuality that do not position us in a privileged position of 'having' a sexuality that 'they' did not.

1. Setting the Stage: Metaphor

1 Dekker's cony-catching pamphlet, written in 1608, is reprinted in Arthur F. Kinney's edition on *Rogues, Vagabonds, and Sturdy Beggars.*

2 In 'Forgetting Foucault,' 108, Halperin suggests that 'what historically distinguishes "homosexuality" as a sexual classification is its unprecedented combination of at least three distinct and previously uncorrelated conceptual entities: (1) a psychiatric notion of a perverted or pathological *psychosexual orientation* ... (2) a psychoanalytic notion of same-sex *sexual object-choice* or desire ... and (3) a sociological notion of sexually *deviant behavior* ...' If the very idea of 'sexuality' indicates a fixed confluence of inner psychology and external behaviour, then my analysis of the rhetorical (and therefore *unfixed*) underpinnings of desire argues against the stultification of these terms, both in the Renaissance and in the present day. As such 'sexuality' becomes both less sacred and more historically discrete.

3 In his analysis of the T-shirt urging 'Americans' not to be 'Saddam-ized,' Jonathan Goldberg has amply shown that 'sodomy,' for instance, is as much a political and xenophobic position as it is a statement of sexual 'fact,' and that it *continues to be so* in current parlance (*Sodometries*, 1). This continuance not only collapses the absolute distinction between sodomy and homosexuality, but it also brands them with the identical sin of rhetorical shape shifting. What might be thought of as an identity belonging exclusively to the realm of the sexual – a male homosexual is a man who has sex with other men – is also a slur that like sodomy, takes on several, seemingly unrelated, prejudices of the day. One needs only to look at recent political events to notice the way in which current rhetoric continues to echo the rhetoric of sodomy circulating during the Renaissance. Witness the post–September 11 peace rally in Baltimore, where rallyists were accused of being 'unAmerican' 'faggots.' Or the Harley website listing Osama bin Laden as a 'faggot punk' who likes to 'Take it up the Ass,' and who wears 'high heels, a dress and a diaper on his head.' Not only is this 'Most Wanted' man a criminal, but he is also a criminally cross-dressed faggot. As though to clarify the enormity of this fact and to distinguish themselves from such faggot punks, the Harley bikers end the page with an example of *their* political beliefs: HELMET LAWS SUCK. If we assume that to the Harley bikers, bin Laden is evil because he is a 'terrorist,' then it is clear that his ability to produce 'terror' is based firmly on an assumption about his sexuality. Even if bin Laden really 'were' gay, then his homosexuality becomes the most effective conduit for the expression of hatred. As though agreeing with this collapse between homosexuality and horror, a New Yorker expressed his conviction

that 'Allah is a faggot,' even as Jerry Falwell blamed September 11 on the existence of homosexuals and abortionists (for websites where these and similar collapses of homosexuality with nationalism, racism, and xenophobia take place, go to http://fando.blogspot.com; http://harleytrike.com/camel/bin.html; and www.boomercafe.com/nyc0901.htm). Like sodomy, homosexuality is a term susceptible to varied and often criminal misuse; what unites these two terms is their mutual imbrication in the field of rhetorical production.

4 Jonathan Goldberg is the single and singular exception to this general trend. Critics who pay attention to rhetoric and sexuality individually, but do not necessarily make a sustained connection between the two include Patricia Parker's work on rhetoric, especially in *Literary Fat Ladies*, which focuses on the connections between rhetoric and gender rather than sexuality. In his work on *Textual Intercourse* Jeffrey Masten pays attention to the realm of textual production – especially as it manifests itself in relation to collaborative authorship – in his theorizations of sexuality. Some critics insist on the irreducible difference between (early modern) 'acts' and (modern) 'identities,' and despite producing fine scholarship, tend not to privilege rhetoric as a productive site for thinking about sexuality; in this latter category belong DiGangi, *The Homoerotics of Early Modern Drama*, and Harriette Andreadis, *Sappho in Early Modern England* (Chicago: University of Chicago Press, 2001), among others.

5 Despite the large number of scholarly studies that take Foucault's periodization as axiomatic (Alan Bray's among others), several scholars have also sought to nuance their understanding of this schema. Among them is Carolyn Dinshaw, who notes in relation to medieval sexuality, that 'what [is] seen to be Hollywood's latest, from the hot-hot-hot Quentin Tarantino, [can turn] out indeed to be an old, old story' (*Getting Medieval*, 184); Guido Ruggiero states in his *Boundaries of Eros* (4) that 'with apologies to Michel Foucault, sexuality was not a discovery of the modern world'; and Ian Frederick Moulton, in his discussion of Vignali's mid-sixteenth-century text *La Cazzaria*, notes that 'Foucault sees *scientia sexualis* as grounded both in the act of confession and in medical and scientific discourse; he claims that it came into being only in the nineteenth century. Clearly, however, Vignali's text subjects sexual activity to a humanist discourse of inquiry which, while prescientific, nonetheless sees sexuality as a site of power and knowledge as well as pleasure' ('Bawdy Politic,' 238). In his essay on 'Forgetting Foucault,' David M. Halperin argues against the positivistic interpretation of Foucault's much-quoted passage on the 'difference' between sodomy and homosexuality, or between sexual 'acts' and 'identities.' Even though I

disagree with many elements of Halperin's argument, I find compelling his suggestion that 'it is a matter of considerable irony that Foucault's influential distinction between the discursive construction of the sodomite and the discursive construction of the homosexual, which had originally been intended to open up a domain of historical inquiry, has now become a major obstacle blocking further research into the rudiments of sexual identity formation in premodern and early modern European societies' (109). Clarifying instead that Foucault speaks in both cases of the discursive *production* of sexuality, Halperin states: 'Foucault's radical take on sexuality consists in approaching it from the perspective of the history of discourses, treating it accordingly not as a positive thing but as an instrumental effect, not as a physical or psychological reality but as a social and political device: Foucault is not trying to describe what sexuality is but to specify what it does and how it works in discursive and institutional practice' (110). This discursive production, I argue, emerges in the Renaissance as a specific effect of discourse about discourse, of language about language. Whether or not that language describes sexuality in terms of homo- and heterosexuality is of less interest to me than the more important discussion of how this rhetorical understanding of sexuality modifies 'our' understanding of sexual desire. In other words, both Renaissance and current ideas of sexuality are, in my understanding, terms that are in flux. By presuming on the fixity of the latter, we might find ourselves implicated in the homophobic discourse of essential difference that most work on Renaissance sexuality seeks to *avoid*. The 'difference' between acts and identities, then, I argue, is less helpful than an analysis of the rhetorically similar modes of sexual production.

6 Goldberg, *Sodometries*, 10, 22.
7 Even though Goldberg is sceptical of an uncritical adherence to Foucault's 'history,' he nonetheless tends to abide by it, not only in *Sodometries*, but also in his pioneering edited collection, *Queering the Renaissance*. Interestingly, however, the overwhelmingly 'historicist' Stephen Greenblatt is now writing that 'language is the slipperiest of human creations; like its speakers, it does not respect borders, and, like the imagination, it cannot ultimately be predicted or controlled' ('Racial Memory and Literary History,' *PMLA* 116:1 [January 2001], 62). One of these 'borders' that needs to be violated is the border of chronological division by which both Foucault and scholars of the Renaissance set so much store.
8 Goldberg, *Writing Matter*, 309. In this book, Goldberg argues in intricate detail about the theoretical link between acts of writing and conceptions of sexuality. He focuses on the instruments – the materiality – of writing, a

focus that develops in *Sodometries* into the link between rhetoric and sexuality.

9 De Man, *The Resistance to Theory*, 7.

10 Goran V. Stanivukovic argues that 'instead of treating rhetoric as a stylistic ornament which supports reading – thematic criticism [posing] ... as "the rhetoric of ..." – ... rhetoric itself, the structure of argumentation, renders meaning.' In his essay on 'Troping Desire in Shakespeare's *Venus and Adonis*,' Stanivukovic goes on to argue that 'the real subject of *Venus and Adonis* is desire in rhetoric, not the rhetoric of desire. This desire is transcribed as rhetorical pattern which in itself captures the nature and structure of desire' (290).

11 Dekker, *Rogues, Vagabonds, and Sturdy Beggars*, 218.

12 Edelman, 'Post-Partum.'

13 De Grazia, 'World Pictures, Modern Periods, and the Early Stage,' 12.

14 Marcus, 'Renaissance/Early Modern Studies,' 42.

15 I deal more fully with this idea of repetition in the epilogue on *Henry VIII*.

16 White, *Metahistory*, x.

17 Butler, *Bodies that Matter*, 16.

18 Marcus, 'Renaissance/Early Modern Studies,' 45.

19 Wayne Rebhorn includes a section from Vives's *De causis corruptarum artium*, itself part of the larger *De disciplinis libri XX*, in his translated and edited collection, *Renaissance Debates on Rhetoric*. This quotation is from 88–9.

20 Rebhorn. *The Emperor of Men's Minds*, 208.

21 Cartwright, *Theatre and Humanism*, 1. Paul Yachnin makes a similar point in *Stage-Wrights*, 27, when he notes that the academic humanist tradition frequently used drama to teach rhetoric.

22 The earliest definition of metaphor is from Aristotle's *Poetics*, 21.7: 'the movement (*epiphora*) of an alien (*allotrois*) name from genus to species or from species to genus or from species to species by analogy.'

23 It must be noted, however, that the tropological nature of rhetoric was not the primary concern of either the Greek or Latin rhetoricians, and became a commonplace only towards the end of the sixteenth century. Among the Greeks, only Gorgias held that rhetoric is all things, linguistic and otherwise (for which he faced the brunt of Plato's scorn). The Latin texts (like the Greek ones before them) were primarily interested in the link between rhetoric and 'civil' (or public) discourse. The 'aim' of Quintilian's text, for instance, is to train effective lawyers who will then go on to fashion a more civil society. The rhetorical handbooks were all aimed at developing effective *orators*, even though as the sixteenth century moved on and the lan-

guage of the texts changed, the emphasis began to shift from speaking persuasively to writing well.

24 The *Ad Herennium* treats its tropes like the 'forensic cases' of the first three books. Puttenham divides his figures into auricular (zeugma, prolepsis), sensible (metaphor, catachresis), and sententious (prosopopeia, omiosis); and Wilson lists the things he will be speaking about (for instance: 'Prudence or wisedome, Justice, Manhood, temperaunce') before going on to detail what he means by these categories.

25 Ricoeur, *The Rule of Metaphor*, 20. In this exhaustive study, he discusses the aspect of alien-ness (*allotrois*) that is so crucial to Aristotle's definition of metaphor, and notes that since it is always seen as a figure of deviation, metaphor can never merit uncensored praise.

26 The attribution of the *Ad Herennium* to Cicero is disputed by many scholars, who claim the work is unworthy of the mature Cicero. Though many now attribute the text to a rhetorician named Cornificius, the issue is yet to be conclusively settled. For details of the controversy, see the Introduction, by Harry Caplan, to the Harvard University Press edition of the *Rhetorica Ad Herennium*.

27 In her pioneering *Handbook to Sixteenth-century Rhetoric*, Lee Sonnino notes Jonson's remark as representative of English Renaissance reliance on classical texts of rhetoric. Other classical and continental texts popular in Renaissance England include Susenbrotus's *Epitome troporum ac schematum*, Sturm's *Scholia ad rhetorica Aristotelis*, and Scaliger's *Poetices libri septem*.

28 In addition to the medieval investment in preceptive rhetoric, the link between sexuality and rhetorical usage that I study in English Renaissance drama is also present in Chaucer's *Canterbury Tales*, and *Troilus and Criseyde*, for instance, as it is in Dante's topography of hell. For more information about medieval understandings and uses of classical rhetoric, see James J. Murphy, *Rhetoric in the Middle Ages* (Berkeley and Los Angeles: University of California Press, 1974); James J. Murphy, ed., *Three Medieval Rhetorical Arts* (Berkeley and Los Angeles: University of California Press, 1971); Robert O. Payne, *The Key to Remembrance: A Study of Chaucer's Poetics* (Westport, CT: Greenwood Press, 1963); and John M. Hill and Deborah Sinnreich-Levi, eds, *Reconstructive Polyphony: Studies in the Rhetorical Poetics of the Middle Ages* (Madison, NJ: Fairleigh Dickinson University Press, 2000).

29 Puttenham, *The Arte of English Poesie*, lxxxiii. The editor of Puttenham's text asserts that 'Book III took its final shape about 1585, just at the topmost point of the rhetorical curve ... In the latter eighties and throughout the nineties the curve declines. Fewer new books and editions of older ones are called for. Rhetoric retreats from the world to the school.' Paul Ricoeur

claims that rhetoric 'died' towards the middle of the nineteenth century when it ceased to be part of the college syllabus (*The Rule of Metaphor*, 9). See also Johnson, *Nineteenth-Century Rhetoric in North America*, for more details.

30 See Halpern, 'A Mint of Phrases: Ideology and Style Production,' in his *Poetics of Primitive Accumulation* for a critique that this emphasis was distinctly elitist in nature.

31 This is not, however, to imply that Bacon is himself immune to the lure of rhetoric. In *The Advancement of Learning*, for instance, he states that 'it is eloquence that prevaileth in an active life' ([Oxford: Clarendon Press, 1957], 177). Rather than abolishing rhetoric, Bacon wanted to tame it as an instrument for the pursuit of (real) knowledge. See also Vickers, 'On the Practicalities of Renaissance Rhetoric,' for the 'practical' (as opposed to the 'theoretical') aspects of rhetoric.

32 Richard Halpern cites Cambridge don and pedant, Gabriel Harvey, as another critic of the 'words-over-content' camp (*Poetics of Primitive Accumulation*, 20). This, however, is an ironic instantiation, since Harvey was himself frequently ridiculed (notably by Nashe, with whom he had a running feud later in life) for using too many words to little effect.

33 Greene, *The Light in Troy*, 1. One of the modes of distinction that the *Ad Herenium* adopts is that of nationality and language. In a move that has widely been recognized as faulty, the author of the *Ad Herennium* prefaces his book on style by arguing against a 'Greek' practice of using examples borrowed from other writers. To compensate for this 'fault,' the author promises to use examples of his own creation except where he cannot help it, but as soon as the preface ends, and the actual book on style begins, he contradicts himself not only by using borrowed examples (many of them Greek), but also by failing to provide references for them. While the Romans tried to assert their authority against the anxiety of Greek influence, the English texts neither escaped the Latin influence nor claimed to escape it, and identified themselves as mere 'translations.' Greene has pointed out that the (sometimes unstated) English consciousness of the 'inferiority' of their own tongue parallels the Roman consciousness of being less developed than the Greek (60), and marks another stage in the cultural anxiety that language produces. As Brian Vickers notes: 'The fact that Latin was the normal language of instruction in rhetoric ma[d]e English abnormal (*Some Reflections on the Rhetoric Textbook*, 88). Therefore, English handbooks, viewed as deviant outgrowths of a tradition that had reached its zenith in a different tongue, emphasized the inability of a translation to approximate the original (whether English to Latin or Latin to Greek). This endlessly deconstruc-

tive mode marked the 'proper' handbooks both before and during the Renaissance as being unable to approach the 'real' text. The *Institutio Oratoria*, for instance, stresses substantive clarity, but this claim is soon undercut by its form, which is a translation of Greek ideas into Latin; the text first uses Greek terms and phrases to describe the various tropes and brings in its Latin definitions only later. This linguistic duplicity is embodied by metaphor, not only as it translates into *translatio*, but also because it is accorded pride of place by almost every handbook as the defining trope of rhetorical language.

For more on translation as an art that acquired particular importance during the Renaissance, see Mathiessen, *Translation: An Elizabethan Art*. Matthiessen argues that without translation, the Renaissance would never have reached England.

34 This is outlined in the 1570 posthumous publication of *The Scholemaster*. In addition to being widespread, Ascham's method of teaching children was also, curiously enough, 'revolutionary' because it advocated a sparing use of the rod as a method of instilling knowledge. For the sodomitical possibilities generated by translation, see Jonathan Goldberg, 'Spenser's Familiar Letters,' in *Sodometries*, 79, where he states: 'Roger Ascham, pausing to memorialize his student John Whitney, now dead, and to bid him farewell, recalls, in his book of double translation, this scene of instruction: "John Whitney, a young gentlemen, was my bedfellow, who, willing by good nature and provoked by mine advice, began to learn the Latin tongue." The text chosen for this double translation "out of Latin into English and out of English into Latin again" was "Tully *De amicitia*." A proper choice. The scene fulfills the dictates of Erasmian pedagogy to the letter, as the teacher incites the pupil to learn by loving imitation within the specular relationship of similarity and simulation.'

35 See Rhodes, *The Power of Eloquence*, for more on this subject.

36 See Jonathan Gil Harris's chapter, '"To stop her mouth with Truths authority": The Poisonous Tongue of the Witch and the Word of God,' in *Foreign Bodies and the Body Politic*, where he remarks on the Renaissance difficulty in distinguishing between godly and satanic tongues. The duplicity of the tongue ensured that its solution too involved a measure of duplicity; the 'problems presented by a mode of containment ... potentially replicated the social pathologies which it was designed to combat' (109). See also Carla Mazzio's essay, 'Sins of the Tongue,' in *The Body in Parts*, ed. Hillman and Mazzio, 52–79, where she states that 'representations of the tongue in the early modern period often encode crises of logic, of language, and of sense' (53).

37 Cave, *The Cornucopian Text*, 82.

38 See Hillman and Mazzio, *The Body in Parts*, xviii: 'In early modern representations ... even ... as a fantasy of the "whole body" emerges, the body is at the same time always, and perhaps inevitably, a body in parts.'

39 De Man, *Allegories of Reading*, 131.

40 In his anecdote, ambiguity resides in the use of (at least) two words: 'weemen' (women/we men) and 'anie' (any/a nie). Polemon, an honest 'plaine' country gentleman, is at his wit's end about how to approach the king for a favour. Philino ('a lover of wine and a merry companion in Court') offers to help, and his advice takes the form of a riddle:

> Your best way to worke – and mark my words well,
> Not money: nor many,
> Nor any: but any,
> Not weemen, but weemen beare the bell. (135)

Polemon, not quite sure how to interpret this speech, takes the 'pleasanter construction,' and routes his request through his daughter. The 'plaine' suit, adorned with advice that is ambiguous on both the rhetorical and sexual fronts, gets a positive response from the 'effeminate' king who takes kindly to Polemon's daughter's request, and everyone lives happily ever after. For pioneering analyses of this passage, see Kegl, '"Those Terrible Approches,"' and Jonathan Goldberg, 'The Making of Courtly Makers,' in *Sodometries*.

41 De Man, *Allegories of Reading*, 107.

42 While the rhetorical tradition, from St Augustine to Erasmus, would agree on the alienated nature of the Word, Reformation leaders, following Luther, would insist on its transparency. However, as Kenneth Graham argues, this insistence was compromised even as it 'ran into internal exegetical crises over, for instance, the "meaning" of the Lord's Supper' (*The Performance of Conviction*, 53).

43 The roots of 'Orientalism' obviously reach far back into Roman rhetorical debates, even though the Asia in 'Asiatic' refers not to the 'East' as we know it today, but rather to countries in Asia Minor, including Rhodes. Interestingly, Cicero, Quintilian's acknowledged hero, was condemned for being too bountifully Asiatic in his style.

44 The Latin version reads: 'Castratam morte Africani rem publicam,' and 'Stercus curiae Glauciam.'

45 For a similar comment in a different setting, this time in relation to the link between a rhetorical text and its preface, see Dunn, *Pretexts of Authority*. Commenting on the deep suspicion with which rhetorical handbooks

viewed the implications of their own project, Dunn notes: 'Classical rhetoric houses in its very presuppositions a decided prejudice against its own project, a prejudice made abundantly clear in its theoretical pronouncements about the preface ... In particular, classical theorizing about forensic rhetoric, with its assumption of a public sphere in which human action is fully intelligible and meaningful, tends to view with suspicion prefatory attempts upon the jury's ability to interpret what ought to be transparent facts' (1).

46 In 'The Epistemology of Metaphor,' de Man seems surprised that Locke should use 'manslaughter, incest, parricide, and adultery' as examples to illustrate the language of 'mixed modes,' even as we might be able to view this choice as perhaps being an inevitable one (*Aesthetic Ideology*, 41n5).

47 Quintilian at times seems to take personal responsibility for, even as he stresses the inevitability of, the corruption of language: 'We have perverted the purity of language by our own corruption, and there is no course left to us but to give ground before the victorious advance of vice' (VIII.iii.45).

48 Fineman, 'The History of the Anecdote,' 74. Fineman goes on to say (in terms that are familiar from his *Shakespeare's Perjured Eye*) that 'for Shakespeare ... language, either as a theme or as a performed practice, does not figure or "embody," to use Greenblatt's metaphor, some biologized erotic impulse ... rather, for Shakespeare, desire is the very literal consequence of the figurality of language – a figurality or "wantonness" that Shakespeare characteristically imagines in terms of the "duplicity" of language, where "duplicity" not only carries with it the erotic metaphorics of the anatomic double "fold" but is at the same time the motivating mechanism of erotic intentionality' (74).

49 See Lezra, '"The Lady was a Little Peruerse."' Lezra notes 'the insistence with which Puttenham returns to the issue of sexual difference – principally in stories of rape, seduction, or instruction ... – constitutes already a perverse reformation of rhetorical problems whose resistance to being symbolic externalizations is neither empirical nor formal' (55).

50 For a recent formulation of this idea in the context of 'hate-speech,' see Butler, *Excitable Speech*, where she claims that the link between linguistic and physical 'injury' can only be expressed metaphorically.

51 In *The Power of Eloquence*, Neil Rhodes cites William Webbe who, in *A Discourse of English Poetrie* (1586), explains that 'both Eloquence and Poetrie ... [draw] as it were by force the hearers eares even whether soever it lysteth, that Plato affirmeth therein to be contained goeteia an inchauntment as it were to perswade them anie thing whether they would or no' (7). The proximity between witchery and rhetoric carries down into the Renaissance,

one instance of which is the endlessly fascinating title of Raphe Lever's 1573 handbook: *The Arte of Reason, Rightly Termed, Witcraft*.

52 Even a cursory reading of Sidney's *Arcadia* or Spenser's *Faerie Queene* shows how this consciousness of rhetoric was a phenomenon that transcended generic boundaries. However, drama was still in the best position to *enact* the consequences of a language with fluid boundaries.

53 As testament to its powerful influence in the Renaissance, we only have to note that the *theatrum mundi* – the theatre as the world, and the world as a theatre – was the most widely disseminated rhetorical and poetic metaphor of its day.

54 Puttenham, for instance, advocates that 'we would not have [Ladies] too precise Poets least with their shrewd wits, when they are married *they might become a little too phantasticall* wives' (249, emphasis mine). Poetry, with its dependence on rhetoric, is a dangerous tool in the hands of women because it might cause them to 'phantastically' try and alter their (God-given) status in life.

55 Rhodes, *The Power of Eloquence*, 18.

56 In an attempt to defend the theatre against what he considered abuses of a legitimately glorious form, Thomas Heywood, in a vein reminiscent of Shakespeare's Jaques, says: 'The world's a theatre, the earth a stage, / Which God and nature doth with actors fill: / ... He that denyes then theatres should be, / He may as well deny a world to me' (*An Apology for Actors*, 13).

57 See among others, Bray, *Homosexuality in Renaissance England*; Goldberg, *Sodometries*; Bredbeck, *Sodomy and Interpretation*; Masten, *Textual Intercourse*; and DiGangi, *The Homoerotics of Early Modern Drama*.

58 Wayne Rebhorn has detailed what he calls the 'gender' of rhetoric as being alternately male and female, in short, hermaphroditic. It is male when it assumes (or wants to assume) mastery over the world, and when its detractors invest it with the absolute power to control life. It is female when, like Puttenham's embodiment of metaphor, it is clothed in gorgeous apparel (*Emperor of Men's Minds*, 143–4). However, Rebhorn quotes Brian Vicker's sense that the predominant notion of rhetoric is 'as an enticing, wanton, deceptive, [overdressed] woman – in short, a harlot or prostitute' (140). The sexual appeal of the prostitute captures the sense of illegality and sensuous physicality that rhetoric is invested with.

59 Fineman, *The Subjectivity Effect*, 19.

60 Fineman, *Shakespeare's Perjured Eye*, 231.

61 Crewe, *Unredeemed Rhetoric*, 20. Crewe also notes the link between rhetoric and drama: 'To put the case as uncontentiously as possible, critics have

found it convenient to approach the literature of the early English Renaissance through models of play (theatrical play, rhetorical performance, festivity, *sprezzatura*, praise of folly), while the same has not applied equally to the later, primarily devotional, works of the seventeenth century' (10). Then again, he states that 'there is a clearly established continuity in the period between rhetorical performance and debate on the one hand, and theater on the other' (22).

2. Performance Anxiety: Metonomy, *Richard II*, *The Roaring Girl*

1 Aristotle, *On Rhetoric*, trans. Kennedy, 41, 1357a.
2 Lanham, *The Motives of Eloquence*, 7.
3 'Sappho to Philaenis,' in *The Complete English Poems of John Donne*, ed. Patrides.
4 For a slightly different reading of the poem, see Janel Mueller, 'Lesbian Erotics: The Utopian Trope of Donne's "Sappho to Philaenis," in *Homosexuality in Renaissance and Enlightenment England: Literary Representations in Historical Context*, ed. Claude J. Summers (New York: Haworth Press, 1992): 103–34. Mueller sees this poem as Donne's exploration of a socio-politico-sexual utopia, in which differences of gender and property can be set aside in a triumphant moment of female-female bonding; for her, Donne 'projects the lesbianism of "Sappho to Philaenis" into a fully utopian moment for human possibility' (125). Even as Mueller sees 'common sense' nagging 'at the heels of the superbly hyperbolic logic' in phrases like 'my *all*, my *more*,' my reading of it differs in the sheer emphasis I place on this and all other 'hyperbole.' The rhetoric of sameness in this text does not, for me, undermine the rhetoric of difference as much as it points out that these two cannot, in any final form, be easily distinguished from one another.
5 In his *Homographesis*, Lee Edelman initiates a discussion on the link between metaphor and metonymy in relation to sexuality by noting: 'Sexuality, as we use the word to designate a systematic organization and orientation of desire, comes into existence when desire – which Lacan, unfolding the implications of Freud's earlier pronouncements, explicitly defines as a metonymy – is misrecognized or tropologically misinterpreted as a metaphor' (8).
6 The *Ad Herennium* never uses the term metalepsis, even though it speaks of the confusion between cause and effect as a marker of metonymy.
7 Bray, *Homosexuality in Renaissance England*, 26.
8 Quintilian's use of 'even' to denote his text is rather puzzling here. The detailing of metonymy, he says, is too intricate *even* for a text that does *not*

deal with the training of an orator ('Quae singula persequi minutioris est curae *etiam non oratorem instruentibus*' emphasis mine), which his does.

9 The shoe is Freud's example of an object that becomes fetishized by virtue of its spatial contiguity to the female genitals. In his *Three Essays on Sexuality*, Freud has this to say about the fetish: 'What is substituted for the sexual object is some part of the body (such as the foot or the hair) which is in general very inappropriate for sexual purposes, or some inanimate object which bears an assignable relation to the person whom it replaces and preferably to that person's sexuality (e.g., a piece of clothing or underlinen).' See 'Fetishism,' in *Three Essays on the Theory of Sexuality*, 19, 21n1.

10 The metonymic concerns of the classical and Renaissance rhetoricians are echoed by (at least) three twentieth-century thinkers whose work has been crucial in attempting a re-reading of both rhetoric and sexuality. The most recent of the three, Paul de Man, notes the difficulty of pinning down metonymy, and links this to the larger (and perhaps equally futile) endeavour of trying to control the workings of language: 'Classical rhetoric generally classifies synecdoche as metonymy, which leads to difficulties characteristic of all attempts at establishing a taxonomy of tropes; tropes are transformational systems rather than grids' (*Allegories of Reading*, 63n8). The metaphor of the grid, of something that can be coordinated and plotted on a graph is, of course, precisely the wrong one for metonymy, since metonymy does not proceed along the lines of a (mathematical) correlation between x and y. For de Man, 'the contingency of ... metonymy [is] based only on the casual encounter of two entities that could very well exist in each other's absence' (63). Much like casual sex, metonymy does not forge a lasting bond, but it does suggest possibilities.

De Man speaks of the link between metaphor and metonymy in terms of necessity and contingency, echoing Roman Jakobson's classic formulation of these two tropes in the *Fundamentals of Language*, where Jakobson begins by explaining the reason why metonymy has been given such short shrift in comparison to metaphor: 'Similarity in meaning connects the symbols of a metalanguage with the symbols of the language referred to. Similarity connects a metaphorical term with the term for which it is substituted. Consequently, when constructing a metalanguage to interpret tropes, the researcher possesses more homogenous means to handle metaphor, whereas metonymy, based on a different principle, easily defies interpretation. Therefore nothing comparable to the rich literature on metaphor can be cited for the theory of metonymy' (26–7). While metaphor can be seen as a stable entity furthering the aim of knowledge (however much that might be a simplification of metaphoric powers), metonymy eludes such epistemological endeavours primarily because it is based on continually shifting ground. The 'homogenous' means that metaphor requires are freely available while the 'different principle' required for metonymy 'easily defies interpretation.' The grounded (and grounding) metaphor is far preferred by the rhetorician over the slippery and unstable metonymy, but even as this preference is translated into critical practice, metonymy defies extinction by continuing to exist without an adequate language to express its nature. For David Lodge, this attempt at self-preservation is doomed to failure: 'Although the metonymic text retards and resists the act of interpretation which will convert it into a total metaphor, it cannot postpone that act indefinitely ... In the metalanguage of criticism, metonymy ultimately yields to metaphor – or is converted to it' (*Modes of Modern Writing*, 110–11). There will be more to say about this 'conversion' with reference to *Richard II*, but what is interesting to note here is the critical speed with which rhetoricians are able to underestimate metaphoric subtlety and overstate the case for its totalitarian tendencies.

The structural link between desire and metonymy has been made by Jacques Lacan for whom desire, because it is based on a chain of association, each of whose parts can be substituted by another part, is metonymic. Elaborating on Freud's theory of the fetish, Lacan sees the desiring subject as 'caught on the rails – eternally stretching forth towards the *desire for something else* – of metonymy' (*Ecrits*, 167). The fetishized shoe can be replaced by the fetishized hat without causing any *essential* disruption of desire. Metonymic desire forever tries to approach itself through contiguous links in a signifying chain, but finds, to use Lacan's example, that each chain is itself only a link in a larger necklace (or metaphoric knot). Despite being 'motivated by a constitutive tendency to pretend the opposite' (*Allegories of Reading*, 71), metaphor and metonymy are always linked to one another.

11 'An Horatian Ode upon Cromwell's Return from Ireland,' in *The Complete English Poems of Andrew Marvell*, ed. Donno.

12 In *Richard II: A Casebook*, Nicholas Brooke reprints C.E. Montague's review of F.R. Benson playing Richard in 1899, which states: 'Shakespere meant to draw in Richard not only a rake and muff on a throne and falling off it but, in the same person, an exquisite poet: to show with one hand how kingdoms are lost and with the other how the creative imagination goes about its work; to fill the same man with the attributes of a feckless wastrel, in high place and with the quite distinct but not incompatible attributes of a typical, a consummate artist' (64).

13 Bloom, *William Shakespeare's 'Richard II,'* 1.

14 *The Riverside Shakespeare*, 845.

15 Mahood, *Shakespeare's Wordplay*, 73.

16 For criticism that accepts metaphor as a premise from which to read the play, see among others, E.M.W. Tillyard, *Shakespeare's History Play* (London: Chatto and Windus, 1944); Harrier, 'Ceremony and Politics in *Richard II*'; Traversi, *Shakespeare: From* Richard II *to* Henry V; Gillespie, *The Age of Richard II*; Rebhorn, *The Emperor of Men's Minds*; Rhodes, *The Power of Eloquence*; Jeanie Grant Moore, 'Queen of Sorrow, King of Grief: Reflections and Perspectives in *Richard II*,' in *In Another Country: Feminist Perspectives on Renaissance Drama*, ed. Dorothea Kehler and Susan Baker (Metuchen, NJ and London: Scarecrow Press, 1991), 19–35; and Miriam Gilbert, '*Richard II* at Stratford: Role-Playing as Metaphor,' in *Shakespeare: The Theatrical Dimension*, ed. Philip C. McGuire and David A. Samuelson (New York: AMS Press, 1979), 85–102. In 'Anger, Wounds, and the Forms of Theater in *King Richard II*, Murray M. Schwartz speaks of the central importance of the garden scene in *Richard II*.

17 *The Riverside Shakespeare*, 845.

18 Parker, *Literary Fat Ladies*, 36.

19 Ziolkowski, *Alan of Lille's* Grammar of Sex, 14. The word 'homosexual' is used only in the modern translation; its existence would have been unthinkable in the twelfth century. Interestingly, the homosexuality that so annoys Lady Nature springs from the heterosexual excesses of Venus, whose adulterous affair with a scoundrel named Antigamus results in the birth of an illegitimate child, Iocus. This is the event that triggers the deviant sexuality so lamented in the text.

In a different translation of the same text by James J. Sheridan (Toronto: Pontifical Institute of Mediaeval Studies, 1980), Lady Nature spells out human depravity by using a grammatical metaphor: 'The active sex shudders in disgrace as it sees itself degenerate into the passive sex. A man turned woman blackens the fair name of his sex. The witchcraft of Venus turns him into a hermaphrodite. He is subject and predicate: one and the same term is given a double application. Man here extends too far the laws of grammar' (67–8). See also Elizabeth Pittenger, 'Explicit Ink,' in *Premodern Sexualities*, ed. Louise Fradenburg and Carla Freccero (New York and London: Routledge, 1996), 226, where she comments on the sex-text link in terms of a power dynamic that seeks to establish control over an otherwise seething mass of contradictory possibilities: 'Nature's complaint and her teaching are supported by an array of grammatical analogies (*analogia, anastrophe, syneresis, tmesis*) that describe sexual aberrations in terms of textual error. The effect of the shift from sexual to textual is far-reaching, for it implies that ethical problems can be handled in terms of technical rules, that there *are* rules in the first place and that they can be enforced by correct training.'

20 Despite Richard's deposition, the play seems loath to give up on his royalty, and so the last act of the play uniquely represents (and nominates) two 'kings' in its text.

21 In the Renaissance understanding of the word, 'lust' covered a broader range of activities and could just as easily refer to desire for political advancement as to sexual desire. However, in all cases, it signified a desire that is both in excess of present conditions, and that seeks to bend (or invert) the framework that constrains its advancement. As such, it becomes more than plausible that Richard's 'lust,' explicitly linked to feeding and then connected to Venus's pleasures, is sexual in nature, and unnaturally so.

22 The gardener-king is, of course, a nice riff on Plato's ideal philosopher-king, and the parallel is not unmerited since both kings fail to materialize from the depths of their metaphors.

23 This is an argument that has dramatic precedent. In *Woodstock*, which is often considered a prelude to *Richard II*, and which is organized on the principle of the morality plays, Woodstock leads the king's uncles in urging Richard onto the path of virtue, while the 'weeds,' Bushy and Green, tempt him to vice. For more details on the link between the two plays, see Cubeta, *Twentieth-Century Interpretations of* Richard II.

24 Page, '*Richard II': Text and Performance*, 49.

25 Bloom, *Modern Critical Interpretations*, 2.

26 Gaudet, 'The "Parasitical" Counsellors in Shakespeare's *Richard II*,' 147, 143. For details of theatrical productions of *Richard II*, see Page, '*Richard II': Text and Performance*, and Gilbert, '*Richard II* at Stratford.'

27 The favourites are really only three in number because the earl of Wiltshire never physically appears in the play. This 'trinity' is in keeping with Richard's assessment of his friends as 'three Judases' (III.ii.132) when he first thinks they have betrayed him and defected to Bullingbrook.

28 Metonymic detail is read in the garden scene as a code for unintelligibility, and then translated figurally as a corruption that resides in weeds, caterpillars, and trees. A metaphoric reading is forced to impose a straight path out of this morass of corruption for the ideal king to follow; for the not-so-straight king, however, there is nothing but eternal damnation. That these two kings are not as clearly distinguishable from each other as the gardener might like to think is evidenced by the metonymic cast of Bullingbrook's speech in which he claims that 'nearness' of blood, rather than incontro-

vertible 'proof' of metaphoric lineage, legitimates his claim to Richard's love and throne. Richard and Henry are themselves linked metonymically, but in order for his metaphoric grand design to succeed, the gardener has to ignore these signs of seepage and diligently keep the two tropes and the two kings apart.

29 Suddenly, the 'crimes' in play proliferate from one to two to many. We are speaking now not only of Richard's crimes in the play, but also of the critic's crime in reading the play. A straightforward reading of the first is mirrored by the metaphorical practice of the second. Perhaps there is no more sufficient example of metonymic insidiousness.

30 For an article that captures this Miltonic tone of the play, see Clayton G. MacKenzie, 'Paradise and Paradise Lost in *Richard II*,' *Shakespeare Quarterly* 37.3 (1986): 318–39.

31 Quoted in Simon Shepherd, *Amazons and Warrior Women: Varieties of Feminism in Seventeenth-Century Drama* (New York: St Martin's Press, 1981): 84.

32 All references to *The Roaring Girl* are from the text in Fraser and Rabkin, *Drama of the English Renaissance II*.

33 Nakayama, *The Life and Death of Mrs. Mary Firth*, xiii.

34 Nakayama, *Life*, 3. It is interesting that another 'roaring girl,' Margaret Cavendish, duchess of Newcastle, insists on a similar containment of virtue within defiance. Just as Moll's 'autobiography' insists on the neatness of her home and person, and the assiduity with which she hunted down sexual incontinence, so too does Cavendish seek to undermine the effect of her own scandal. In an essay on Cavendish's 'Assaulted and Pursued Chastity,' in *Menacing Virgins: Representing Virginity in the Middle Ages and Renaissance*, ed. Kathleen Lynne Kelly and Marina Leslie (Newcastle: University of Delaware Press, 1999), 197, Leslie argues that 'the peculiar combination of ... masculine habits and her feminine virtues ... made her ... utterly incomprehensible to her contemporaries. In her youth, she was by her own report so shy and awkward in her service of Henrietta Maria that she was taken for "a Natural Fool" by the more polished and worldly attendants of the court. But, she adds, "I rather chose to be accounted a Fool, than to be thought rude or wanton ..." Thus it is that the entry on Cavendish in the *Dictionary of National Biography* concludes that 'her occasional appearances in theatrical costume, and her reputation for purity in life ... contributed to gain her a reputation for madness.'

35 It is important that Moll's reputation *precedes* her dramatic appearance, so the play can expend its energies in defending what it does not need to describe in any detail.

36 Sebastian responds to Moll's exclamation of incredulity by stating: 'I'd kiss

such men to choose, Moll / Methinks a woman's lip tastes well in a doublet' (IV.i.48–9).

37 In 'Sex and Social Conflict: The Erotics of *The Roaring Girl*,' in *Erotic Politics*, ed. Zimmerman, 185, Jean Howard notes that 'Moll never denies her sexuality. She has and acknowledges her sexual dreams; she has and acknowledges her "instrument," that viol with which she is so insistently linked, the fingering of which seems to symbolize her skill at clitoral masturbation, as well as her potential skill at manual stimulation of the male penis.'

In 'The Logic of the Transvestite,' 221, Marjorie Garber makes a related point about female sexuality by pointing to patriarchy's inability to provide pleasure: 'the play's anxiety about clothing and fashion, which is omnipresent, is indeed conjoined with a related anxiety about sexuality, but that anxiety is not so much based upon women's emancipatory strategies as upon the sexual inadequacies of men.'

38 John Webster, *The White Devil*, ed. Christina Luckyj; 2nd ed. (London: A & C Black, 1996). The scene in which Vittoria stands trial is called 'The Arraignment of Vittoria,' and is the only 'titled' scene in a Renaissance play, as though the text, aware of its own rhetorical importance, were calling attention to itself.

39 Fraunce, *The Arcadian Rhetoric*, 4ff.

40 A similar movement takes place in *Twelfth Night*, where the 'discovery' of Viola's disguise clears the way for heterosexual unions. However, despite the marriages at the end of both plays, Viola in *Twelfth Night*, and Moll in *The Roaring Girl*, remain on stage dressed as men. Mary, whose marriage the whole play tends toward, is appropriately costumed and wedded at the comic conclusion.

41 Middleton and Dekker, *The Roaring Girl*, V.i.64.

42 De Man, *Allegories of Reading*, 63.

43 Ganymede, of course, no longer exists, but Phebe nowhere indicates she is *averse* to Rosalind without the male disguise.

44 For a recent article that looks at the same passage, see Tracey Sedinger, '"If sight and shape be true": The Epistemology of Crossdressing on the London Stage,' *Shakespeare Quarterly* 48:1 (1997): 63–80. Sedinger states that 'the crossdresser is not a visible object but rather a structure enacting the failure of a dominant epistemology in which knowledge is equated with visibility' (64).

3. First Night: Metalepsis, *Romeo and Juliet*, *All's Well that Ends Well*

1 Lacan, *Feminine Sexuality*, 152.

2 Evans, *The Osier Cage*, 12.

3 Three early manuscripts identify the earl of Rochester as the author, but this attribution has been contested. There have been attempts at fixing the authorship at lesser doors, but none of these latter claims has been sustainable. Current scholarship prefers the attribution to Rochester, and that is how the matter stands. For further details, see *The Works of John Wilmot, Earl of Rochester*, ed. Love, 497–8. In some editions, the play is titled *The Farce of Sodom, or The Quintessence of Debauchery.*

4 Harold Love, *The Works of John Wilmot*, 496, notes that '*Sodom*, though indisputably indecent, is not in its primary intention a work of pornography, but a *hilarotragedia* or burlesque.' All references are to this edition.

5 Interestingly, the only images of pleasurable sex in this text are of those between men.

6 Barkan, *Transuming Passion*, 70–1.

7 Like Freud's later model of repression, metalepsis has to be *untraceable* in order to be successful; it has to be invisible in order to cloak the extent of its presence.

8 The author of the *Ad Herennium* deals only with the transposition of words, as exhibited by tropes like hyperbaton, which 'upset the word order by means either of Anastrophe or Transposition' (337), rather than with their transumption.

9 Hawkes, *Metaphor*, 4.

10 See the *Lewis and Short Latin Dictionary*. In *Transuming Passion*, 44, Leonard Barkan glosses Quintilian's example: 'Though he is discussing a trope that removes meaning in a specially remote way, his example is of the most immediate kind: the activity he is himself performing, and in the first person. Nor is it coincidental that the track on which the figural motion is taking place is precisely that of speech, poetry, and (by implication) writing ... The special force of transumption, in other words, is that by accumulating, juxtaposing, and even betraying tropic meanings, it succeeds in calling attention to its own figural activity and therefore to the acts of the imagination and the culture made up of such acts; at the same time its own metaphoricity underlines the phenomenological basis for figures.'

11 Erasmus cites the Virgilian example for metalepsis in his *Copia*, 31: 'Similar to *abusio* is *metalepsis*, which is called *transumptio* by the Latins. This is when we proceed by steps to that which we wish to express, as: he hid in dark caves. For the connotation is of black caves, from black, obscure, and from this finally, extreme depth.'

12 This distinction between masculine and feminine rhetoric ties in nicely with the Attic/Asiatic distinction that was current in Quintilian's day. See chapter 1 for more details on this division.

13 Several readings of *Romeo and Juliet* have taken note of the play's invest-

ment in homoerotic male bonding and anal eroticism. See, for instance, Joseph Porter, *Shakespeare's Mercutio* (Chapel Hill: University of North Carolina Press, 1988), and Eric Partridge, *Shakespeare's Bawdy* (London: Routledge, 1990). For a compelling reading of the play's sexuality that is different from my own but informed by similar concerns, see Goldberg, '*Romeo and Juliet*'s Open Rs.'

14 Discussing the balcony scene and noting the inevitability of the '*contretemps*' that for him, ensures the play's tragedy, Derrida states that 'this drama belongs to the night because it stages what is not seen, the name; it stages what one calls because one cannot see or because one is not certain of seeing what one calls. Theater of the name, theater of night' (*Acts of Literature*, 425). For other commentaries on the balcony scene, see, among others, Lucking, 'That Which We Call a Name'; Catherine Belsey, 'The Name of the Rose in *Romeo and Juliet*,' in *Critical Essays on Shakespeare's* Romeo and Juliet, ed. Joseph A. Porter, 64–81 (New York: G.K. Hall and Co., 1997); and Whittier, 'The Sonnet's Body and the Body Sonnetized in *Romeo and Juliet*.'

15 The aubade, or dawn song, is a trope frequently used in medieval literature to signify the dangers and pleasures of love. It is characteristically sung by lovers (whose love is, in some way, illegitimate, either because one of them is married, or because rank separates them) who have just been reminded that they must part since delay will mean discovery and ruin. As soon as the sun rises, the lovers sing a song of welcome to the dawn which also serves as their song of farewell to each other. The aubade, as Gale Sigal has pointed out, 'like dawn itself, is Janus-faced: it commemorates and prolongs a love affair while its subject is love's dissolution' (*Erotic Dawn-Songs* 1). Dawn marks the *transition* from night to day, and is the metaleptic trope that mediates between those two, diametrically opposed, periods of time. Dawn, like the threshold to Juliet's bedroom, marks a liminal state: between two worlds, yet belonging to neither of them; delivering the break of day, but itself disappearing in the bloody afterbirth. The aubade both celebrates the night of love just past and laments the day of distance just dawned, but almost all of the song's passion and pathos stems from the fact that the love being celebrated is *illegitimate*. If the lovers were legitimate, they would not need to lament the dawn of day since it would merely signify another period of time to be spent together. But since a threatening husband or wife looms in the distance, the sun signifies an end to night's revels. Even if there is no threatening spouse around, as is the case with Chaucer's Criseyde, the dawn song nonetheless marks the point at which the pleasure principle surrenders to reality.

Troilus and Criseyde, that other pattern of lovers, sing a dawn song that sets up an interesting framework within which to read Romeo and Juliet's similar 'song' of lamentation. In Book III of *Troilus and Criseyde*, the lovers have just consummated their love when the sun rises:

> But cruel day – so wailaway the stounde! –
> Gan for t'aproche, as they by sygnes knew,
> For which hem thoughte feelen dethis wownde.
> So wo was hem that chaungen gan hire hewe,
> And day they gonnen to despise al newe,
> Callyng it traitour, envyous, and worse,
> And bitterly the dayes light thei corse. (III.1695–701)

The rising sun forces their passion to set, and is therefore despised as an enemy to love. The sun sheds light on that which the lovers want to keep in the dark, and Troilus and Criseyde draw even closer to one another in reproaching the common enemy, whose 'chaung(ing) hewe' forces a change in the colour of their love, and mars their lustre with its own.

A few lines later, however, in Troilus's song about love, the sun takes on an entirely different role. It is now no longer the enemy to love, but in fact, becomes the guarantor of love's truth:

> That, that the world with feith which that is stable
> Diverseth so his stowndes concordynge,
> That elementz that ben so discordable
> Holden a bond perpetuely durynge,
> That Phebus mote his rosy day forth brynge,
> And that the mone hath lordshipe over the nyghtes:
> Al this doth Love, ay heried be his myghtes! (III.1751–7)

The constancy of the sun and the government of the moon are here cited as examples of the truth and durability that love inspires in a world of change. In fact, the rhetoric of the passage suggests that the sun *must* rise in order for love to be true. Phoebus, once so vilified, is now glorified by the lover in his paean to love. If, on the one hand, the condition for the continuance of Troilus and Criseyde's love is that the sun should not rise, and if, on the other hand, the sun's rising is a mark of the constancy of love, then either their love will not last or it will not be constant. As it turns out, both these things come true. The rhetorical damnation that these passages produce in conjunction with each other makes visible the darkness surrounding the sublunary activities presided over by Venus: clear and sunny danger lurks at the heart of blind love.

The aubade is thus, at the very least, a two-edged sword that cuts both ways. The sun, like language itself, both guarantees presence and takes it away. Troilus and Criseyde want to build a passage from stolen lust to lasting love, but the rhetorical device of the aubade is unable, as we see, to put up such a permanent structure. Sex, that highly contested and *private* sign, has to signify in an *appropriate* manner to be transformed into public love, but the aubade, by insisting on the *privacy* of sex, makes it rhetorically impossible for Troilus and Criseyde publicly to sanctify their love in the light of day.

16 The tradition of the First Night, while it ostensibly did not exist in Renaissance England, flourished in medieval France and continues to thrive in several countries today.

17 Hollander, *The Figure of Echo*, 140.

18 In *A Map of Misreading* (New York: Oxford University Press, 1975), 138, Harold Bloom asserts that 'transumption murders time, for by troping on a trope, you enforce a state of rhetoricity or word-consciousness, and you negate fallen history.'

19 Hollander, *Figure of Echo*, 115.

20 There is something reminiscent of the Virgin Mary in Helena's miraculous cure, both of the French king's ailment, and of her own predicament, which demands immaculate conception. Also, Helena supposedly embarks on a 'religious' pilgrimage soon after hearing that Bertram has fled the country, reinforcing the spiritual aura that surrounds her person in the play.

21 For a fascinating account of some of the rhetorical stakes inherent in the names in *Romeo and Juliet*, see Iselin, '"What Shall I Swear By?"'

22 For more details on the links between Boccaccio and Shakespeare, see Cole, *The* All's Well *Story from Boccaccio to Shakespeare*; and Hodgdon, 'The Making of Virgins and Mothers.'

23 Hodgdon, 'The Making of Virgins and Mothers, 55.

24 In this scene, Bertram is already in some trouble since he is unable to explain how he has Helena's ring on his finger. The French king, who gave her the ring, recounts Helena's promise that she would never take it off her finger unless the matter were extremely pressing.

As an earlier confirmation of Bertram's behaviour, we have Parolles's letter to Diana, which is intercepted by the soldiers who ambush him:

When he swears oaths, bid him drop gold, and take it;
After he scores, he never pays the score.
Half won is match well made; match, and well make it;
He ne'er pays after-debts, take it before,
And say a soldier, Dian, told thee this:
Men are to mell with, boys are not to kiss;

For count of this, the Count's a fool, I know it,
Who pays before, but not when he does owe it. (IV.iii.223–30)

Bertram, interestingly, does not have much fodder with which to refute
Parolles's claims, and the Count's sleaze, we may safely assume, is well
grounded in fact.

25 A play like *Pericles* literalizes the riddling nature of desire by couching its
original sin – the incestuous relationship between Antiochus and his
daughter – in a riddle that the daughter's suitors have to solve:

I am no viper, yet I feed
On mother's flesh, which did me breed.
I sought a husband, in which labor
I found that kindness in a father.
He's father, son, and husband mild;
I mother, wife – and yet his child.
How they may be, and yet in two,
As you will live, resolve it you. (I.i.64–71)

As Pericles knows, 'solving' this riddle is a two-edged sword, since either
way he will be killed. Unlike in *All's Well*, the 'clear answer' to Antiochus's
riddle is precisely the answer that cannot be spoken. Pericles manages to
extricate himself from this particular sticky situation by fleeing but the text
continues to be haunted by images of incestuous father-daughter relationships and rhetorical puzzles where the answer seems to matter less than the
question.

26 McCandless, 'Helena's Bed-Trick,' 463.

27 In her introduction to the play in the *Riverside* edition, Anne Barton notes
that '[Helena's] distrust of disembodied words is plain from the start ... She
forces language to become fact and confronts Bertram at the end not with
words but with two talismanic *things*: the ring and the child she has conceived' (535–6; emphasis mine). But Helena, as we have seen, is the arch
manipulator of words and of rhetoric. She is able to take Bertram's verbal
impossibilities and twist them to suit her own convenience. Thus it is that
even though she is *not* the one who has Bertram's ring at the end (it is Diana
who brings it to the court), Helena is nonetheless able to convince people
that she has fulfilled both her husband's conditions.

4: Cast in Order of Appearance: Catachresis, *Othello*, *King John*

1 Eagleton, *William Shakespeare*, 8. Also cited in Rose, *The Expense of Spirit*,
144. Needless to say, Eagleton does *not* approve of the kind of linguistic

freedom that leads to such prolific abuse, even though his mixed metaphor, summoning up, as it does, the image of a necrophiliac orgy (dead letters inbreeding), is an instructively implosive moment of deconstruction.

2 For Lemuel Johnson's discussion of *Hamlet*, see his *Shakespeare in Africa*, esp. 92–4.

3 Orgel, *The Jonsonian Masque*, 34.

4 The title page of the *Masque of Blacknesse* reads: 'Two royall Masques. The one of BLACKNESSE, The other of BEAVTIE, personated By the most magnificent of Queenes ANNE Queene of great Britaine, &c. With her honorable Ladyes ...'

5 For a recent article that looks at the impact of humoral-climatic theory on the political and racial constructions in *The Masque of Blacknesse*, see Mary Floyd-Wilson, 'Temperature, Temperance, and Racial Difference in Ben Jonson's *The Masque of Blackness*,' *ELR* 28.2 (1998):183–209.

6 All references to the *Masque of Blacknesse* are from Jonson, *Complete Works*, vol. 7.

7 'Coolness' indicates both a drop in temperature and a rise in fashionability. While the latter meaning was not current in the Renaissance, the move to Albion certainly imparts a sense of moving up in the world of fashionable beauty.

8 See also an earlier passage, in which 'fair' Niger is praised, who, along with his daughters, 'prove that beauty best, / Which not the colour, but the feature / Assures unto the creature' (106–8). For a similar, and funnier, version of the same sentiment, see the film, *Bhaji on the Beach*, where Zora Sahgal, one of the grand matriarchs upholding Indian 'purity' in England, defends her racist dislike of an Indian girl's West Indian boyfriend by saying her objection 'is not colour, it is culture.'

9 It should come as no surprise that the *Masque of Beavtie* really does not solve any of the contradictions that *Blacknesse* sets up. At first sight, when the Nigerian nymphs come back with 'their beauties varied,' their (newfound) chastity is stressed; a 'world of little Loues, and chast Desires' (133) replaces the universe of foamy sex that the earlier masque seemed immersed in. Thus far, with fairness and chastity replacing blackness and sexuality, *Beavtie* seems to be following through on, and clarifying, the (il)logic that animated *Blacknesse*, but very soon, this edifice crumbles to reveal the rot beneath. The king, as an inserted note tells us, 'incited ... by his own liking,' asks his wife and courtiers to repeat their dances for his viewing pleasure. Before they come on again for their repeat performance, the masque gives us three songs, the first of which, sung by a treble, runs as follows:

If all these Cvpids, now, were blind
As is their wanton brother;
Or play should put it in their mind
To shoot at one another:
What prettie battaile they would make,
If they their objects should mistake
And each one wound his *mother*. (341–7)

This kind of jesting is obviously extremely popular, and ultimately, after a great deal more of dancing and singing, Ianvarivs, the presiding deity of the masque, pleased with the spectacle before him, renews the 'happy rites' that have celebrated the return of the beautiful nymphs. These 'happy rites' take the princesses right back to the unspeakable rites in *Blacknesse*, and point powerfully to the fact that ultimately there is very little to differentiate the two states of being. 'Whiteness' is as closely linked to sexuality as 'blackness' is, and the common denominator is the inevitable and unstable nature of sexual desire.

10 Serpieri, 'Reading the Signs,' 135.

11 The Latin reads: 'Neque enim quisquam putat luxuriam et liberalitatem idem significare ...' It is interesting that the two words that Quintilian chooses are *luxuriam* and *liberalitatem*, since, in addition to signifying 'prodigality,' *luxuriam* routinely carries with it associations of sexual excess. It is really only by opposing such excess to *liberalitatem* that we can see the shades of gray between the two concepts.

12 In *On Copia of Words and Ideas*, 30, Erasmus makes it clear that he uses this example because the Latin term for a bathing pool is *piscina*, literally, a 'fish pond.'

13 Okri, 'Meditations on Othello.' Also cited in Loomba, *Gender, Race, Renaissance Drama*, 61. Okri makes his comment in the context of attending a performance of *Othello*, where his own physiognomy is read in a particular way by other members of the audience. So even if, he states, *Othello* is not a play about 'race,' the protagonist's blackness has certainly come to be identified as the major thrust of the (dramatic) performance.

14 See Little, '"An Essence That's Not Seen,"' where he states: 'Othello has a black protagonist' (306). Little goes on to question what 'this black inscription' means, and arrives at a set of conclusions somewhat similar to mine, but only in that they take note of the fundamental link between sexuality and colour: 'The scene of intercourse between [Othello and Desdemona] functions, for the on- and offstage audiences alike, as the sexual site and sight of the play's racial anxieties ... [T]he way the play responds to and cre-

ates these anxieties is by mocking the sexual coupling of Othello and Desdemona and by associating it with other culturally horrifying scenes of sexuality, especially bestiality and homosexuality' (306). While this is an interesting argument, it does not take account of *why* these two counters – race and sexuality – should have been used, and does not reckon with the particular force of this choice.

15 There has, of course, been a consistently racist *critical* tradition that has accompanied readings of *Othello*. From Thomas Rymer's caution in 1693, to all 'Maidens of Quality' not to elope with 'Blackamoors,' to Coleridge's 'liberal' argument that Othello was not a 'veritable negro,' to Ridley's 'elevation' of Othello's features to a European classical perfection, the critical tradition has always been fascinated with Othello's colour.

16 For discussions of the play that hinge on the confluence of race and gender, see, among others, Karen Newman's classic essay, '"And wash the Ethiop White": Femininity and the Monstrous in *Othello*,' in her *Fashioning Femininity and English Renaissance Drama*; and Ania Loomba's essay, 'Sexuality and Racial Difference,' in her *Gender, Race, Renaissance Drama*.

17 See Patricia Parker's important essay, 'Shakespeare and Rhetoric: "Dilation" and "Delation" in *Othello*,' in *Shakespeare and the Question of Theory*, ed. Patricia Parker and Geoffrey Hartman.

18 In his essay on *Othello*, '"An Essence That's Not Seen,"' Arthur Little explores the way in which colour is a 'primal' force in the play. While the idea of the 'primal scene' is an interesting one, I revert to the Freudian investment in sexuality and suggest that in *Othello*, race should be read through the lens of sexuality, rather than vice versa.

19 The textual situation of *Othello*, as all its editors remind us, is more than usually fraught. Most modern editions follow F1 with a generous sprinkling of Q1; the two texts have more than a thousand verbal variants, and there are about 160 lines found only in F1. 'Producted' is the use from the First Folio of 1623, which the *Riverside* edition follows, while Q1 (1622) has 'produc'd.' It seems rather significant that, even if the change resulted from scribal incompetence in transcribing the 'foul papers,' that this should be the *only* instance of its use. For further details on the textual situation of *Othello*, see, among others, the Riverside's 'Note on the Text,' M.R. Ridley's introduction to the New Arden *Othello*; and Greg's *The Shakespeare First Folio*.

20 For Iago as self-fashioner, see Stephen Greenblatt, 'The Improvisation of Power,' in his *Renaissance Self-Fashioning*.

For clear textual evidence that Iago too sees himself as a self-fashioner, see I.iii.319 onwards: 'Virtue? a fig!' tis in ourselves that we are thus or thus.'

Our bodies are our gardens, to the which our wills are gardeners; so that if we will plant nettles or sow lettuce, set hyssop and weed up [tine], supply it with one gender of herbs, either to have it sterile with idleness or manur'd with industry – why, the power and corrigible authority of this lies in our wills. If the [beam] of our lives had not one scale of reason to poise another of sensuality, the blood and baseness of our natures would conduct us to most prespost'rous conclusions.' It is, as always, fascinating to note Iago's obsession with sexuality as that which has the potential to undermine the gardens of our bodies. Iago tries to separate 'will' from lust, but since it is connotatively imbricated in it, the separation between the two is a difficult one (for him) to make.

21 The other instances can be found in *The Merry Wives of Windsor* (3), *The Merchant of Venice* (1), and *Richard III* (1). Interestingly, this variant is not used in those other great plays that crucially pivot around jealousy: *Much Ado About Nothing*, and *The Winter's Tale*.

22 Bartels, '*Othello* and Africa,' 63.

23 Orkin, '*Othello* and the "Plain Face" of Racism,' 184. For similar discussions of 'race,' both within and beyond the Renaissance, see Hall's influential *Things of Darkness*; Gates, Jr., '*Race,' Writing, and Difference*; Hendricks and Parker, *Women, 'Race,' and Writing in the Early Modern Period*.

24 Note that in the *Masque of Blacknesse*, Aphrodite's birthplace is, conveniently, the foam off the shore of 'Britania.'

25 As Arthur Little has pointed out, this story was circulated during the period in George Best's *Discourse*, initially published in 1578, and subsequently reprinted in Hakluyt's influential and widely read *Principal Navigations* in 1600. Another essay that discusses the Ham story is Newman, '"And Wash the Ethiop White."' For more discussion of period tracts on darkness and its implications, see Emily Bartels's important essay on '*Othello* and Africa.'

26 As far as I am aware, none of the studies on *Othello* and race cites this particular biblical passage, although almost all cite the story from Best's *Discourse*.

27 In an astute reading of 'The Sound of O in *Othello*,' Joel Fineman details how Shakespeare's play is a story of a 'man named desire,' since Othello's very name, derived etymologically from the Greek for 'desire,' marks the tragedy not only as inevitable, but also as inevitably sexual. Fineman looks at the structures of desire that permeate the text, whittling down the verbal echo of that desire to the use of the 'O.' One of the questions that animates his meditation is why, 'for Shakespeare, is the story of the man named desire a story that is tragic and not, for example, something pastoral, or

comic, or romantic?' (*The Subjectivity Effect*, 146). One of his answers, which he locates in Desdemona's Willow Song, is: 'What there is in a Shakespearean name that makes it Shakespearean [is] specifically the *O*, calling to us from an elsewhere that is other, that determines the Shakespearean subject as the difference between the subject of a name and the subject of full being' (158). The tragedy of *Othello*, by being inscribed within and as the tragedy of a name, is at the same time, unbearably present and unutterably alien. My interest in this project of 'naming,' of course, extends to both the catachrestic obsession with names, and Iago's ability, supremely and devastatingly, to name people and things according to his own vocabulary.

28 I am grateful to one of the University of Toronto Press readers for pointing out to me that Othello's self-accusation exists in the twin registers of foreignness and foreign sexuality.

29 Dollimore, '*Othello*: Sexual Difference and Internal Deviation,' in *Sexual Dissidence*, 158. In the same chapter, Dollimore recommends that we 'forget Iago's homosexuality': 'Iago's and/or Othello's jealousy may well have a homoerotic component, if only because the homoerotic, like other forms of eroticism, might in principle be anywhere, attached to anyone, and in an indeterminate number of contexts. But we would be mistaken to conclude that "repressed homosexuality" is the "real" motivation of the homosocial bond since such a conclusion would obscure much and reveal little' (158). Even as I do not see Iago's 'homosexuality' as the 'real' reason behind his 'motiveless malignity,' it would, I think, be foolish not to note that the cast of Iago's speech is continually motivated by images of horrific sexuality, and that, interestingly, this image is considerably softened in his description of Cassio's dream, which has almost a lyrical and lovable quality about it. Whether or not this means that Iago is sexually 'attracted' to Cassio is, ultimately, not a very important question; what *is* crucial is that Iago's imagination is fired, at all times, by all manner of things sexual.

30 Rose, *The Expense of Spirit*, 153.

31 In her essay on 'Iago as Deconstructionist,' Bonnie Melchior points out the pun on 'lie' as part of her larger point on how Iago achieves his rhetorical effects: '[Iago's] words themselves are true, but somehow, a lie ... [T]he speech act he actually performs is at odds with what the words themselves seem to indicate' (70).

32 Serpieri, 'Reading the Signs,' 141.

33 Iago prefers to forget that like sexuality, blackness too is susceptible to the instability of language. The point, as Derrida notes in reference to racism, 'is not that acts of racial violence are *only* words but rather that they have to have a word' ('Racism's Last Word,' 292; emphasis mine).

34 The visibility that Iago so craves for his malevolence *requires* a physicality that sexuality is unable to provide. De Man points to this very necessity in one of his many treatments of catachresis: 'The trope which coins a name for a still unnamed entity, *which gives face to the faceless is*, of course, catachresis' (*The Resistance to Theory* 44; emphasis mine).

35 *Pericles*, v.i.118–19.

36 All the history plays, by virtue of their subject matter, are obsessed with questions of legitimacy and lineage, and fascinatingly plot how the royal line gets interpreted and interrupted (*Richard II, Richard III*). Unlike *King John*, the other history plays, no matter how much they call the king's name into question, nonetheless continue to function with a stable (even when it is shifting) concept of kingship. Even as all of Shakespeare's history plays, to varying degrees, call legitimacy into question (the simultaneous existence of 'King Richard' and 'King Henry' in the text of *Richard II* being a case in point), *King John* refuses to even superficially gloss over these schisms, and instead chooses to explore them in a ruthlessly relentless manner.

37 *King John* is a scarcely read play. Although the text is 'very verbal,' it is, the *Riverside* informs us, 'marked by tumid rhetoric,' and is a 'puzzling and uneven play' (806). It is, in addition, one of the least popular history plays (*Richard III*, Al Pacino reminds us in *Looking for Richard*, is the most frequently staged Shakespeare play, and both *Richard II*, and *Henry V*, at different times, have been put to ideological use by people who thought them particularly apposite to their cause), so that *King John* has languished on the sidelines of history, scarcely meriting a footnote in the great accompt of English bravery. It is interesting, however, to look at the way in which the sixteenth century recreated John as a much-celebrated Protestant martyr, and as the great precursor of Henry VIII. As Carole Levin notes, 'The recreation of John as a hero was one part of the changing of historical images and the propaganda campaign of the English Reformation ... King John, regarded for centuries as a monster (was) transformed into a hero to suit the new religious and political climate' (*Propaganda in the English Reformation*, 2). Even the anonymous *Troublesome Reign of John, King of England*, published in two parts in 1591, and acknowledged as Shakespeare's source play, glorifies John as a Protestant martyr, who 'set himself against the Man of Rome.'

38 De Man, *Allegories of Reading*, 120, 122.

5. Encore! Allegory, *Volpone, The Tempest*

1 Hazlitt, *Lectures on the English Poets*, 49.

2 Jonson, *Complete Works*, vol. 7, 570. Also cited in Greenblatt, 'The False Ending in *Volpone*,' 91.

3 Fineman, 'The Structure of Allegorical Desire.'

4 Johnson, *Discoveries*, 593.

5 It is interesting that the *Ad Herennium* does not use Clodia or Caelius's speech as examples of allegory. Could this be another indicator that the *Ad Herennium* might, in fact, *not* be Ciceronian?

6 I have derived information on Clodia from the *Oxford Classical Dictionary*, and from the introduction to Catullus's *Poems*, ed. Kenneth Quinn (London: Macmillan, 1970).

7 In his essay, 'The Rhetoric of Temporality,' in *Blindness and Insight*, de Man comments on 'the implicit and rather enigmatic link between allegory and irony,' by stating that the two share a structure in which 'the relationship between sign and meaning is discontinuous ... In both cases, the sign points to something that differs from its literal meaning and has for its function the thematization of this difference' (209).

8 In 'The Structure of Allegorical Desire,' 26, Joel Fineman says something similar: 'The notion of structure, especially of literary structure, presupposes the same system of multiply articulated levels as does that of allegory [and] the possibility of such coherently polysemic significance originates out of the same intention – what I call desire – as does allegorical narrative. I speak of desire in deference to the thematics of allegory and to describe the self-propelling, digressive impulse of allegorical movement.'

9 See, for instance, Slavoj Žižek, *The Plague of Fantasies* (London: Verso, 1997), particularly 'The Seven Veils of Fantasy,' 3–44.

10 Quilligan, *The Language of Allegory*, 26. Quilligan makes the link between punning and allegory the basis of her brilliant book. Explaining the genesis of her theory, she states: 'I noticed that William Langland punned a great deal; that he would, in fact, stop everything for the fatal Cleopatra of a "quibble," as Dr. Johnson said of Shakespeare. So I began reading allegory, counting puns. In the course of reading later literature, I discovered that many other works I had not thought of as allegory also played with words to remarkably similar effect. From this shared fact – the generation of narrative structure out of wordplay – the members of the (allegorical) genre grouped themselves' (21–2). While I fully agree with Quilligan's link between wordplay and allegory, I would hesitate to make that link the basis of a *formal* correspondence. Rather, I think the resemblance ends at the fact of twinning; that apart, punning hides completely different meanings under one form while allegory suggests a deep and abiding link between fiction and the 'truth' it allegedly veils.

11 After speaking of the 'qualities' of cruelty and miserliness, for instance, Machiavelli states: 'It is not necessary for a prince to have all of the above-mentioned qualities, but it is very necessary for him *to appear to have them*' (*The Prince*, 59, emphasis mine).

12 Salman Rushdie, *Midnight's Children* (New York: Avon Books, 1980), 19. Rushdie has frequently been accused of sacrificing 'content' to revel in style and nowhere more than in this book which, after all, charts the course of an independent nation's history. For a criticism of Rushdie's tendency to use style as an indicator of substance, see among others, Feroza F. Jussawalla's chapter, 'Beyond Indianness: The Stylistic Concerns of *Midnight's Children*,' in *Family Quarrels: Towards a Criticism of Indian Writing in English* (New York: Peter Lang, 1985), 133–56.

13 See, for instance, Dolan, '"We must here be fixed"'; Manlove, 'The Double Vision in *Volpone*'; and Leggatt, '*Volpone*: The Double Plot Revisited.'

14 Barbour, '"When I Acted Young Antinuous,"' 1009.

15 For studies that look at the homoerotic element in the play, see, among others, Marchitello, 'Desire and Domination in *Volpone*'; DiGangi, 'Asses and Wits'; Barbour, '"When I Acted Young Antinuous"'; and Ronald Huebert, '"A Shrew Yet Honest": Manliness in Jonson,' *Renaissance Drama* 20 (1984): 31–68.

16 In his *Arte of English Poesie*, Puttenham makes a link between poetry and medicine, and suggests that in some instances, poets should act *like* physicians, 'not onely by applying a medicine to the ordinary sicknes of mankind, but by making the very greef it selfe (in part) cure of the disease' (61–2). He adds later that poets have sought to appease sorrows 'not with any medicament of a contrary temper, as the *Galenistes* use to cure [*contraria contraries*] but as the *Paracelsians*, who cure [*similia similibus*] making one dolour to expel another, and in this case [of lamentation], one short sorrowing the remedie of a long and grievous sorrow' (63).

17 Corvino draws a chalk circle around Celia and threatens her with dire consequences if she steps out of that circumference. This myth of female containment within a circle is a transcultural one. In India, for instance, the central mythological text of *The Ramayana* is fuelled by the transgression of the 'Laxman Rekha' (the chalk circle drawn by Laxman) by his sister-in-law Sita, who is then abducted, triggering off a war between her husband and her captor, allegorized as the battle between Good and Evil.

18 For a brilliant analysis of the link between allegory and gender, see Barbara Johnson's essay, 'Women and Allegory,' in *The Wake of Deconstruction* (Oxford: Blackwell, 1994), 52–75.

19 In 'Allegory, Materialism, Violence,' Gordon Teskey's thesis revolves

around this split that is constitutive of allegory. For him, allegory tries 'to conceal the fundamental disorder out of which the illusion of absolute order is raised. It is ... out of this struggle at the rift that the whole process of allegorical figuration is generated, thus creating a veil of analogies behind which we imagine is placed, like the vanishing point in linear perspective, the singularity of absolute truth' (302).

20 See, for instance, Fletcher, *Allegory*, 304–59.

21 In his article on the 'false ending' in *Volpone*, Stephen Greenblatt notes that the 'deadness' the play leaves us with 'has all along been lurking just beneath the glittering surface of Volpone's existence, and ... in the pause after the Fox's triumph, it is revealed. We suddenly glimpse that dark thing which lay hidden behind all of the frenetic activity – not criminality, or satanic evil but something subtler and more insidious: emptiness, boredom, the void' ('The False Ending in *Vapone*,' 93). The *endlessness* of allegory in *Volpone* defies closure in much the same way as it defies 'openings' or 'illumination.' Even though the trope generates enough light to dazzle attention *away* from the void of disease, the *name* for that void, tropologically protected by a glittering veil and endlessly circuitous is, nonetheless, sexuality.

22 Quoted in Vaughan and Vaughan, *Shakespeare's Caliban*, 263–4.

23 An interesting link between *Volpone* and *The Winter's Tale* lies in the connection between Julio Romano, that 'rare Italian master' of the latter play, and Aretino, of whose pornography Lady Would-Be displays her knowledge in the former text. Romano made a series of illustrations for Aretino's treatise on sexual positions (an Italian *Kama Sutra*), which was known in Italy as *I Modi*.

24 De Man, *Aesthetic Ideology*, 51.

25 Plutarch, *De Garrulitate*, in *Moralia*, trans. W.C. Hembold, vol. 6 (Cambridge, MA.: Harvard University Press, 1939), 403.

26 For studies that look at *The Tempest* as an allegory for colonialism, see, among others, Greenblatt, *Shakespearean Negotiations*; Peter Hulme, 'Hurricans in the Caribbees: The Constitution of the Discourse of English Colonisation,' in *1642: Literature and Power in the Seventeenth Century*, ed. Francis Barker, et al. (Colchester: University of Essex Press, 1981); Leslie A. Fiedler, *The Stranger in Shakespeare* (New York: Stein and Day, 1972); and Brown, '"This thing of darkness I acknowledge mine." For studies that question this paradigm see, among others, David Scott Kastan, '"The Duke of Milan/And his brave son": Dynastic Politics in *The Tempest*,' in *Critical Essays on Shakespeare's* The Tempest, ed. Vaughan and Vaughan, 91–103.

27 For a critique of the America-centredness of postcolonial readings of the play, see Brotton, '"This Tunis, sir, was Carthage."'

28 Brown, '"This thing of darkness I acknowledge mine,"' 58.

29 This fact from critical/theatrical history is cited in Alden T. Vaughan's comprehensive study of the symbolic potential of Caliban in 'Caliban in the "Third World": Shakespeare's Savage as Sociopolitical Symbol,' in *Critical Essays on Shakespeare's* The Tempest, ed. Vaughan and Vaughan, 247.

30 In the opening sentence of 'The Structure of Allegorical Desire,' Joel Fineman states that the 'of' in his title should be read as both 'objective and subjective genitive.' In keeping with the allegorical imperative, Fineman's 'of' serves both to speak of the desire *of* allegory and the desire *for* allegory. His structure expresses both a longing for allegory and the framework within which allegory longs. Fineman goes on to suggest that desire is by its very nature allegorical since both desire and allegory originate in 'the possibility of coherently polysemic significance' (26). This polysemy – structurally necessary to allegory – is the reason why neither allegory nor sexuality can come to rest at any one reading or interpretation.

31 Barker and Hulme, '"Nymphs and reapers heavily vanish,"' 203.

32 For George Lamming's description of this accusation as 'the Lie,' see Jonathan Goldberg's discussion in *The Generation of Caliban*, 24. Perhaps Prospero's fondness for and dependence on Ariel stems from the fact that within the scope of the play, this spirit is sexless and so does not pose a threat to the old man of the island.

33 Goldberg, 'The Print of Goodness,' 247.

34 Burnett, '"Strange and Wonderfull Syghts,"' 195.

35 Goldberg, *The Generation of Caliban*, 12.

36 Allegorical readings of texts involve a mode of interpretation that does not take the letter at its word, and all reading is, properly speaking, allegorical in nature, since the subjectivity of the reading enterprise stems from the fact that a text signifies differently for different people even though many of them might share the same ideological/cultural assumptions. To say, therefore, that allegory hinges on more than one level of meaning, is not sufficient to locate the *specificity* of the allegorical mode. Even as this specificity might be (and, I will argue, is) translatable into the critical/ theoretical enterprise *per se*, that does not prevent the fact that a trope called allegory, with particular rhetorical characteristics, exists as its foundation. This trope, I suggest, is isolatable precisely because it repeatedly *forgets* its own signification. In *The Winter's Tale*, allegory is unable to process the passage of linear time because that makes it lose the identity of its presence *as* presence, and gestures instead to the absence that stretches across the sands of

time. Similarly, as *The Tempest* makes abundantly clear, allegory is predicated on a mode of forgetting that eschews beginnings and ends to indulge instead in an endless circle, escape from which is virtually impossible. At times, one can glimpse an image that seems to lie beyond this restrictive circumference, and allegoresis reaches for that image as an instance of what lies outside, only to discover, as we have already seen, that both the veil and the image it hides are contained in an alcove within the greater circle area.

37 Some might suggest this is a self-interested move, but so be it.

After Words: *Henry VIII* and the Ends of History

1 Lord Herbert's *Life and Raigne of King Henry the Eighth* (London: 1672), 1. In this work, which runs into 639 pages of text, the author gestures towards the difficulty of his project in the epistle dedicatory itself, where he says: 'Though as I have endeavoured to set down the truth impartially, I hope they will not be so great or so many, as to exauctorate the rest. I am not yet ignorant that the King, whose History I write, is subject to more obloquies, than any since the worst Roman Emperours times. But I shall little care for censure, as long as the testimonies I use do assure and warrant me; since I intend not to describe him otherwise, either good or bad, but as He really was.' Henry is considered a more difficult subject than the 'worst Roman emperor' and there seems to be something about this king's story that proves particularly challenging to the historian. The text provides a detailed, blow-by-blow account of Henry's reign, in which the trouble with Katherine begins only on p. 244. At the conclusion of this epic, Lord Herbert states in his final line: 'To conclude; I wish I could leave him in his grave.' This desire, of course, comes only after the historian has already exhumed the body of the dead monarch.

In '*Henry VIII* and the Deconstruction of History' Peter L. Rudnytsky quotes the opening paragraph of the *History* to support his argument of Shakespeare's 'deconstruction' of history, a crucial element of which lies in the playwright's attempt to take note of 'several countenances' at once.

2 The most frequently argued contention is for joint Shakespeare-Fletcher authorship. See the Introduction to the *Riverside Shakespeare*'s edition for more details. In his introduction to the *Arden* edition, R.A. Foakes discusses in detail the reasons for a Fletcherian attribution before finally coming down on the side of sole Shakespearean authorship.

3 This is the title that Sir Henry Wotton, writing to Sir Edmund Bacon in 1613, gives the play that burned down the Globe Theatre, and which had 'repre-

sent[ed] some principal pieces of the Reign of *Henry 8*' (Foakes, *The Arden Shakespeare*, xxvi).

4 In his essay on 'Aspects of the Incest Problem in *Hamlet*,' Jason P. Rosenblatt undertakes a detailed analysis of these two biblical texts. While commenting on the injunction in Deuteronomy, Rosenblatt notes, in the context of *Hamlet*, that 'the King's role is a travesty of the *levir*'s. The validity of his marriage to Gertrude actually depends on the absolute severance of the earlier marital union by death and obliteration of all his brother's claims. Yet Claudius opens the play's second scene by pretending that he keeps those claims alive' (352).

5 McCabe, *Incest, Drama, and Nature's Law*, 53.

6 Boehrer, *Monarchy and Incest in Renaissance England*, 44.

7 Ibid., 46.

8 Ibid., 46–7.

9 Ibid., 46.

10 Shell, *The End of Kinship*, 29.

11 For an exhaustive account of the affair, written during the reign of Mary, see Harpsfield, *Treatise on the Pretended Divorce between Henry VIII and Catherine of Aragon*. See also Marc Shell's discussion of the Henry VIII affair(s) in *The End of Kinship*, esp. 110–14; Jason P. Rosenblatt's parallel between *Hamlet* and *Henry VIII* in 'The Incest Problem in *Hamlet*'; and Foakes's introduction to the Arden edition of *Henry VIII*, esp. xliv–liv.

12 R.A. Foakes singles out the courtiers' derisive remarks about Henry's 'conscience' before noting that Henry's slipping conscience reveals him to be 'human and fallible' (lxi), a judgment rather too mild in the context of the play.

13 This is yet another indicator of Elizabeth's 'bastardy': she was possibly conceived before Henry and Anne were married, and certainly before Henry and Katherine were divorced. Also see McCabe, *Incest, Drama, and Nature's Law*, esp. 159–61. McCabe notes that Henry's concern over the lack of a male heir (which for the king bespeaks divine wrath) 'is somewhat disingenuous since the relevant Levitical texts speak of childlessness and not specifically the lack of a male heir' (160). While commenting on Cranmer's speech, with which the play nears its end, McCabe notes that 'perhaps more than any other history play, Henry VIII is pervaded by a keen sense of proleptic irony. As everyone knew, Anne's sumptuous coronation served merely as the prelude to ignominious execution, and the birth of England's virgin queen promised no boys hereafter but an end to the Tudor dynasty' (160).

14 Mary was reinstated into the line of succession in 1543, although placed, along with Elizabeth, behind Edward.

15 Gordon McMullan, '"Swimming on Bladders,"' 222.

16 Kermode, 'What Is Shakespeare's *Henry VIII* About?' 54.

17 Rosenblatt, 'Aspects of the Incest Problem in *Hamlet*,' 361.

18 In his introduction to the Arden *Henry VIII*, R.A, Foakes notes: 'Like all the last plays, *Henry VIII* leaves open the possibility of the repetition of a cycle of events such as it presents' (ixi). He is referring to Henry's penchant for changing wives, but this observation could equally be extended to the idea of incest.

19 This persistence takes the form of repeated terms of similitude in Cranmer's speech: 'As great in admiration,' 'Shall star-like rise as great in fame.'

20 I am very satisfied with the reasons the *Arden* editor cites for sole Shakespearean authorship; see esp. xx–xxvi.

21 Kermode, 'What Is Shakespeare's *Henry VIII* About?' 48.

22 Foakes, *The Arden Shakespeare*, xxii.

23 For an argument that collaboration was constitutive rather than exceptional in the English Renaissance theatre, see Masten, *Textual Intercourse*.

24 Rudnytsky, '*Henry VIII* and the Deconstruction of History,' 47.

25 In the *Arden* introduction, Foakes rehearses the arguments that have been put forth for the Shakespeare-Fletcher collaboration. These arguments include detailed act and scene divisions between the two alleged authors. By this reckoning, Cranmer's scene of benediction at Elizabeth's christening, in which the phoenix makes its appearance (v–iv), was not even written by 'Shakespeare.'

26 McCabe, *Incest, Drama, and Nature's Law*, 161.

27 These stylistic inconsistencies include feminine endings, run-on lines, frequent use of words like 'em and ye, which critics note as typical Fletcherian signatures.

28 Felperin, 'Shakespeare's *Henry VIII*: History As Myth,' 227.

29 One of the reasons the cover of the second edition of the *Riverside Shakespeare* is so fascinating is because it provides us with a cherubic, lace-ruffed bard whom people can identify as the 'author' whose works are contained within the covers of the book. There is also a scene in *Shakespeare in Love* that deals, in a typically smart and hilarious way, with this question of identity: on the verge of consummating their passion, Viola asks Will if he is the author of the plays by William Shakespeare. Without batting an eyelid or skipping a beat, Will lays to rest the ghost of centuries-old speculation and answers: 'I am'!

30 Masten, *Textual Intercourse*, 107.

31 Taylor, *Shakespeare's Darker Purpose*, 122.

32 Foakes, *The Arden Shakespeare*, xlii.

33 Ibid.

34 In his formulation of the notion of the 'dangerous supplement,' Jacques
    Derrida, in *Acts of Literature*, notes that 'the supplement is maddening
    because it is neither presence nor absence' (96) and that 'the concept of the
    supplement is a sort of blind spot ... the not-seen that opens and limits visi-
    bility' (108). This blind spot so enraged an editor like Boyle that, as Foakes
    notes, he fully excised *Henry VIII* from the Shakespearean canon (xlvi);
    Foakes is a notable exception to this general tendency to view *Henry VIII* as
    both inferior to and vastly different from, Shakespeare's other plays. This
    blind spot is also at play in the critical tradition surrounding *Henry VIII*,
    which insists that its artistic 'inferiority' is to blame for the text's troubled
    (and incestuous) relation to history.

35 Gordon McMullan makes a similar point while commenting on the wide-
    spread use of third-party narrative in this play: 'The act of witnessing is
    demonstrated to be essential to the construction of history, and it is history
    as construct, rather than as event, which is emphasised throughout'
    ('Shakespeare and the End of History,' 17).

36 Henry's 'tool' was probably a matter of some pride since it was always rep-
    resented by means of an exaggerated codpiece in his portraits.

37 Even though, as Judith Anderson notes, '*Henry VIII* is commonly regarded
    as being more "historical" than is typical of Shakespeare's major history
    plays [since] [m]any passages in it seem versified Holinshed' (*Biographical
    Truth*, 131). Such an observation, while granting historical verifiability to
    the play, nonetheless relies on such verifiability or its lack as the point of
    departure for interest in the text. If *Henry VIII* is *more* 'historical' than
    Shakespeare's other history plays, then in my argument, that would mean
    an even greater lack of fixity within the category of the historical.

38 *The Riverside Shakespeare*, 1022.

39 'The Globe' itself has come to figure an 'authentic' history, which is pre-
    sumably the primary reason for rebuilding it on the banks of the Thames.
    This recreation of an 'original' space by the aptly named Sam Wanamaker is
    aimed at enhancing the experience of the audience as it sits in the 'same'
    space as its predecessors did four centuries ago.

Bibliography

Abel, Elizabeth, ed. *Writing and Sexual Difference*. Chicago: University of Chicago Press, 1980.

Adelman, Janet. 'Iago's Alter Ego: Race as Projection in *Othello.'* *Shakespeare Quarterly* 48 (1997): 125–44.

– *Suffocating Mothers: Fantasies of Maternal Origin in Shakespeare's Plays*, Hamlet to The Tempest. New York and London: Routledge, 1992.

Anderson. Judith H. *Biographical Truth: The Representation of Historical Persons in Tudor-Stuart Writing*. New Haven and London: Yale University Press, 1984.

– *Words that Matter: Linguistic Perception in Renaissance English*. Stanford: Stanford University Press, 1996.

Aristotle. *On Rhetoric*. Trans. George A. Kennedy. New York: Oxford University Press, 1991.

– *The Poetics*. Ed. T.E. Page. Cambridge, MA.: Harvard University Press, 1927.

Ascham, Roger. *The Scholemaster*. London: Edward Arber, 1870.

Aubrey, James R. 'Race and the Spectacle of the Monstrous in *Othello.'* *CLIO* 22.3 (1993): 221–38.

Bakhtin, Mikhail. *Rabelais and His World*. Trans. Helene Iswolsky. Bloomington: Indiana University Press, 1984.

Barber, C.L. *Shakespeare's Festive Comedy*. Cleveland: Meridian, 1967.

Barbour, Richard. '"When I Acted Young Antinuous": Boy Actors and the Erotics of Jonsonian Theater.' *PMLA* 110.5 (October 1995): 1006–22.

Barish, Jonas A. *The Antitheatrical Prejudice*. Berkeley: University of California Press, 1981.

– 'The Uniqueness of Elizabethan Drama.' In *Drama in the Renaissance*, ed. Clifford Davidson, C.J. Grianakaris, and John H. Stroupe, 1–10. New York: AMS Press, 1986.

Barkan, Leonard. *Transuming Passion: Ganymede and the Erotics of Humanism.* Stanford: Stanford University Press, 1991.

Barker, Deborah E., and Ivo Kamps, eds. *Shakespeare and Gender: A History.* London: Verso, 1995.

Barker, Francis. *The Tremulous Private Body: Essays on Subjection.* Ann Arbor: University of Michigan Press, 1995.

Barker, Francis, and Peter Hulme. '"Nymphs and reapers heavily vanish": The Discursive Con-texts of *The Tempest*.' In *Alternative Shakespeares*, ed. John Drakakis, 191–205. London: Methuen, 1985.

Bartels, Emily. 'Making More of the Moor: Aaron, Othello, and Renaissance Refashionings of Race.' *Shakespeare Quarterly* 41.4 (1990): 433–54.

– '*Othello* and Africa: Postcolonialism Reconsidered.' *William and Mary Quarterly* 54.1 (January 1997): 45–64.

Barton, Anne. *Essays, Mainly Shakespearean.* Cambridge: Cambridge University Press, 1994.

– *The Names of Comedy.* Toronto: University of Toronto, 1990.

Baumlin, Tita French. '"All yet seems well, and if it ends so meet": Ambiguity and Tragic Language in *All's Well That Ends Well*.' *Explorations in Renaissance Culture* 17 (1991): 125–43.

Berger Jr., Harry. *The Allegorical Temper.* New Haven: Yale University Press, 1957.

Blake, N.F. *A History of the English Language.* New York: New York University Press, 1996.

Blamires, Alcuin, ed. *Woman Defamed and Woman Defended: An Anthology of Medieval Texts.* Oxford: Clarendon Press, 1992.

Bloom, Harold. *A Map of Misreading.* New York: Oxford University Press, 1975.

– ed. *William Shakespeare's 'Richard II': Modern Critical Interpretations.* New York: Chelsea House, 1988.

Blum, Abbe. '"Strike all that look upon with mar[b]le": Monumentalizing Women in Shakespeare's Plays.' In *The Renaissance Englishwoman in Print: Counterbalancing the Canon*, ed. Anne M. Haselkorn and Betty S. Travitsky, 99–118. Amherst: University of Massachusetts Press, 1990.

Bly, Mary. 'Bawdy Puns and Lustful Virgins: The Legacy of Juliet's Desire in Comedies of the Early 1600s.' *Shakespeare Survey* 49 (1996): 97–109.

Boehrer, Bruce. *Monarchy and Incest in Renaissance England.* Philadelphia: University of Pennsylvania Press, 1992.

Bradby, G.F. *Short Studies in Shakespeare.* New York: Macmillan, 1929.

Bray, Alan. 'Homosexuality and the Signs of Male Friendship in Elizabethan England.' In *Queering the Renaissance*, ed. Jonathan Goldberg, 40–61. Durham and London: Duke University Press, 1994.

– *Homosexuality in Renaissance England*. London: Gay Men's Press, 1982.

Bredbeck, Gregory W. *Sodomy and Interpretation: Marlowe to Milton*. Ithaca: Cornell University Press, 1991.

Breitenberg, Mark. *Anxious Masculinity in Early Modern England*. Cambridge: Cambridge University Press, 1996.

Brereton, Geoffrey. *Principles of Tragedy*. Coral Gables: University of Miami Press, 1970.

Bristow, Joseph. *Sexuality*. New York and London: Routledge, 1997.

Brook, G.L. *The Language of Shakespeare*. London: Andre Deutsch, 1976.

Brooke, Christopher N.L. *The Medieval Idea of Marriage*. Oxford: Oxford University Press, 1989.

Brooke, Nicholas, ed. *Richard II: A Casebook*. London: Macmillan, 1973.

Brotton, Jerry. '"This Tunis, sir, was Carthage": Contesting Colonialism in *The Tempest*.' In *Post-Colonial Shakespeares*, ed. Ania Loomba and Martin Orkin, 23–42. London: Routledge, 1998.

Brown, Paul. '"This thing of darkness I acknowledge mine": *The Tempest* and the Discourse of Colonialism.' In *Political Shakespeare: New Essays in Cultural Materialism*, ed. Jonathan Dollimore and Alan Sinfield, 48–71 Ithaca: Cornell University Press, 1985.

Bryant, Donald C. *The Rhetorical Idiom: Essays in Rhetoric, Oratory, Language, and Drama*. Ithaca: Cornell University Press, 1958.

Bullough, Vern L., and Bonnie Bullough. *Cross Dressing, Sex, and Gender*. Philadelphia: University of Pennsylvania Press, 1993.

Burckhardt, Sigurd. *Shakespearean Meanings*. Princeton: Princeton University Press, 1968.

Burnett, Mark Thornton. '"Strange and Wonderfull Syghts": *The Tempest* and the Discourses of Monstrosity.' *Shakespeare Survey* 50 (1997): 187–99.

Burt, Richard, and John Michael Archer, eds. *Enclosure Acts: Sexuality, Property, and Culture in Early Modern England*. Ithaca: Cornell University Press, 1994.

Butler, Judith. *Bodies That Matter: On the Discursive Limits of 'Sex.'* New York and London: Routledge, 1993.

– *Excitable Speech: A Politics of the Performative*. New York: Routledge, 1997.

Calderwood, James L. *Shakespearean Metadrama*. Minneapolis: University of Minnesota Press, 1971.

Callaghan, Dympna. *Woman and Gender in Renaissance Tragedy*. Atlantic Highlands, NJ: Humanities Press International, 1989.

Campbell, Lily B., ed. *The Mirror for Magistrates*. New York: Barnes & Noble, 1960.

Carroll, William C. *The Great Feast of Language in* Love's Labour's Lost. Princeton: Princeton University Press, 1976.

Cartwright, Kent. *Theatre and Humanism: English Drama in the Sixteenth Century.* Cambridge: Cambridge University Press: 1999.

Cave, Terence. *The Cornucopian Text: Problems of Writing in the French Renaissance.* Oxford: Clarendon Press, 1979.

Cavell, Stanley. *Disowning Knowledge in Six Plays of Shakespeare.* Cambridge: Cambridge University Press, 1987.

Cavendish, Margaret. *The Blazing World and Other Writings.* Ed. Kate Lilley. London: Penguin, 1992.

Césaire, Aimé. *A Tempest.* Trans. Richard Miller. New York: Ubu Repertory Theater Publications, 1969.

Chaucer, Geoffrey. *The Riverside Chaucer.* Ed. Larry Benson et al. Boston: Houghton Mifflin,1987.

Cheyfitz, Eric. *The Poetics of Imperialism: Translation and Colonization from* The Tempest *to* Tarzan. Philadelphia: University of Pennsylvania Press, 1991.

Cicero, Marcus Tullius (?). *Rhetorica Ad Herennium.* Trans. Harry Caplan. Cambridge, MA: Harvard University Press, 1954.

Cole, Douglas. *Christopher Marlowe and the Renaissance of Tragedy.* Westport, CT: Praeger, 1995.

Cole, Howard C. *The* All's Well *Story from Boccaccio to Shakespeare.* Chicago: University of Illinois Press, 1981.

Colie, Rosalie L. *Shakespeare's 'Living Art.'* Princeton: Princeton University Press, 1974.

Collier, Jeremy. *A Short View of the Immorality and Profaneness of the English Stage.* Munich: Wilhelm Fink Verlag, 1967.

Comensoli, Viviana, and Anne Russell, eds. *Enacting Gender on the English Renaissance Stage.* Urbana and Chicago: University of Illinois Press, 1999.

Cooper, David E. *Metaphor.* London: Basil Blackwell, 1986.

Crane, William G. *Wit and Rhetoric in the Renaissance.* New York: Columbia University Press, 1964.

Crewe, Jonathan V. *Unredeemed Rhetoric: Thomas Nashe and the Scandal of Authorship.* Baltimore: Johns Hopkins University Press, 1982.

Cubeta, Paul M., ed. *Twentieth Century Interpretations of* Richard II. Englewood Cliffs, NJ: Prentice-Hall, 1971.

Davis, Lloyd.'"Death-Marked Love": Desire and Presence in *Romeo and Juliet.'* *Shakespeare Survey* 49 (1996): 57–67.

Davis, Lloyd, ed. *Sexuality and Gender in the English Renaissance: An Annotated Edition of Contemporary Documents.* New York: Garland, 1998.

Deats, Sara Munson. *Sex, Gender, and Desire in the Plays of Christopher Marlowe.* Newark: University of Delaware Press, 1997.

De Grazia, Margreta. 'World Pictures, Modern Periods, and the Early Stage.' In *A New History of Early English Drama*, ed. John D. Cox and David Scott Kastan, 7–21. New York: Columbia University Press, 1997.

Dekker, Thomas. 'Lantern and Candle-Light.' In *Rogues, Vagabonds, and Sturdy Beggars: A New Gallery of Tudor and Early Stuart Rogue Literature*, ed. Arthur F. Kinney, 207–60. Amherst: University of Massachusetts Press, 1990.

– *The Magnificent Entertainment*. London: 1603.

de Man, Paul. *Aesthetic Ideology*. Minneapolis: University of Minnesota Press, 1996.

– *Allegories of Reading: Figural Language in Rousseau, Nietzsche, Rilke, and Proust*. New Haven: Yale University Press, 1979.

– *Blindness and Insight: Essays in the Rhetoric of Contemporary Criticism*. Minneapolis: University of Minnesota Press, 1983.

– 'Pascal's Allegory of Persuasion.' In *Allegory and Representation*, ed. Stephen Greenblatt, 1–25. Baltimore and London: The Johns Hopkins University Press, 1981.

– *The Resistance to Theory*. Minneapolis: University of Minnesota Press, 1986.

Derrida, Jacques. *Acts of Literature*. Ed. Derek Attridge. New York: Routledge, 1992.

– *Dissemination*. Trans. Barbara Johnson. Chicago: University of Chicago Press, 1981.

– 'Racism's Last Word.' *Critical Inquiry* 12 (1985): 290–9.

– 'White Mythology.' Trans. F.C.T. Moore. *New Literary History* 6:1 (1974): 5–74.

Digangi, Mario. 'Asses and Wits: The Homoerotics of Mastery in Satiric Comedy.' *ELR* 25.2 (spring 1995): 179–208.

– *The Homoerotics of Early Modern Drama*. Cambridge: Cambridge University Press, 1997.

Dinshaw, Carolyn. *Getting Medieval: Sexualities and Communities, Pre- and Postmodern*. Durham: Duke University Press, 1999.

Doherty, Gerald. 'The Art of Appropriation: The Rhetoric of Sexuality in D.H. Lawrence.' *Style* 30:2 (summer 1996): 289–308.

Dolan, Frances. '"We must here be fixed": Discovering a Self behind the Mask in *Volpone*.' *Iowa State Journal of Research* 60.3 (February 1986): 355–67.

Dollimore, Jonathan. *Death, Desire and Loss in Western Culture*. New York: Routledge, 1998.

– *Radical Tragedy*. Durham: Duke University Press, 1993.

– *Sexual Dissidence: Augustine to Wilde, Freud to Foucault*. Oxford: Clarendon Press, 1991.

Donawerth, Jane. *Shakespeare and the Sixteenth-Century Study of Language*. Chicago: University of Illinois Press, 1984.

Donne, John, *The Complete English Poems of John Donne*. Ed. C.A. Patrides. London: Dent, 1985.

Dunn, Kevin. *Pretexts of Authority: The Rhetoric of Authorship in the Renaissance Preface*. Stanford: Stanford University Press, 1994.

Dutton, Richard. *Licensing, Censorship and Authorship in Early Modern England*. New York: Palgrave, 2000.

Eagleton, Terry. *William Shakespeare*. Oxford and New York: Basil Blackwell, 1986.

Edelman, Lee. *Homographesis: Essays in Gay Literary and Cultural Theory*. New York: Routledge, 1994.

– 'Post-Partum.' *Narrative* 10.2 (May 2002), 183.

Elam, Keir. *Shakespeare's Universe of Discourse: Language-Games in the Comedies*. New York: Cambridge University Press, 1984.

Eliot, T.S. *Selected Essays*. London: Faber and Faber, 1934.

Elliott, John. 'The Ethics of Repression: Deconstruction's Historical Transumption of History.' *New Literary History* 23 (1992):727–45.

Embler, Weller. *Metaphor and Meaning*. DeLand, FL: Everett/Edwards, 1966.

Empson, William. *Seven Types of Ambiguity*. Harmondsworth: Penguin, 1973.

Enterline, Lynn. '"You speak a language that I understand not": The Rhetoric of Animation in *The Winter's Tale*.' *Shakespeare Quarterly* 48.1: (1997): 17–44.

Erasmus, Desiderius. *The Colloquies*. Trans. N. Bailey. London: Reeves and Turner, 1878.

– *On Copia of Words and Ideas*. Trans. Donald B. King and H. David Rix. Milwaukee, WI.: Marquette University Press, 1963.

Evans, Robert O. *The Osier Cage: Rhetorical Devices in* Romeo and Juliet. Lexington: University of Kentucky Press, 1966.

Farley-Hills, David. *Shakespeare and the Rival Playwrights, 1600–1606*. London: Routledge, 1990.

Felperin, Howard. 'Political Criticism at the Crossroads: The Utopian Historicism of *The Tempest*.' In *The Tempest*, ed. Nigel Wood, 29–66. Buckingham and Philadelphia: Open University Press, 1995.

– 'Shakespeare's *Henry VIII*: History as Myth.' *Studies in English Literature 1500–1900* 6 (winter 1966): 225–46.

– '"Tongue-tied out queen?": The Deconstruction of Presence in *The Winter's Tale*.' In *Shakespeare and the Question of Theory*, ed. Patricia Parker and Geoffrey Hartman, 3–18. New York: Methuen, 1985.

Ferguson, Margaret, et al., eds. *Rewriting the Renaissance: The Discourses of Sexual Difference in Early Modern Europe*. Chicago: University of Chicago Press, 1986.

Ferris, Lesley, ed. *Crossing the Stage: Controversies on Cross-Dressing*. London: Routledge, 1993.

Fineman, Joel. 'The History of the Anecdote: Fiction and Fiction.' In *The New Historicism*, ed. H. Aram Veeser, 49–76. New York and London: Routledge, 1989.

– *Shakespeare's Perjured Eye: The Invention of Poetic Subjectivity in the Sonnets*. Berkeley: University of California Press, 1986.

– 'The Structure of Allegorical Desire.' In *Allegory and Representation*, ed. Stephen Greenblatt, 26–60. Baltimore: Johns Hopkins University Press, 1981.

– *The Subjectivity Effect in Western Literary Tradition: Essays toward the Release of Shakespeare's Will*. Cambridge, MA: MIT Press, 1991.

Finney, Gail, ed. *Look Who's Laughing: Gender and Comedy*. Langhorne, PA: Gordon and Breach, 1994.

Finucci, Valeria, and Regina Schwartz, eds. *Desire in the Renaissance: Psychoanalysis and Literature*. Princeton: Princeton University Press, 1994.

Fischlin, Daniel. 'Metalepsis and the Rhetoric of Lyric Affect.' *English Studies in Canada* 22.3 (1996): 315–35.

Fletcher, Angus. *Allegory: The Theory of a Symbolic Mode*. Ithaca: Cornell University Press, 1964.

Foakes, R.A., ed. *The Arden Shakespeare: King Henry VIII*. London: Methuen, 1957.

Foucault, Michel. *The History of Sexuality*. Vol. 1. Trans. Robert Hurley. New York: Vintage Books, 1990.

Fradenburg, Louise, and Carla Freccero, eds. *Premodern Sexualities*. New York and London: Routledge, 1996.

Franceschina, John. *Homosexualities in the English Theatre: From Lyly to Wilde*. Westport, CT: Greenwood Press, 1997.

Fraser, Russell A., and Norman Rabkin, eds. *Drama of the English Renaissance*. Vol. 2. *The Stuart Period*. New York: Macmillan, 1976.

Fraunce, Abraham. *The Arcadian Rhetoric*. Menston: Scolar Press, 1969.

Freud, Sigmund. *Three Essays on the Theory of Sexuality*. Trans. and ed. James Strachey. New York: Harper Collins, 1962.

Froissart, Jean. *Chronicles*. Trans. and ed. Geoffrey Brereton. London: Penguin, 1968.

Frye, Northrop. *Myth and Metaphor: Selected Essays, 1974–1988*. Ed. Robert D. Denham. Charlottesville, VA: University of Virginia Press, 1990.

– *A Natural Perspective*. New York: Columbia University Press, 1965.

Garber, Marjorie. 'The Logic of the Transvestite.' In *Staging the Renaissance: Reinterpretations of Elizabethan and Jacobean Drama*, ed. David Scott Kastan and Peter Stallybrass, 221–34. New York: Routledge, 1991.

Gates, Jr., Henry Louis, ed. *'Race,' Writing, and Difference*. Chicago: University of Chicago Press, 1986.

Gaudet, Paul. 'The "Parasitical" Counselors in Shakespeare's *Richard II*: A Problem in Dramatic Interpretation.' *Shakespeare Quarterly* 33.2 (1982): 142–54.

Gillespie, James L., ed. *The Age of Richard II*. New York: St Martin's Press, 1997.

Gillies, John. *Shakespeare and the Geography of Difference*. Cambridge: Cambridge University Press, 1994.

Goldberg, Jonathan. *The Generation of Caliban*. Vancouver: Ronsdale Press, 2002.

– 'The Print of Goodness.' In *The Culture of Capital*, ed. Henry S. Turner, 231–54. New York and London: Routledge, 2002.

– '*Romeo and Juliet*'s Open Rs.' In *Queering the Renaissance*, ed. Jonathan Goldberg, 215–35. Durham: Duke University Press, 1994.

– *Sodometries: Renaissance Texts, Modern Sexualities*. Stanford: Stanford University Press, 1992.

– *Writing Matter: From the Hands of the English Renaissance*. Stanford: Stanford University Press, 1990.

Goodman, Anthony. *A History of England from Edward II to James I*. London: Longman, 1977.

Gosson, Stephen. *The Schoole of Abuse*. London: Shakespeare Society, 1841.

Grady, Hugh. *Shakespeare's Universal Wolf: Studies in Early Modern Reification*. Oxford: Clarendon Press, 1996.

Graham, Kenneth J.E. *The Performance of Conviction: Plainness and Rhetoric in the Early English Renaissance*. Ithaca: Cornell University Press, 1994.

Granville-Barker, Harley. *More Prefaces to Shakespeare*. Ed. Edward M. Moore. Princeton: Princeton University Press, 1974.

– *Prefaces to Shakespeare*. Princeton: Princeton University Press, 1958.

Greenblatt, Stephen J. 'The False Ending in *Volpone*.' *Journal of English and Germanic Philology* 75 (1976): 90–104.

– *Learning to Curse: Essays in Early Modern Culture*. New York and London: Routledge, 1990.

– *Renaissance Self-Fashioning: From More to Shakespeare*. Chicago: University of Chicago Press, 1980.

– *Shakespearean Negotiations: The Circulation of Social Energy in Renaissance England*. Berkeley: University of California Press, 1988.

Greenblatt, Stephen J., ed. *Allegory and Representation: Selected Papers from the English Institute, 1979–80*. Baltimore: Johns Hopkins University Press, 1981.

Greene, Thomas M. *The Light in Troy: Imitation and Discovery in Renaissance Poetry*. New Haven: Yale University Press, 1982.

Greg, W.W. *The Shakespeare First Folio: Its Bibliographical and Textual History*. Oxford: Clarendon Press, 1955.

Habicht, Werner, D.J. Palmer, and Roger Pringle, eds. *Images of Shakespeare: Proceedings of the Third Congress of the International Shakespeare Association*. Newark: University of Delaware Press, 1988.

Hale, David George. *The Body Politic: A Political Metaphor in Renaissance English Literature*. The Hague: Mouton, 1971.

Hall, Kim F. *Things of Darkness: Economies of Race and Gender in Early Modern England*. Ithaca: Cornell University Press, 1995.

Haller, Robert S., ed. *Literary Criticism of Dante Alighieri*. Lincoln: University of Nebraska Press, 1973.

Halperin, David M. 'Forgetting Foucault: Acts, Identities, and the History of Sexuality.' *Representations* 63 (summer 1998): 93–120.

Halpern, Richard. '"The Picture of Nobody": White Cannibalism in *The Tempest*.' In *The Production of English Renaissance Culture*, ed. David Lee Miller, Sharon O'Dair, and Harold Weber, 262–92. Ithaca: Cornell University Press, 1994.

– *The Poetics of Primitive Accumulation: English Renaissance Culture and the Genealogy of Capital*. Ithaca: Cornell University Press, 1991.

Hamilton, A.C. *The Structure of Allegory in* The Faerie Queene. Oxford: Clarendon Press, 1961.

Hamilton, Donna B. *Virgil and The Tempest: The Politics of Imitation*. Columbus: Ohio State University Press, 1990.

Harbage, Alfred. *Shakespeare without Words and Other Essays*. Cambridge, MA.: Harvard University Press, 1972.

Harpsfield, Nicholas. *A Treatise on the Pretended Divorce between Henry VIII and Catherine of Aragon*. 1555. Camden Society, vol. 21. Westminster, 1878.

Harrier, Richard. 'Ceremony and Politics in *Richard II*.' In *Shakespeare: Text, Language, Criticism*, ed. Bernhard Fabien and Kurt Tetzeli von Rosador, 80–97. New York: Olms-Weidman, 1987.

Harris, Jonathan Gil. *Foreign Bodies and the Body Politic: Discourses of Social Pathology in Early Modern England*. Cambridge: Cambridge University Press, 1998.

– 'This Is Not a Pipe: Water Supply, Incontinent Sources, and the Leaky Body Politic.' In *Enclosure Acts: Sexuality, Property, and Culture in Early Modern England*, ed. Richard Burt and John Michael Archer, 203–28. Ithaca: Cornell University Press, 1994.

Hartman, Geoffrey. *Beyond Formalism*. New Haven: Yale University Press, 1975.

Haste, Helen. *The Sexual Metaphor*. Cambridge, MA.: Harvard University Press, 1994.

Hawkes, Terence. *Metaphor*. London: Methuen, 1972.

Hazlitt, William. *Lectures on the English Poets and the English Comic Writers*. London: Bell and Daldy, 1870.

Hedley, Jane. *Power in Verse: Metaphor and Metonymy in the Renaissance Lyric*. University Park: Pennsylvania State University Press, 1988.

Hendricks, Margo, and Patricia Parker, eds. *Women, 'Race,' and Writing in the Early Modern Period*. London and New York: Routledge, 1994.

Heywood, Thomas. *An Apology for Actors*. London: Shakespeare Society, 1841.

– *The Fair Maid of the West*. Parts I and II. Ed. Robert K. Turner. Lincoln: University of Nebraska Press, 1967.

Hillman, David, and Carla Mazzio, eds. *The Body in Parts: Fantasies of Corporeality in Early Modern Europe*. New York and London: Routledge, 1997.

Hillman, Richard. *Self-Speaking in Medieval and Early Modern English Drama: Subjectivity, Discourse and the Stage*. New York: St Martin's Press, 1997.

Hirsch, James. 'Cynicism and the Futility of Art in *Volpone*.' In *New Perspectives on Ben Jonson*, ed. James Hirsch, 106–27. London: Associated University Press, 1997.

Hodgdon, Barbara. 'The Making of Virgins and Mothers: Sexual Signs, Substitute Scenes and Doubled Presences in *All's Well That Ends Well*.' *Philological Quarterly* 66.1 (1987): 47–71.

Holinshed, Raphael. *Chronicles of England, Scotland, and Ireland*. New York: AMS Press, 1965.

Hollander, John. *The Figure of Echo: A Mode of Allusion in Milton and After*. Berkeley: University of California Press, 1981.

Holman, Hugh C., and William Harmon. *A Handbook to Literature*. New York: Macmillan, 1986.

Honig, Edwin. *Dark Conceit: The Making of Allegory*. New York: Oxford University Press, 1966.

Honigmann, E.A.J. *The Texts of* Othello *and Shakespearian Revision*. London and New York: Routledge, 1996.

Hoskins, John. *Direccions for Speech and Style*. Ed. H. Hudson. Princeton: Princeton University Press, 1935.

Hotson, Leslie. *The Death of Christopher Marlowe*. Cambridge, MA.: Harvard University Press, 1925.

Hughes, Richard E., and Albert Duhamel. *Rhetoric: Principles and Usage*. Englewood Cliffs, NJ: Prentice-Hall, 1962.

Hunt, Maurice. 'Shakespeare's *King Henry VIII* and the Triumph of the Word.' *English Studies* 75.3 (1994): 225–45.

– *Shakespeare's Romance of the Word*. London and Toronto: Associated University Press, 1990.

Iselin, Pierre. '"What Shall I Swear By?": Rhetoric and Attitudes to Language in *Romeo and Juliet*.' In *'Divers toyes mengled': Essays on Medieval and Renaissance Culture*, ed. Michael Bitot, 261–80. Tours: Université François Rabelais, 1996.

Jakobson, Roman, and Morris Halle. *Fundamentals of Language.* Janua Linguarum, Series Minor, 1. The Hague: Mouton, 1965.

Johnson, Barbara. *The Critical Difference: Essays in the Contemporary Rhetoric of Reading.* Baltimore: Johns Hopkins University Press, 1980.

Johnson, Lemuel A. *Shakespeare in Africa (and Other Venues): Import and the Appropriation of Culture.* Trenton, NJ and Asmara, Eritrea: Africa World Press, 1998.

Johnson, Nan. *Nineteenth-Century Rhetoric in North America.* Carbondale: Southern Illinois University Press, 1991.

Johnson, Nora. 'Body and Spirit, Stage and Sexuality in *The Tempest*.' *English Literary History* 64.3 (1997): 683–701.

Johnson, Samuel. *Poetry and Prose of Samuel Johnson.* Ed. Mona Wilson. London: Beekman, 1969.

Jonson, Ben. *The Complete Works of Ben Jonson.* Ed. C.H. Herford, Percy Simpson, and Evelyn Simpson. 11 vols. Oxford: Clarendon Press, 1952.

Jordan, Mark. *The Invention of Sodomy in Christian Theology.* Chicago: University of Chicago Press, 1997.

Joseph, B.L. *Elizabethan Acting.* London: Oxford University Press, 1951.

Joseph, Miriam. *Shakespeare's Use of the Arts of Language.* New York: Columbia University Press, 1947.

Justice, Steven. *Writing and Rebellion: England in 1381.* Berkeley: University of California Press, 1994.

Kahn, Victoria. *Rhetoric, Prudence, and Skepticism in the Renaissance.* Ithaca: Cornell University Press, 1985.

Kaplan, Lindsay M., and Katherine Eggert. '"Good queen, my lord, good queen": Sexual Slander and the Trials of Female Authority in *The Winter's Tale*.' *Renaissance Drama* 25 (1994): 89–118.

Kegl, Rosemary. '"Those Terrible Aproches": Sexuality, Social Mobility, and Resisting the Courtliness of Puttenham's *The Arte of English Poesie*.' *English Literary Renaissance* 20 (1990): 179–208.

Kelley, Theresa M. *Reinventing Allegory.* Cambridge: Cambridge University Press, 1997.

Kelly, Henry Ansgar. *The Matrimonial Trials of Henry VIII.* Stanford: Stanford University Press, 1976.

Kermode, Frank. 'What Is Shakespeare's *Henry VIII* About?' *Durham University Journal*, new series, 9 (March 1948): 48–55.

Kernan, Alvin. 'Two Renaissance Mythmakers: Christopher Marlowe and Ben Jonson.' In *Selected Papers from the English Institute, 1975–76*, ed. Alvin Kernan, 41–69. Baltimore: Johns Hopkins University Press, 1977.

Kiefer, Frederick. *Writing on the Renaissance Stage: Written Words, Printed Pages, Metaphoric Books.* Newark: University of Delaware Press, 1996.

Kittay, Eva Feder. *Metaphor: Its Cognitive Force and Linguistic Structure*. Oxford: Clarendon Press, 1987.

Knights, L.C. *Shakespeare: The Histories*. London: Longmans, Green and Co., 1962.

Knowles, Ronald, ed. *Shakespeare and Carnival*. London: Macmillan, 1998.

Kokeritz, H. *Shakespeare's Pronounciation*. New Haven: Yale University Press, 1953.

Kritzman, Lawrence D. *The Rhetoric of Sexuality and the Literature of the French Renaissance*. Cambridge: Cambridge University Press, 1991.

Krook, Dorothea. *Elements of Tragedy*. New Haven: Yale University Press, 1969.

Lacan, Jacques. *Ecrits: A Selection*. Trans. Alan Sheridan. New York: W.W. Norton, 1977.

– *Feminine Sexuality: Jacques Lacan and the école Freudienne*. Ed. Julie Mitchell and Jacqueline Rose, and trans. Jacqueline Rose. New York: W.W. Norton, 1982.

– *The Four Fundamental Concepts of Psycho-Analysis*. Trans. Alan Sheridan. New York: W.W. Norton, 1981.

Lane, Robert. '"The Sequence of Posterity": Shakespeare's *King John* and the Succession Controversy.' *Studies in Philology* 92.4 (1995): 460–81.

Lanham, Richard A. *The Motives of Eloquence: Literary Rhetoric in the Renaissance*. New Haven: Yale University Press, 1976.

Laqueur, Thomas. *Making Sex: Body and Gender from the Greeks to Freud*. Cambridge, MA: Harvard University Press, 1990.

Larmour, David, et al., eds. *Rethinking Sexuality: Foucault and Classical Antiquity*. Princeton: Princeton University Press, 1998.

Lauter, Paul, ed. *Theories of Comedy*. New York: Anchor Books, 1964.

Lawrence, Natalie Grimes, and J.A. Reynolds, eds. *Sweet Smoke of Rhetoric: A Collection of Renaissance Essays*. Miami: University of Miami Press, 1964.

Leggatt, Alexander. '*Volpone*: The Double Plot Revisited.' In *New Perspectives on Ben Jonson*, James Hirsch, ed., 89–105. London: Associated University Press, 1997.

Levenson, Jill L. 'Shakespeare's *Romeo and Juliet*: The Places of Invention.' *Shakespeare Survey* 49 (1996): 45–55.

Levin, Carole. *Propaganda in the English Reformation: Heroic and Villainous Images of King John*. Lewiston, NY, and Queenston, ON: Edwin Mellen Press, 1988.

Levin, Carole, and Karen Robertson, eds. *Sexuality and Politics in Renaissance Drama*. Lewiston, NY, and Queenston, ON: Edwin Mellen Press, 1991.

Levin, Carole, and Jeannie Watson, eds. *Ambiguous Realities: Women in the Middle Ages and Renaissance*. Detroit: Wayne State University Press, 1987.

Levin, Samuel R. *Metaphoric Worlds: Conceptions of a Romantic Nature*. New Haven: Yale University Press, 1988.

Levine, Laura. *Men in Women's Clothing: Anti-Theatricality and Effeminization, 1579– 1642*. Cambridge: Cambridge University Press, 1994.

Lewis, C.S. *The Allegory of Love*. Oxford: Oxford University Press, 1936.

Lezra, Jacques. '"The Lady Was a Litle Peruerse": The "Gender" of Persuasion in Puttenham's *Arte of English Poesie*.' In *Engendering Men: The Question of Male Feminist Criticism*, ed. Joseph A. Boone and Michael Cadden, 53–65. New York: Routledge, 1990.

Lindley, Arthur. *Hyperion and the Hobbyhorse: Studies in Carnivalesque Subversion*. Newark: University of Delaware Press, 1996.

Lindsey, Karen. *Divorced, Beheaded, Survived: A Feminist Reinterpretation of the Wives of Henry VIII*. New York: Addison-Wesley, 1995.

Little, Arthur L. '"An Essence That's Not Seen": The Primal Scene of Racism in *Othello*.' *Shakespeare Quarterly* 44.3 (1993): 304–24.

Lodge, David. *The Modes of Modern Writing: Metaphor, Metonymy, and the Topology of Modern Literature*. Ithaca: Cornell University Press, 1977.

Londré, Felicia Hardison, ed. Love's Labour's Lost: *Critical Essays*. New York and London: Garland, 1997.

Loomba, Ania. *Gender, Race, Renaissance Drama*. Manchester: Manchester University Press, 1989.

Loomba, Ania, and Martin Orkin, eds. *Post-Colonial Shakespeares*. London: Routledge, 1998.

Lucking, David. '"And all things change them to the contrary": *Romeo and Juliet* and the Metaphysics of Language.' *English Studies* 78.1 (1997): 8–18.

– 'Putting Out the Light: Semantic Indeterminacy and the Deconstitution of Self in *Othello*.' *English Studies* 75.2 (1994): 110–22.

– 'That Which We Call a Name: The Balcony Scene in *Romeo and Juliet*.' *English* 44.178 (1995): 1–16.

Machiavelli, Niccolo. *The Prince*. Ed. Peter Bondanella. Oxford: Oxford University Press, 1979.

Mack, Peter, ed. *Renaissance Rhetoric*. London: Macmillan, 1994.

Maclean, Hugh, and Anne Lake Prescott, eds. *Edmund Spenser's Poetry*. New York and London: W.W. Norton, 1993.

MacQueen, John. *Allegory*. London and New York: Methuen, 1970.

Madsen, Deborah L. *Rereading Allegory: A Narrative Approach to Genre*. New York: St Martin's Press, 1994.

Mahood, M.M. *Shakespeare's Wordplay*. London: Methuen, 1957.

Manlove, C.N. 'The Double Vision in *Volpone*.' *Studies in English Literature 1500–1800* 19 (1979): 239–52.

Maquerlot, Jean-Pierre. *Shakespeare and the Mannerist Tradition*. Cambridge: Cambridge University Press, 1995.

Marchitello, Howard. 'Desire and Domination in *Volpone*.' *Studies in English Literature 1500–1800* 31.2 (1991): 287–308.

– *Narrative and Meaning in Early Modern England: Browne's Skull and Other Histories*. Cambridge: Cambridge University Press, 1997.

Marcus, Leah S. 'Renaissance/Early Modern Studies.' In *Redrawing the Boundaries: The Transformation of English and American Literary Studies*, ed. Stephen Greenblatt and Giles Gunn, 41–63. New York: MLA, 1992.

– *Unediting the Renaissance: Shakespeare, Marlowe, Milton*. London: Routledge, 1996.

Marshburn, Joseph H. *Murder and Witchcraft in England, 1550–1640*. Norman: University of Oklahoma Press, 1971.

Marston, John. *The Plays of John Marston*. Ed. H. Harvey Wood. London: Oliver and Boyd, 1938.

Marvell, Andrew. *The Complete English Poems of Andrew Marvell*. Ed. Elizabeth Story Donno. New York: St Martin's Press, 1972.

Masten, Jeffrey. *Textual Intercourse: Collaboration, Authorship, and Sexualities in Renaissance Drama*. Cambridge: Cambridge University Press, 1997.

Matheson, Mark. 'Venetian Culture and the Politics of *Othello*.' *Shakespeare Survey* 48 (1995): 123–33.

Mathew, Gervase. *The Court of Richard II*. London: John Murray, 1968.

Matthiessen, F.O. *Translation: An Elizabethan Art*. New York: Octagon Books, 1965.

Matz, Robert. 'Slander, Renaissance Discourses of Sodomy, and *Othello*.' *English Literary History* 66.2 (1999): 261–76.

Maus, Katharine Eisaman. 'Horns of Dilemma: Jealousy, Gender, and Spectatorship in English Renaissance Drama.' *English Literary History* 54 (1987): 561–83.

Mazzeo, Joseph Anthony. *Renaissance and Seventeenth-Century Studies*. New York: Columbia University Press, 1964.

McCabe, Richard A. *Incest, Drama, and Nature's Law, 1550–1700*. Cambridge: Cambridge University Press, 1993.

McCandless, David. 'Helena's Bed-Trick: Gender and Performance in *All's Well That Ends Well*.' *Shakespeare Quarterly* 45.4 (winter 1994): 449–68.

McGuire, Philip C., and David A. Samuelson, eds. *Shakespeare: The Theatrical Dimension*. New York: AMS, 1979.

McKeon, Richard. *Rhetoric: Essays in Invention and Discovery*. Ed. Mark Backman. Woodbridge, CT: Ox Bow Press, 1987.

McMullan, Gordon. 'Shakespeare and the End of History.' In *The Endings of Epochs: Essays and Studies*, ed. Laurel Brake, 16–37. Cambridge: D.S. Brewer, 1995.

– '"Swimming on Bladders": The Dialogics of Reformation in Shakespeare and Fletcher's *Henry VIII*.' In *Shakespeare and Carnival: After Bakhtin*, ed. Ronald Knowles, 211–27. New York: St Martin's Press, 1998.

Meagher, John C. *Method and Meaning in Jonson's Masques*. Notre Dame: University of Notre Dame Press, 1966.

Melchior, Bonnie. 'Iago as Deconstructionist.' *Publications of the Arkansas Philological Association* 16 (1990): 63–81.

Miall, David S., ed. *Metaphor: Problems and Perspectives*. Sussex: Harvester Press, 1982.

Michell, John. *Who Wrote Shakespeare?* London: Thames and Hudson, 1996.

Mikalachki, Jodi. 'Gender, Cant, and Cross-Talking in *The Roaring Girl*.' *Renaissance Drama* 25 (1994): 119–43.

Miller, Carl. *Stages of Desire: Gay Theatre's Hidden Identity.* London: Cassell, 1996.

Miller Owen, 'Necessary Metaphors and Contingent Metonymies: The Interpretation of Tropes.' *Dalhousie French Studies* 38 (spring 1997): 103–8.

Montrose, Louis. 'Of Gentlemen and Shepherds: The Politics of Elizabethan Pastoral Form.' *English Literary History* 50 (1983): 415–59.

Moulton, Ian Frederick. 'Bawdy Politic: Renaissance Republicanism and the Discourse of Pricks.' In *Opening the Borders: Inclusivity in Early Modern Studies. Essays in Honor of James V. Mirollo*, ed. Peter C. Herman, 225–42. Newark: University of Delaware Press, 1999.

Murrin, Michael. *The Veil of Allegory.* Chicago: University of Chicago Press, 1969.

Murry, Middleton. *The Problem of Style*. London: Oxford University Press, 1965.

Nakayama, Randall S., ed. *The Life and Death of Mrs. Mary Firth, Commonly Called Moll Cutpurse*. New York: Garland, 1993.

Neely, Carol Thomas. *Broken Nuptials in Shakespeare's Plays*. New Haven: Yale University Press, 1985.

– '*The Winter's Tale*: The Triumph of Speech.' In The Winter's Tale: *Critical Essays*, ed. Maurice Hunt, 243–57. New York and London: Garland, 1995.

Neill, Michael. *Putting History to the Question: Power, Politics, and Society in English Renaissance Drama*. New York: Columbia University Press, 2000.

Newman, Karen. *Fashioning Femininity and English Renaissance Drama*. Chicago: University of Chicago Press, 1991.

Nuttall, A.D. *Two Concepts of Allegory.* London: Routledge and Kegan Paul, 1967.

Okri, Ben. 'Meditations on Othello.' *West Africa*, 23 March 1987, 562–4.

Orgel, Stephen. *Impersonations: The Performance of Gender in Shakespeare's England*. Cambridge: Cambridge University Press, 1996.

– *The Jonsonian Masque*. Cambridge, MA: Harvard University Press, 1967.

– 'The Poetics of Incomprehensibility.' *Shakespeare Quarterly* 42.4 (1991): 431–7.

Orkin, Martin. 'Othello and the "Plain Face" of Racism.' *Shakespeare Quarterly* 38.2 (1987): 166–88.

Osgood, Charles G. *Boccaccio on Poetry.* Princeton: Princeton University Press, 1930.

Ovid. *Metamorphoses*. Trans. David R. Slavitt. Baltimore: Johns Hopkins University Press, 1994.

Page, Malcolm. *'Richard II': Text and Performance*. Atlantic Highlands, NJ: Humanities Press International, 1987.

Parker, Andrew, and Eve Kosofsky Sedgwick, eds. *Performativity and Performance*. New York and London: Routledge, 1995.

Parker, Patricia. *'All's Well That Ends Well*: Increase and Multiply.' In *Creative Imitation: New Essays on Renaissance Literature in Honor of Thomas M. Greene*, ed. David Quint et al., 355–90. Binghamton, NY: Medieval and Renaissance Texts and Studies, 1992.

– *Literary Fat Ladies: Rhetoric, Gender, Property*. London and New York: Methuen, 1987.

– 'On the Tongue: Cross Gendering, Effeminacy, and the Art of Words.' *Style* 23.3 (1989): 445–65.

Parker, Patricia, and Geoffrey Hartman, eds. *Shakespeare and the Question of Theory.* New York: Methuen, 1985.

Patterson, Annabel. '"All Is True": Negotiating the Past in *Henry VIII*.' In *Elizabethan Theater: Essays in Honor of S. Schoenbaum*, ed. R.B. Parker and S.P. Zitner, 147–66. Newark: University of Delaware Press, 1996.

Peacham, Henry. *The Garden of Eloquence*. Gainesville, FL: Scolars' Facsimiles and Reprints, 1954.

Pechter, Edward. '"Have you not read of some such thing?": Sex and Sexual Stories in *Othello*.' *Shakespeare Survey* 49 (1996): 201–16.

Pirnie, Karen. '"In Changed Shapes": The Two Jonsons' *Volpones* and Textual Editing.' *Comitatus* 27 (1996): 42–55.

Plato. *Gorgias*. Trans. Terence Irwin. Oxford: Clarendon Press, 1979.

– *The Republic*. Trans. Francis Cornford. London: Oxford University Press, 1941.

Porter, Joseph A., ed. *Critical Essays on Shakespeare's* Romeo and Juliet. New York: G.K. Hall and Co., 1997.

Prynne, William. *Histrio-Mastix; The Player's Scourge or, Actor's Tragedy.* New York: Johnson Reprint, 1972.

Puttenham, George. *The Arte of English Poesie.* Ed. Gladys Willcock and Alice Walker. Cambridge, Cambridge University Press, 1936.

Quilligan, Maureen. *The Language of Allegory: Defining the Genre.* Ithaca: Cornell University Press, 1979.

Quintilian, *Institutio Oratoria.* Trans. J.S. Watson. London: George Bell and Sons, 1907.

Rackin, Phyllis. 'Androgyny, Mimesis, and the Marriage of the Boy Heroine on the English Renaissance Stage.' *PMLA* 102 (January 1987): 29–41.

– *Stages of History: Shakespeare's English Chronicles.* Ithaca: Cornell University Press, 1990.

Radcliff-Umstead, Douglas, ed. *Human Sexuality in the Middle Ages and Renaissance.* Pittsburgh: University of Pittsburgh Publications on the Middle Ages and the Renaissance, 1978.

Rebhorn, Wayne A. *The Emperor of Men's Minds: Literature and the Renaissance Discourse of Rhetoric.* Ithaca: Cornell University Press, 1995.

Rebhorn, Wayne A., trans. and ed. *Renaissance Debates on Rhetoric.* Ithaca: Cornell University Press, 2000.

Rex, Richard. *Henry VIII and the English Reformation.* New York: St Martin's Press, 1993.

Rhodes, Neil. *The Power of Eloquence and English Renaissance Literature.* New York: St Martin's Press, 1992.

Richards, I.A. *The Philosophy of Rhetoric.* London: Oxford University Press, 1936.

Ricoeur, Paul. *The Rule of Metaphor: Multi-Disciplinary Studies of the Creation of Meaning in Language.* Trans. Robert Czerny. Toronto: University of Toronto Press, 1997.

Rogers, Robert. *Metaphor: A Psychoanalytic View.* Berkeley: University of California Press, 1978.

Roof, Judith. *Come As You Are: Sexuality and Narrative.* New York: Columbia University Press, 1996.

Rose, Mary Beth. *The Expense of Spirit: Love and Sexuality in English Renaissance Drama.* Ithaca: Cornell University Press, 1988.

– 'Women in Men's Clothing: Apparel and Social Stability in *The Roaring Girl*.' *English Literary Renaissance* 14.3 (1984): 367–91.

Rosenblatt, Jason P. 'Aspects of the Incest Problem in *Hamlet*.' *Shakespeare Quarterly* 29.3 (1978): 349–64.

Rudnytsky, Peter L. '*Henry VIII* and the Deconstruction of History.' *Shakespeare Survey* 43 (1991): 43–57.

Ruggiero, Guido. *The Boundaries of Eros: Sex Crime and Sexuality in Renaissance Venice.* New York and Oxford: Oxford University Press, 1985.

Schwartz, Murray M. 'Anger, Wounds, and the Forms of Theater in *King Richard II*: Notes for a Psychoanalytic Interpretation.' *Assays* 2 (1982): 115–29.

Schwartz, Murray M., and Coppelia Kahn, eds. *Representing Shakespeare: New Psychoanalytic Essays.* Baltimore: Johns Hopkins University Press, 1980.

Serpieri, Alessandro. 'Reading the Signs: Towards a Semiotics of Shakespearean Drama.' In *Alternative Shakespeares*, ed. John Drakakis, 119–43. London: Methuen, 1985.

Shakespeare, William. *The Riverside Shakespeare.* Ed. G. Blakemore Evans, et al. 2nd ed. Boston: Houghton Mifflin, 1997.

Shapiro, James. *Rival Playwrights: Marlowe, Jonson, Shakespeare.* New York: Columbia University Press, 1991.

Shell, Marc. *The End of Kinship: 'Measure for Measure,' Incest, and the Ideal of Universal Siblinghood.* Stanford: Stanford University Press, 1988.

Shepherd, Simon. *Amazons and Warrior Women: Varieties of Feminism in Seventeenth-Century Drama.* New York: St Martin's Press, 1981.

Sidney, Philip. *An Apology for Poetry (or The Defence of Poesy).* Ed. R.W. Maslen. 3rd ed. Manchester: Manchester University Press, 2002.

Sigal, Gale. *Erotic Dawn-Songs of the Middle Ages: Voicing the Lyric Lady.* Miami: University Press of Florida, 1996.

Skulsky, Harold. 'Cannibals vs. Demons in *Volpone.*' *Studies in English Literature 1500–1800* 29.2 (1989): 291–308.

Smith, Bruce R. *Homosexual Desire in Shakespeare's England: A Cultural Poetics.* Chicago: University of Chicago Press, 1991.

– 'Prickly Characters.' In *Reading and Writing in Shakespeare*, ed. David M. Bergeron, 25–44. Newark: University of Delaware Press, 1996.

Snow, Edward A. 'Sexual Anxiety and the Male Order of Things in *Othello.*' *English Literary Renaissance* 10.3 (1980): 384–412

Sonnino, Lee A. *A Handbook to Sixteenth-Century Rhetoric.* London: Routledge and Kegan Paul, 1968.

Spedding, James. 'Who Wrote Shakespeare's *Henry VIII*?' *Gentleman's Magazine* 178 (August–October 1850), 115–24.

Spevack, Marvin. *A Complete and Systematic Concordance to the Works of Shakespeare.* Hildesheim and New York: Georg Olms Verlag, 1980.

Stanford, Bedell. *Greek Metaphor: Studies in Theory and Practice.* London: Johnson Reprint, 1972.

Stanivukovic, Goran V. 'Troping Desire in Shakespeare's *Venus and Adonis.*' *Forum for Modern Language Studies* 33.4 (1997): 289–301.

Stanton, Donna C., ed. *Discourses of Sexuality: From Aristotle to AIDS*. Ann Arbor: University of Michigan Press, 1992.

Steinmann Jr., Martin, ed. *New Rhetorics*. New York: Charles Scribner's Sons, 1967.

Stoler, Ann Laura. *Race and the Education of Desire*. Durham: Duke University Press, 1995.

Stubbes, Philip. *Anatomy of the Abuses in England in Shakespeare's Youth*. Vaduz: Kraus Reprint, 1965.

Summers, Claude J., ed. *Homosexuality in Renaissance and Enlightenment England: Literary Representations in Historical Context*. New York: Haworth, 1992.

Sweeney, John. '*Volpone* and the Theater of Self-Interest.' *English Literary Rennaissance* 12.2 (1982): 220–41.

Talvacchia, Bette. 'The Rare Italian Master and the Posture of Hermione in *The Winter's Tale*.' *Literature, Interpretation, Theory* 3 (1992): 163–74.

Taylor, Mark. *Shakespeare's Darker Purpose: A Question of Incest*. New York: AMS Press, 1982.

Tennenhouse, Leonard. *Power on Display: The Politics of Shakespeare's Genres*. New York: Methuen, 1986.

Teskey, Gordon. 'Allegory, Materialism, Violence.' In *The Production of English Renaissance Culture*, ed. David Lee Miller, Sharon O'Dair, and Harold Weber, 293–318. Ithaca: Cornell University Press, 1994.

Thompson, Ann, and John O. Thompson. *Shakespeare: Meaning and Metaphor*. Iowa City: University of Iowa Press, 1987.

Traub, Valerie. *Desire and Anxiety: Circulations of Sexuality in Shakespearean Drama*. London: Routledge, 1992.

Traversi, Derek. *Shakespeare: From* Richard II *to* Henry V. Stanford: Stanford University Press, 1957.

Trousdale, Marion. 'Reading the Early Modern Text.' *Shakespeare Survey* 50 (1997): 135–45.

– *Shakespeare and the Rhetoricians*. Chapel Hill: University of North Carolina Press, 1982.

Tudeau-Clayton, Margaret. *Jonson, Shakespeare, and Early Modern Virgil*. Cambridge: Cambridge University Press, 1998.

Turner, Denys. *Eros and Allegory*. Kalamazoo, MI: Cistercian Press, 1995.

Vaughan, Alden T., and Virginia Mason Vaughan, eds. *Shakespeare's Caliban: A Cultural History*. Cambridge: Cambridge University Press, 1991.

Vaughan, Virginia Mason, and Alden T. Vaughan, eds. *Critical Essays on Shakespeare's* The Tempest. New York: G.K. Hall and Co., 1998.

Vickers, Brian. *Classical Rhetoric in English Poetry*. London: Macmillan, 1970.

– 'On the Practicalities of Renaissance Rhetoric.' In *Rhetoric Revalued*, Brian

Vickers, 247–66. Binghamton, NY: Medieval and Renaissance Texts and Studies, 1982.

– 'Some Reflections on the Rhetoric Textbook.' In *Renaissance Rhetoric*, ed. Peter Mack, 81–102. London: Macmillan, 1994.

Walch, Gunter. '"What's past is prologue": Metatheatrical Memory and Transculturation in *The Tempest*.' In *Travel and Drama in Shakespeare's Time*, ed. Jean-Pierre Maquerlot and Michele Willems, 223–38. Cambridge: Cambridge University Press, 1996.

Wall, Wendy. 'Reading for the Blot: Textual Desire in Early Modern English Literature.' In *Reading and Writing in Shakespeare*, ed. David M. Bergeron, 131–59. Newark: University of Delaware Press, 1996.

Warnicke, Retha. 'Conflicting Rhetoric about Tudor Women: The Example of Anne Boleyn.' In *Political Rhetoric, Power, and Renaissance Women*, ed. Carole Levin and Patricia A. Sullivan, 39–54. Albany: SUNY Press, 1995.

Wells, Stanley, Gary Taylor, et al. *William Shakespeare: A Textual Companion*. Oxford: Clarendon Press, 1987.

Westermarck, Edward. *A Short History of Marriage*. New York: Humanities Press, 1968.

Wheeler, Richard P. *Shakespeare's Development and the Problem Comedies: Turn and Counter-Turn*. Berkeley: University of California Press, 1981.

White, Hayden. *Metahistory: The Historical Imagination in Nineteenth-Century Europe*. Baltimore: Johns Hopkins University Press, 1973.

Whittier, Gayle. 'The Sonnet's Body and the Body Sonnetized in *Romeo and Juliet*.' *Shakespeare Quarterly* 40 (1989): 27–41.

Wilde, Oscar. *Complete Works*. London: Collins, 1967.

Wilmot, John, Earl of Rochester. *The Works of John Wilmot, Earl of Rochester*. Ed. Harold Love. Oxford: Oxford University Press, 1999.

Wilson, Thomas. *Arte of Rhetorique*. Ed. G.H. Mair. Oxford: Clarendon Press, 1919.

Yachnin, Paul. *Stage-Wrights: Shakespeare, Jonson, Middleton, and the Making of Theatrical Value*. Philadelphia: University of Pennsylvania Press, 1997.

Zimmerman, Susan. *Erotic Politics: Desire on the Renaissance Stage*. New York: Routledge, 1992.

Ziolkowski, Jan. *Alan of Lille's Grammar of Sex: The Meaning of Grammar to a Twelfth-Century Intellectual*. Cambridge, MA: Medieval Academy of America, 1985.

Index

Adams, Thomas: *Mystical Bedlam*, 54

Alan of Lille: *Grammar of Sex*, 43

allegory, 33, 127–48, 150–6, 202nn7–8, 10, 203nn18–19, 204n21, 205nn30, 36

Anderson, Judith, 209n36

Andreadis, Harriet, 175n4

Anne, queen of England, 94, 96

antitheatricality, 10, 12, 28, 30, 31

Aretino, Pietro, 204n23

Aristotle, 15, 16, 28, 29, 120, 177n22, 178n25; *On Rhetoric*, 35

Arthur, Prince, brother of Henry VIII, 105–6, 160

Ascham, Roger, 16–17, 180n34

Augustine, Saint, 20, 181n42

Bacon, Edmund, 206n3

Bacon, Francis, 16, 179n31

Barbour, Richard, 203nn14–15

Barkan, Leonard, 72, 191nn6, 10

Barker, Francis, 150

Bartels, Emily, 107–8, 199n25

Barton, Anne, 195n27

Belsey, Catherine, 192n14

Benson, F.R., 186n12

Best, George: *Discourse*, 108–9, 199nn25–6

Bloom, Harold, 42, 51, 194n18

Boccaccio, 194n22

Boehrer, Bruce, 159

Boleyn, Anne, 105, 158–60, 164, 166, 207n13

Braithwaite, Edward Kamau, 145–6

Branagh, Kenneth, 103

Bray, Alan, 5, 39, 175n5, 183n57

Brecht, Bertolt, 28

Bredbeck, Gregory, 183n57

Brooke, Nicholas, 186n12

Brotton, Jerry, 205n27

Brown, Paul, 147–8, 204n26

Burnett, Mark Thornton, 153–4

Butler, Judith, 9, 182n50

Campbell, Lily B., 169

Caplan, Harry, 178n26

Carroll, William, 173n2

Cartwright, Kent, 12

Castiglione, Baldessare, 138

catachresis, 33, 97–123, 201n34

Catherine of Aragon. *See* Katherine of Aragon

Catullus, 132

Cave, Thomas, 20
Cavendish, Margaret, 189n34; *The
    Blazing World*, 11–12
Chaucer, Geoffrey, 178n28; *Troilus
    and Criseyde*, 192–4n15
Cicero, 15, 16, 24, 138, 181n43; *De
    Inventione*, 15; *De Oratore*, 12, 13
Cole, Howard C., 194n22
Coleridge, Samuel Taylor, 106,
    198n15
Cox, Leonard: *The Arte or Crafte of
    Rhetoryke*, 16
Cranmer, Thomas, archbishop of
    Canterbury, 158, 167, 170
Crewe, Jonathan, 33, 183–4n61

Dante Alighieri, 138, 178n28
De Grazia, Margreta, 8
Dekker, Thomas: *Lantern and Candle-
    Light*, 5, 7, 31; *The Roaring Girl* (*see*
    Thomas Middleton)
Derrida, Jacques, 192n14, 200n33,
    209n34
DiGangi, Mario, 175n4, 183n57,
    203n15
Dinshaw, Carolyn, 173n4, 175n5
Dolan, Frances E., 203n13
Dollimore, Jonathan, 109, 200n29
Donne, John, 165; 'Sappho to Philae-
    nis,' 35–8, 72
Dowden, Edward, 168
Drummond, William, 16
Dudley, John, 19
Dunn, Kevin, 181–2n45

Eagleton, Terry, 94
Edelman, Lee, 8, 184n5
Edward VI, king of England,
    207n14
Elizabeth I, queen of England, 106,
    159, 160, 163–4, 165–6, 167, 168,
    169–70, 207nn13–14
Erasmus, 181n42; *Copia Verborum ac
    Rerum*, 3, 13, 17, 27, 75, 99–100,
    191n11, 197n12
Evans, Robert O., 68, 76

Felperin, Howard, 168
Fiedler, Leslie A., 204n26
Fineman, Joel, 26, 31, 32, 112, 199–
    200n27, 202n8, 205n30
Firth, Mary: *The Life and Death of
    Mary Firth*, 55, 57
Fishburne, Laurence, 103
Fletcher, Angus, 204n20
Fletcher, John, 166, 167, 168–9
Floyd-Wilson, Mary, 196n5
Foakes, R.A., 167, 169
Foucault, Michel, 6, 175n5, 176n7
Fradenburg, Louise, 173n4
Fraunce, Abraham: *Arcadian Rhetoric*,
    4, 9, 63
Freccero, Carla, 173n4
Freud, Sigmund, 33, 51, 54, 104,
    185n9, 186n10, 191n7, 198n18

Garber, Marjorie, 190n37
Gates, Henry Louis, Jr, 199n23
Gaudet, Paul, 51
Gilbert, Miriam, 187n16
Gillespie, James, 187n16
Goldberg, Jonathan, 4, 6, 153, 173n4,
    174n3, 175n4, 176nn6, 7, 180n34,
    181n40, 183n57, 192n13, 205n32
Gosson, Stephen: *Schoole of Abuse*, 27,
    29
Graham, Kenneth, 181n42
Greenblatt, Stephen, 176n7, 198n20,
    204nn21, 26
Greene, Thomas M., 179n33

Greg, W.W., 198n19

Hall, Kim F., 199n23
Halperin, David, 173n2, 175–6n5
Halpern, Richard, 179nn30, 32
Harpsfield, Nicholas: *Treatise on the Pretended Divorce Between Henry VIII and Catherine of Aragon*, 105–6
Harrier, Richard, 187n16
Harris, Jonathan Gil, 180n36
Harvey, Gabriel, 179n32
Hawkes, Terence, 73
Hazlitt, William, 124, 135–6, 137
Hendricks, Margo, 199n23
Henry VIII, king of England, 105–6, 157–60, 164, 166, 168, 169–70, 207n13, 209n36
Herbert of Cherbury, Lord: *Life and Raign of King Henry the Eighth*, 157–9, 165
heterosexuality, 9, 36, 53, 58, 65, 68, 187n19, 190n40
Heywood, Thomas: *Apology for Actors*, 10, 183n56
Hill, John M., 178n28
Hillman, David, 181n38
history, 6–9, 22, 26, 33–4, 103, 115–16, 119, 121, 157–60, 162, 165, 168–71, 206n1, 207n13, 209nn34–9
Hodgdon, Barbara, 88, 194n22
Holinshed, Raphael: *Chronicles*, 45, 51, 52
Hollander, John, 85, 86
Howard, Jean, 190n37
Homer: *Odyssey*, 142
homosexuality, 5–6, 39, 43, 51, 174n2, 174–5n3, 175–6n5, 187–8n19, 200n29
Howard, Catherine, 159
Huebert, Ronald, 203n15

Hulme, Peter, 150, 204n26

incest, 43, 69, 158–67, 170, 182n46, 195n25, 207nn4, 13, 209n34
Iselin, Pierre, 194n21

Jakobson, Roman, 185n10
James I, king of England, 95, 96, 98, 164, 165, 166, 167, 168, 170
Johnson, Barbara, 203n18
Johnson, Lemuel, 196n2
Johnson, Nan, 179n29
Jonson, Ben, 16, 138, 146; *Bartholomew Fair*, 145; *Masques of Blacknesse and Beautie*, 94–7, 114, 121; *Timber, or Discoveries*, 124, 130; *Volpone*, 130, 140–5, 146–7, 154, 155–6
Jussawalla, Feroza F., 203n12

Kastan, David Scott, 204n26
Katherine of Aragon, 105–6, 158, 160
Kegl, Rosemary, 181n40
Kermode, Frank, 163, 166–7
Knight, G. Wilson, 166, 169

Lacan, Jacques, 54, 68, 135, 186n10
Lamming, George, 205n32
Lanham, Richard: *The Motives of Eloquence*, 35
Leggatt, Alexander, 203n13
lesbian, 35, 130–3, 145, 184n4
Leslie, Marina, 189n34
Lever, Raphe, 183n51
Lezra, Jacques, 182n49
Little, Arthur, 104, 197–8n14, 198n18, 199n25
Locke, John, 182n46
Lodge, David, 186n10
Loomba, Ania, 198n16

Love, Harold, 191n4
Lucking, David, 192n14
Luther, Martin, 181n42

Machiavelli, Niccolo, 138, 203n11
Mackenzie, Clayton G., 189n30
de Man, Paul, 7, 21, 22, 120, 146,
    182n46, 185n10, 201n34, 202n7
Marchitello, Howard, 203n15
Marcus, Leah, 8, 10
Marlowe, Christopher, 27; *Edward II*,
    51
Marvell, Andrew: 'An Horatian
    Ode,' 42
Mary, queen of England, 105, 158–9,
    207n14
Mary, queen of Scots, 164
Masten, Jeffrey, 168, 175n4, 183n57,
    208n23
Mathiessen, F.O., 180n33
Mazzio, Carla, 180n36, 181n38
McCabe, Richard, 158, 167, 207n13
McCandless, David, 91
McMullan, Gordon, 163, 169, 209n34
Melchior, Bonnie, 200n31
metalepsis, 33, 68–9, 71–8, 82, 84–93,
    145, 191nn7, 11, 192n15
metaphor, 13–15, 17, 20–5, 27–33, 43,
    45–7, 53, 56–60, 144, 156, 157, 160,
    164, 171, 177n22, 178n25, 179–
    80n33, 182n46, 184n5, 185–6n10,
    188–9n28
metonymy, 33, 36–42, 53–4, 60–7, 118,
    184n5, 184–5n8, 185–6n10, 188–
    9n28
Middleton, Thomas: and Thomas
    Dekker, *The Roaring Girl*, 7, 33, 39,
    54–64, 67
Milton, John: *Paradise Lost*, 19
Mirrour for Magistrates, 44, 45

Montague, C.E., 186n12
Moore, Jeannie Grant, 187n16
Moulton, Ian Frederick, 175n5
Mueller, Janel, 184n4
Murphy, James J., 178n28
mystery plays, 124, 126

Nashe, Thomas, 33, 179n32
Newman, Karen, 198n16, 199n25
Nietzsche, Friedrich, 120

Okri, Ben, 103
Olivier, Laurence, 51
Orkin, Martin, 108

Parker, Patricia, 43, 104, 173n4,
    175n4, 199n23
Partridge, A.C., 166
Partridge, Eric, 192n13
Payne, Robert O., 178n28
performativity, 6–7, 12
Pittenger, Elizabeth, 187–8n17
Plato, 14, 27, 28, 177n27, 188n22
Plutarch: *De Garrulitate*, 146
Porter, Joseph, 192n13
postcolonialism, 147–8, 205n27
procreative sexuality, 68
Prynne, William: *Histrio-Mastix*, 27,
    29
Pseudo-Cicero. See *Rhetorica ad
    Herennium*
Puttenham, George: *Arte of English
    Poesie*, 4, 12, 16, 20–3, 25, 26, 27, 39,
    41, 76–8, 85, 98, 100–1, 102, 115,
    131, 137–8, 178n24, 183n54, 203n16

queer, 5, 7–8, 31, 51
Quilligan, Maureen, 136–7, 202n10
Quintilian: *Institutio Oratoria*, 3, 4, 12,
    13–16, 18, 21, 23, 24–6, 27, 28, 31,

32, 39–40, 56, 73–7, 81–2, 98–100,
103, 106–7, 114, 115, 130–5, 136, 138,
140, 145, 154, 177n23, 180n33,
181n43, 182n47, 191n10, 197n11

race, 97, 103–4, 107–8, 111–16, 118,
122–3, 151, 197–8n14, 198n16,
200n33
Rebhorn, Wayne, 12, 183n58,
187n16
Renaissance, 8–9, 49, 123, 137, 152,
165, 182–3n51, 188n21
rhetoric: classical (see Aristotle,
Cicero, Plato, Plutarch, Quintilian,
Rhetorica ad Herennium); medieval,
15, 178n28; Renaissance (see Cox,
Leonard, Erasmus, Fraunce, Abra-
ham, Puttenham, George, Wilson,
Thomas). See also allegory, cata-
chresis, metalepsis, metaphor,
metonymy
Rhetorica ad Herennium, 3, 14–15, 21,
27, 39, 40, 73, 97–8, 99, 134–5, 136,
178nn24, 26, 179n33, 184n6, 191n8,
202n5
Rhodes, Neil, 182n51, 187n16
Ricoeur, Paul, 14, 178–9n29
riddles, 131–4, 181n40, 195n27
Ridley, M.R., 198nn15, 19
Rochester, earl of: Sodom and Gomor-
rah, 33, 68–72, 74
Romano, Julio, 204n23
Rose, Mary Beth, 110
Rosenblatt, Jason, 163
Rudnytsky, Peter L., 167, 206n1
Ruggiero, Guido, 175n5
Rushdie, Salman, 203n12; Midnight's
Children, 139–40
Rymer, Thomas, 198n15
Sahgal, Zora, 196n8

Sappho, 132
Schwartz, Murray M., 187n16
Second Shepherds' Play, 124–30, 135, 146
Sedinger, Tracey, 190n44
Serpieri, Alessandro, 97, 112
sexuality, 3–11, 16, 26, 31–4, 36, 38–9,
42, 44, 51–4, 58, 61, 64, 71, 83–4,
86, 88, 93, 97, 106–7, 109–16, 118,
121–3, 128–30, 134–6, 138, 142–3,
145–50, 152–6, 167, 173n4, 174n2,
175n4, 175–6n5, 176–7n8, 178n28,
184n5, 185n9, 185–6n10, 190n37,
191–2n13, 196–7n9, 197–8n14,
198n18, 198–9n20, 200nn28, 33,
201n34, 204n21, 205n30. See also
heterosexuality, homosexuality,
lesbian, queer, sodomy
Shakespeare, William, 26, 27, 138; All
is True (see King Henry VIII); All's
Well that Ends Well, 72, 77, 85–93;
As You Like It, 65–7, 183n56; Hamlet,
4, 94, 102, 196n2; Henry IV, Part 1,
116; Henry V, 201n37; Henry VIII,
158–71; King John, 97, 99, 107, 116–
22; Love's Labour's Lost, 3–4, 6, 12,
26, 32, 90, 136; Macbeth, 7, 125, 170;
Merchant of Venice, 199n21; Merry
Wives of Windsor, 199n21; Much Ado
About Nothing, 107, 199n21; Othello,
33, 97, 99, 102, 103–4, 106–15, 116–
17, 118, 120, 122; Pericles, 115, 119,
195n25; Richard II, 33, 39, 42–54, 61,
64, 201nn36–7; Richard III, 199n21,
201nn36–7; Romeo and Juliet, 72, 77,
78–84, 86, 87–8, 92–3; Tempest, 130,
147–56, 168; Troilus and Cressida, 85;
Twelfth Night, 5, 6–7, 26, 190n40;
Winter's Tale, 107, 146, 199n21,
205n36; and John Fletcher, Two
Noble Kinsmen, 168

Shell, Marc, 159
Sidney, Philip, 66, 183n52; *Apology for Poetry*, 101–2
Sigal, Gale, 192n15
Simpson, O.J., 104
Sinnreich-Levi, Deborah, 178n28
sodomy, 5, 63, 68, 71–2, 74, 174–5n3, 175–6n5
Sonnino, Lee, 178n27
Spedding, James, 166
Spenser, Edmund, 183n52; *Faerie Queene*, 127–8, 129, 133, 138
Stanivukovic, Goran V., 177n10
Stubbes, Philip: *Anatomy of Abuses in England*, 27–8, 29–30
Sykes, H.D., 166

Taylor, Mark, 168
Teskey, Gordon, 203–4n19
Tillyard, E.M.W., 169, 187n16
translation, 179–80n33, 180n34

Vickers, Brian, 179nn31, 33, 183n58

Virgil, 75, 191n11
Vives, Juan Luis, 11

Wakefield Master. See *Second Shepherds' Play*
Wanamaker, Sam, 209n39
Webbe, William, 182n51
Webster, John: *The White Devil*, 62–3
White, Hayden, 9
whiteness, 96–7
Whittier, Gayle, 192n14
Wilmot, John. *See* Rochester, earl of
Wilson, J. Dover, 166
Wilson, Thomas: *Arte of Rhetorique*, 4, 12, 17–20, 22, 23, 27, 40–1, 75, 100
Wotton, Sir Henry, 206n3

Yachnin, Paul, 177n21
Yeats, William Butler, 38

Žižek, Slavoj, 135, 202n9